PLOUGH
&
SCATTER

Dedicated to

Bombardier George C. Kingsland MSM
and
Signaller Cyril F. Bunker

My chief comrades in the Royal Field Artillery,
in appreciation of their long and faithful friendship
in time of war and peace.

PLOUGH & SCATTER

SCATTER

The Diary-Journal of a First World War Gunner

J. Ivor Hanson
Alan Wakefield

Haynes Publishing

First published in October 2009

A catalogue record for this book is available from the British Library

ISBN 978 1 84425 717 1

Library of Congress catalog card no 2009927972

Published by Haynes Publishing,
Sparkford, Yeovil, Somerset BA22 7JJ, UK
Tel: 01963 442030 Fax: 01963 440001
Int.tel: +44 1963 442030 Int.fax: +44 1963 440001
E-mail: sales@haynes.co.uk
Website: www.haynes.co.uk

Haynes North America Inc.,
861 Lawrence Drive, Newbury Park, California 91320, USA

Designed and typeset by Dominic Stickland
Printed and bound in the UK

CONTENTS

Acknowledgements

First I would like to thank Leighton Hanson, Ivor's elder son, who agreed to my editing his father's diary-journal for publication and who stuck with me following a change in publisher, which delayed completion of the project. The publication of his father's wartime account is something Leighton has hoped to achieve for many years and I am pleased that he is satisfied with the finished work.

From my visit to the Hanmer/Bettisfield area where Ivor spent the majority of 1917 in training, I would like to thank the Rev'd Clive Hughes of Hanmer who devised an itinerary that ensured I was able to see key locations mentioned in the diary. As part of this, Clive arranged for me to meet with a number of people holding useful knowledge of the area and its association with the First World War. Of particular assistance was Sir Guy Hanmer, who took time to show me that part of the Bettisfield Park Estate on which the Royal Artillery training camp was located. Also, Dr Joan Daniels, Site Manager of Fenn's, Bettisfield, Cadney, Wem and Whixall Mosses, who gave an extensive tour of Fenn's Moss, including the remnants of the First World War musketry butts on which both Ivor and his friend Abraham trained. At the site of Bettisfield railway station I met Frank Simkiss and local historian Reg Meredith, who both gave me interesting information regarding the locality in both World Wars. In Penley I was indebted to Bert and Ellen Tennant who were on hand so that I could gain access to the last surviving wooden hut from Bettisfield Park Camp, which currently serves as the local Community Centre.

For assistance with endnotes I would like to thank Dr John Bourne, Director of the Centre for First World War Studies at the University of

Birmingham, Mr Bruce Dennis and members of the online Great War Forum. Thanks must also go to Jo Garnier, Glyn Biesty and Max Bonini for assistance with the provision of digital images from the extensive collection held by the Imperial War Museum.

I must also thank my wife Julie, who helped proofread my yearly summaries, assisted with the selection of images and accompanied me on the visit to Hanmer and Bettisfield.

Finally, I would like to thank Ivor Hanson for spending time after his return from the Western Front putting together this account of his war service. Through reading and editing the work and talking to Leighton I have gotten to know Ivor to some extent and I am proud to have been involved in bringing his story to a wider audience.

INTRODUCTION

John Ivor Hanson, always known as Ivor, was born on 26 November 1898 at 11 Maes Y Cwrt, Port Talbot. Two years later his family rented out their house and moved to live with his widowed maternal grandfather at 7 High Street, Taibach. Here they remained until Ivor's grandfather died in 1922. Ivor attended Port Talbot Higher Elementary School, where he developed a lifelong interest in art and literature. He left school aged 15 and became a junior clerk at Port Talbot Steelworks. Outside of school he was a patrol leader in the Boy Scouts. Along with the rest of his family, Ivor attended an English-speaking Presbyterian Church of Wales Chapel. He became friends with a number of divinity students who gave readings and led services at the chapel. One of these students, John Edward 'Eddie' Rogers, who served in the Royal Army Medical Corps during the First World War, went on to marry Ivor's older sister, Nellie.

Ivor's best friend was Abraham Marienberg (always called Abram by Ivor), a Jewish boy whose family had fled from the violent pogroms of Tsarist Russia. They shared many childhood and adolescent experiences together and, after the declaration of war in August 1914, could not wait to come of age and join up. This they did in 1916 and, although they hoped to serve together, Abraham ended up in the infantry, while Ivor was posted to the Royal Field Artillery. Despite serving in different units, the two friends were able to meet each other during their period of military training as both were sent to camps in the Bettisfield/Whitchurch area on the Shropshire–Welsh border. Ivor would spend almost a year at Bettisfield Park Artillery Training Camp as he was too young for overseas service until his nineteenth birthday late in the year. Posted to France in December 1917, he became disillusioned with the war and military life following the news of Abraham's death in action. As with many soldiers, the one thing that sustained Ivor through the harsh realities of life on the Western Front was the comradeship of men with whom he served. Of these, his three best wartime friends, with whom he stayed in touch after 1918, were Cyril Bunker, with whom he trained as a Signaller, Greville Page and George Kingsland, who both served with Ivor in 311 Brigade, Royal Field Artillery.

After demobilisation in 1919, Ivor returned to work at Port Talbot Steelworks, this time as a stocktaker in the Light Plate Mill Office. At this time he also began attending evening classes at Swansea Art School to hone his artistic skills. In 1926 he met his future wife, Margaret Jennet David, with whom he would have two sons, Leighton and Bernard. At the outbreak of the Second World War, Ivor joined the Local Defence Volunteers at the steelworks and also took turns at fire-watching during air raids. During the war, Ivor moved to work in the accounts department of an aluminium factory in the Neath Valley and then as a packing and shipping superintendent at Mansel Tinplate Works. At the war's end he moved to the accounts department and statistics section of the Wern Aluminium Works at Briton Ferry, where he remained until retiring in 1963.

While working at Wern, Ivor began producing articles and sketches for the company paper. He was to take this further through employment as a freelance writer with the *Port Talbot and Neath Guardian*, producing a long-running column entitled 'Sketches from Life'. Each piece followed from an interview with a local figure or celebrity, from which Ivor would produce a potted biography and sketch of the person in question. He also produced quarterly articles for 'The Scribbler', the journal of a writing club of which he was a founder member. Ivor also self-published three books, of which the best seller was *Profile of a Welsh Town*, a history of life in Port Talbot. However, the most prolonged writing project undertaken by Ivor was his diary, which he kept for more than 70 years until his death in 1993, just short of his ninety-fifth birthday.

Of his wartime diary, Ivor wrote:

During my military service in the British Army, my sister, at my request, kept so meticulously all the communications, written from a training camp and from the Western Front, that when I was demobilised at the beginning of 1919, I returned home to find that my letters, postcards and field-cards filled a portmanteau.

Among pastimes engaged in during those early post-war years was the writing up from this correspondence, plus the entries in the pocket diaries I had kept, of the diary-journal that follows.

This work is unlike many First World War memoirs, written by veterans in later life with the benefit of hindsight and at a time when the pervading negative view of the Western Front had been shaped by the work of war poets such as Sassoon and Owen. Instead, this is the product of a young man just returned from the battlefield and based directly on his wartime writings. These present us with an account charting his development from an enthusiastic youth, keen on joining up to 'do his bit', through to his becoming an experienced soldier, increasingly disillusioned by the realities of modern war but knowing that the conflict had to be carried through to victory. As he wrote in later life: 'Regarding our justification in going to war with Germany I had and have no doubts. I was not a pacifist and considered the two wars necessary surgical operations to remove the cancerous growth that was Germany.'

The diary also provides much in the way of detail that cannot be easily found elsewhere. This is particularly the case in relation to Ivor's training as an artillery signaller and to daily life in the Army, both in camp and on active service in France. He also provides a poignant account of the chaos that overwhelmed the British Fifth Army on 21 March 1918, the day Germany launched her all-out offensive on the Western Front.

Ivor records such things as all the artistes he has seen perform at concert parties and mentions every book he read while serving on the Western Front. When the war ends, he is within a few days of his twentieth birthday. It is a testament to him that he kept such a comprehensive and varied account of his war years.

In editing the work I have removed the minimum of diary entries to make the final manuscript conform to the requirements of the publisher. I have standardised spellings, abbreviations and acronyms to conform with accepted practice. The footnotes are a mixture of my own and information provided by Ivor in his original draft. These generally cover events mentioned in the diary, provide short biographical notes on individuals and explain military and other terminology. Finally, to set Ivor's work in context of the wider World War, I have provided an overview for each year of the conflict, outlining key events in each theatre of war and on the British home front. These appear within the body of the diary before Ivor's entries for each year.

My aim has always been to preserve, as far as possible, the integrity of Ivor's work and not to detract from its interest as a complete account of one man's war.

Alan Wakefield, 2009

1914

Despite the murder of Archduke Franz Ferdinand, heir to the Habsburg throne of Austria-Hungary, on 28 June 1914, very few members of the general populace or their political or military leaders foresaw that, within just over a month, the continent would be embroiled in a major war. There had been international crises before, such as the Franco-German dispute over Morocco in 1911, but these had always been ended diplomatically. So, in the summer of 1914 most people simply went on with their daily lives. The holiday season had begun and in Britain, workers from industrial cities headed for seaside resorts, while members of the more affluent middle classes crossed the English Channel to favoured destinations in countries such as France and Italy. Back home, members of the Territorial Force and reserves of the Royal Navy donned uniform for their annual summer camps and manoeuvres. This would prove very fortuitous as the storm clouds gathered in late July.

Although war seemed far from people's minds in 1914, there was an increasingly widespread fascination with the subject. Over preceding years many public figures had uttered pro-war sentiments and mass-circulation newspapers were increasingly jingoistic in tone, publicising international conflicts and preparing their readerships for an impending crisis which, editors argued, could only be settled on the field of battle. In Britain, Germanophobia was not just stoked up by the press but also in popular literature through the publication of many invasion and war-scare stories, including *The Riddle of the Sands* by Erskine Childers (1903) and *The Invasion of 1910* by William le Queux (1906). These filled the public's minds with fear of attack by Germany and created the stereotype of the savage Hun, which was a cause of much of the rabid xenophobia in Britain during the early months of the First World War and paved the way for the internment or deportation of thousands of Austrian and German nationals during the first two months of the conflict.

For those young men who would have to fight the war, their ideals were often moulded through the membership of youth organisations, which burgeoned in many countries of Europe after 1900. In Britain, the Scouts – established after the Boer War by Lieutenant-General Robert Baden-Powell to improve the health of the youth of the Empire by developing an interest in outdoor pursuits – was perhaps the most important, having some 150,000 members by 1913. Alongside the Scouts were found the Boys' Brigade, Church Lads' Brigade and Lads' Drill Association. These groups emphasised patriotism, loyalty and comradeship, all key foundations for possible later military service. Similar sentiments could also be found in Britain's public schools where a traditional commitment to nation, Empire and military service was reinforced through the creation of the Officer Training Corps (OTC). By 1910, more than 150 of the country's public schools had established their own OTC, which would be training grounds for many of the young officers who served during the First World War.

With the European people's increasing acceptance of the concept of war, military and political leaders across the Great Powers held the belief that such a conflict, when it came, would be of short duration. It was felt that modern industrialised nations could not afford the costs inherent in economic dislocation that would result from a protracted conflict. Military strategists backed this up by stressing the superiority of the offensive spirit, where morale and the charge into action with the bayonet or lance would bring victory over superior firepower in a decisive battle. This was, at its basic level, an unwillingness to accept the killing power of modern weapons, such as machine-guns. The short war illusion would have serious effects on the abilities of combatant nations to fight the war once it was realised that a quick victory could not be secured, as there was little interest in building up reserves of manpower, munitions and other war materiel. Luckily for Britain, the Secretary of State for War, Lord Kitchener, was one of the few to foresee a prolonged conflict and took the initiative to call for volunteers to join what would become known as 'Kitchener's Army'. However, this force of civilians required training plus uniforms and equipment and the majority would have to wait until 1916 before they experienced combat.

The international crisis over the summer of 1914 initially developed slowly, with Austria-Hungary biding her time between the Archduke's assassination on 28 June and their delivery of an ultimatum to Serbia on 23 July, the latter country being held responsible for organising the crime. The intervening weeks left many feeling that the incident would blow over or at least remain a localised affair. This certainly could have been the case had Austria-Hungary acted quickly. However, fear of possible Russian backing for Serbia made it vital for the diplomats in Vienna to secure unconditional support from their German ally before moving against the Serbs. Such agreement, popularly known as the 'blank cheque', was given on 5 July by the German Kaiser, Wilhelm II, and his Chancellor, Bethmann-Hollweg. Key to this was the promise of full German diplomatic and military support to Austria-Hungary should she declare war on Serbia, no matter what stance Russia might take. The first step on the road to war had now been taken. Although the Serbs reply to the Austro-Hungarian ultimatum, which included a high level of interference in her foreign and internal affairs, was most accommodating, leaders in Vienna wanted war to rid the empire of the perceived threat of Serbian-led Slav nationalism. A declaration of war followed on 28 July and two days later Russia began to mobilise her forces in a show of strength aimed at making the Austro-Hungarians back down. However, with German support guaranteed, this was not contemplated, making the chances of a limited Austro-Serbian war increasingly unlikely.

Germany now had to make a move in support of her ally. This meant implementing the Schlieffen Plan, which had underpinned her strategy for a European war since its inception in the 1890s. Unfortunately the plan, which called for an overwhelming knock-out blow against Russia's ally, France, before German forces turned eastward to deal with the slower mobilising Russians, meant that a major European war was inevitable. Calls from Germany for Russia to cease mobilisation and for the French not to begin gathering her forces were met with negative and ambivalent replies, giving Germany an excuse for mobilising her armies against France on 1 August. On the same day she declared war on Russia. The following day, lead elements of the German Army invaded Luxembourg to secure vital railheads into France and Belgium.

The invasion of Belgium, a neutral country, was an integral part of the German war plan as it provided the only way by which the Kaiser's troops could pass round the flank of the French Army to encircle the bulk of the French forces, thus securing victory within six weeks. However, this strategic decision led to the likelihood of British involvement in the ever growing conflict. A guarantee of Belgian neutrality had been agreed by the major European powers in 1839 and for Britain this assisted her foreign-policy goal of preventing any potentially aggressive power from controlling the coastline of the Low Countries, from where invasion and attacks on shipping could be threatened. This was considered by German war leaders but the gamble was taken as it was felt the war would be brought to a victorious conclusion well before the potential military strength of the British Empire could affect the outcome. Belgian refusal to allow German troops to move through her territory brought a de facto declaration of war from Germany on the morning of 4 August. This violation of Belgian neutrality unified British public and political opinion. At midnight on 4 August, Britain declared war on Germany. The decision was then made to send the British Expeditionary Force to France. Within a week, what had started as a diplomatic incident in the Balkans had escalated to engulf the Great Powers of Europe in war.

The outbreak of war was greeted with enthusiasm throughout the capitals of Europe. Young men flocked to the colours full of idealism, all wanting to 'do their bit' before the fighting ended. In Britain, Kitchener's call for 100,000 volunteers was met almost immediately and plans were soon afoot to take on more men who would fill the ranks of newly created war-service battalions of existing infantry regiments. A few joined out of a sense of patriotic duty. But the majority were looking for adventure and a chance to escape 'Civvy Street' with its often humdrum work and narrow, confining class and social structure.

Army life seemed to offer men a way out and a return to a healthier, outdoor life, with a chance to see the world while they were still young. Many of these keen volunteers would have to wait until 1915 or 1916 to get their first taste of action. By that time Britain's professional Army, the majority of which formed the British Expeditionary Force, was destroyed helping to stop the initial German advance through Belgium and France. The names Mons, Le Cateau, the Marne and Ypres became known across Britain as the BEF fought the Kaiser's army in the opening engagements of the war.

Germany's ambitious Schlieffen Plan soon broke down and ultimately floundered because of its overly ambitious timetable, which marching infantry and horse-drawn supply transport could not meet. The unexpectedly stubborn resistance of Belgian troops at fortress cities such as Liège and Antwerp delayed the German advance for precious days. The BEF too slowed the German advance and finally supported the French Army in pushing their exhausted enemy back from the River Marne (6–11 September 1914). German commanders now chose to dig in along the line of the River Aisne, a decision that heralded the beginning of trench warfare on the Western Front. Each side began trying to outflank each other in what became known as 'the race to the sea'. These attempts ended in clashes and the digging of trenches, establishing the 450-mile trench system that stretched from the Channel coast to the Swiss frontier and dominated the Western Front for the next four years.

Elsewhere, Russian forces battled with Austro-Hungarian and German armies on the Eastern Front. Again fortunes were mixed for both sides. An offensive launched by the Austro-Hungarians in Galicia on 23 August ended in failure and the Russian counter-offensive pushed Habsburg troops back to the Carpathian Mountains from where an invasion of the rich Hungarian agricultural plains was a real possibility. However, in the north, an advance by the Russian 1st and 2nd Armies was crushed by German forces under Field Marshal Paul von Hindenburg and General Erich Ludendorff at the battles of Tannenberg (28–30 August) and the Masurian Lakes (7–13 September). These victories cleared Russian forces from Prussian territory and gave Germany the upper hand in the east. However, not everything was positive for the Germans as her ally's poor showing in Galicia, and failure on three occasions to knock the increasingly weak Serbia out of the war, led to growing disillusion about Austria-Hungary's ability to make a fair contribution to the war effort.

One diplomatic coup that came the way of Germany was the entry of Turkey into the war on the side of the Central Powers on 29 October 1914. This cut off any chance Britain and France had of shipping war materiel to their Russian ally through the Black Sea. Although major military action against the Turks would come in 1915, Britain did send a small expeditionary force from India in November 1914 to secure the Anglo-Persian oil refinery at Abadan in the Turkish province of Mesopotamia. This source of oil was vital to the Royal Navy whose latest warships were oil rather than coal fired. Against inferior quality Turkish and Arab irregular forces, Indian Expeditionary Force 'D' (IEF 'D') secured a front line some 50 miles forward of Abadan.

Mesopotamia was not the only remote corner of the globe touched by the war in 1914 as forces from Britain, France, Australia, New Zealand, South Africa and Japan invaded Germany's far-flung colonial empire in Africa and the Pacific. Of these colonies only Cameroon, German East Africa and German South West Africa offered continued resistance beyond December 1914.

At sea the Royal Navy's dominance had been somewhat undermined by German battlecruisers shelling east-coast towns, defeat of a British squadron at the Battle of the Coronel (1 November) and the ravaging of commerce by raiding cruisers such as SMS *Emden*. However, victory in the Battle of the Falkland Islands (8 December), the destruction of all but one raiding cruiser and the daring seaplane raid on Cuxhaven had redressed the balance by the end of the year.

Chapter 1

PREPARING FOR WAR

18 July (Saturday)

Present at the laying of foundation stones of the Carnegie Free Library, in Taibach. Councillor William Lewis, Chairman of the Library Committee, laid one of the stones. A supporting speaker was Rev'd D.J. Jones MA, the first Vicar of St Theodore's Church, Port Talbot, who, stressing his belief that one of the chief aims of education was to make people better citizens, referred to his newly born son and said, 'When he comes of age I should not mind too much if he chose to become a chimney-sweep, if that was the job he fancied doing most, but what I should be concerned about is that he became a good chimney-sweep.'

4 August (Tuesday)

Britain has declared war on Germany, so the prophets and the scaremongers were right. Today we had a picnic on the expansive, golden sands of Morfa Mawr, having walked over the Morfa Colliery railroad, which is laid on a bank across the moors, and over the moorlands where rabbits bounced away at our approach, where agitated lapwings resented our invasion, and where the ditchwater is richly coloured with iron.

My sister, Nellie, who is four years my senior, half a dozen of her girl friends, a theological student named W.T. Davies, who preached at our church on Sunday, and who was invited to stay for this picnic, my best companion, a Jewish boy named Abram Gerald Marienberg, myself and my mother, who presided over the food, comprised the happy party.

It was a scorching day and we bathed in a placid, turquoise sea whose single, foamy breaker tumbled on to the sands and in flecked wavelets flung forward in rapid little advances. We played games, ate enormously, but behind all the hilarity loomed the ominous shadow of war. Across the Bristol Channel, Somersetshire and Devonshire were dimly visible and some steamships stood out faintly against the coast. They were too far away for us to determine their class, but Davies, whom everyone calls 'W.T.', thought they were warships, and my heart swelled with pride at the thought of Britain's glorious naval traditions. W.T. said that the government would soon be asking for volunteers for the Army and Navy, and that if necessary he was quite prepared to enlist. Abram and I felt we too would willingly go if required, though we are as yet both only 15 years of age, and the war, they estimate, cannot possibly last more than six months, and some say it will be over by Christmas. The male section gathered firewood, bleached branches and pieces of timber left in a long lane of flotsam and jetsam at the high-tide mark. We savoured the sweet smell of the driftwood fire, and had the kettle boiling in no time, and then ate with relish a tea of bread and butter, cakes and pastries, including tiesen lap,[1] and bananas.

When it was time to return, some delay and much laughter resulted from the girls having hidden W.T.'s shoes and socks. Moths fluttered around us as we returned through the velvet darkness of the cooling night. I found myself paired off with a well-built girl whose first name was Rose, who soon charmed away my boyish unease and shyness by stimulating a happy conversation mostly concerned with our schooldays, which I had shared with her in the same class not so long ago. Before returning to Aberystwyth, W.T. presented me with an elegant little gilt-edged volume of selections from the writings of John Ruskin. At my request, he has also written out a list of books he would like me to read. They are: *Under the Greenwood Tree*, by Thomas Hardy; *Science of Life*, by Benjamin Kidd; *Sesame and Lilies*, by John Ruskin; and *Treasure Island*, by Robert Louis Stevenson.

14 August (Friday)

Today at Port Talbot Steelworks pay office, situated near the steel railway bridge, it was found that paper money had replaced gold. I did not receive any myself as my own wages amount to only 9*s*, less 2*d* deductions, but the

---

1. Literally 'plate cake', a popular currant cake.

notes were shown to me by senior friends. The pound notes were lettered in black and the 10s notes in red.

24 August (Monday)

As yet our church cannot afford to engage the services of a resident Minister, but every Sunday we have Ministers or theological students coming for the day to preach. When they come from a distance, they stay over the weekend, often at our house, and on Saturday nights it is my job to meet them at the railway station and take them home or to wherever they are staying for the weekend. Abram accompanies me on these tasks and by so-doing has come to know and admire several theological students.

29 August (Saturday)

Our home visited by Aunt Eileen Harries of Dafen, near Llanelli. She is a spinster and a schoolmistress. She was immediately 'taken up' with Abram. Discussing the war with him, she seemed shocked at the destruction by the Germans of Louvain Cathedral. Listening, I wondered how it was possible to bombard a city without damaging such large buildings; but partly because I thought my aunt possessed superior knowledge of the facts, and partly to minimise any outrage committed by the enemy would certainly have been considered unpatriotic, I remained silent.

15 September (Wednesday)

The Battle of the Aisne is in full progress on the Western Front. Doris Davies, youngest sister of Sol Davies the barber, whose salon is situated about four doors west of us, has brought me her autograph album with a request for a sketch, so I painted in it, in water colours, the Kaiser in naval uniform, and beneath which I have lettered, 'Our Future Ruler. Perhaps!' The sketch is a copy from the cover of one of the monthly magazines subscribed to by my father.

30 September (Wednesday)

I have been promoted from the Light Bar Mill Office to the Plate Mill Office, but am still considered a junior stocktaker. I am now doing clerical work in rooms which were once bedrooms of what was Daycock's Farm. To balance the half-a-crown increase in my pay I have to start work even earlier than in the Light Bar Mill, for here we commence at 6.30 am. We finish work at 5.30 pm, excepting Saturdays when we finish at 1 pm. We are allowed intervals of half an hour for breakfast and an hour for lunch. Owing to the vagaries of machinery and the class of orders being rolled, work is never proportionately distributed over periods. In short it is either neck or nothing. When say, because of a breakdown, we have little to do, the assorted and animated members of the staff have plenty of time for study. For some the subject is the racing news, for others, reading, sketching, mischievous pranks and a host of other unprofitable activities, judged from the employer's standpoint. One of my pastimes during this leisure has been to compile up to date a list of sunken British and German naval ships, together with their tonnage. The result is illuminating but depressing, for the impartial observer must admit that even on the seas, where we thought ourselves invincible, we are not having it all our own way. This little list of mine has enabled me to modify the unconsidered opinions of not a few people regarding the war at sea. Facts, my dear sir, are stubborn things. About a week ago a German submarine[2] sank three of our armoured cruisers, the *Aboukir*, *Cressy* and *Hogue*, torpedoing them in succession. It was but small consolation to be told by the newspapers that they were old craft. One of my favourite subjects for sketching is naval craft, especially destroyers silhouetted against a moonlit, blue-silver sky.

1 October (Thursday)

The supposed impregnable Belgian forts of Liège and Namur fell in the first month of the war. Bombarded by heavy howitzers, these and other fortifications cracked like eggshells. Refugees have poured into our country and we now have some in Port Talbot.

17 October (Saturday)

We have been thrilled by the sinking of four German destroyers in the

---

2. *U-9* commanded by Otto Weddigen. The action took place on 22 September 1914.

English Channel, and by Beatty's telegrams, the first reading, 'Four enemy destroyers sighted in the Channel', and the second, sent shortly afterwards, 'Sunk the lot'. That had the flavour of our seadog methods.[3] Recently the newspapers contained a picture of British Marines marching briskly into Antwerp. We expect great things of them, for they looked so smart and disciplined. We also think of Kitchener's advice to troops going overseas, 'Beware of wine and women'.

8 November (Sunday)

Carl Lody, a German spy, has been shot in the Tower of London.[4] Locally it is rumoured that found in his possession were plans of the Great Western Railway bridge which crosses the river at Aberafan, and over which passes not only the Great Western Railway but also the Rhondda and Swansea Bay Railway.

26 November (Thursday)

Today I am 16 years of age. Abram, who came to tea, presented me with R.M. Ballantyne's *Fighting the Flames*, a story of the London Fire Brigade. On the flyleaf Abram has written, 'A token of sincere appreciation of friendship.' This volume is another addition to my little library which is growing steadily. In addition to some of the books recommended by W.T. Davies, I have bought Wells's *War in the Air*, Carlyle's *Heroes and Hero Worship*, a short biography of Samuel Taylor Coleridge by S.L. Bensusan, and a book on architecture by Mrs Arthur Bell.

17 December (Thursday)

We are shocked by the news of the bombardment of Hartlepool, Scarborough and Whitby. That German battlecruisers could penetrate our defences and come near enough to bombard our towns seems incredible. Where was the British Fleet?

3. This relates to the sinking of the German destroyers *S115*, *S117*, *S118* and *S119*, which were engaged off Texel Island by the 1st Division of the Royal Navy's 3rd Destroyer Flotilla (HMS *Lance*, HMS *Lennox*, HMS *Legion*, HMS *Loyal*) and the light cruiser HMS *Undaunted*. The action occurred between 2 pm and 4.30 pm on 17 October 1914.

4. Lody was executed by firing squad on 6 November 1914. He had arrived in Britain from Norway on 27 August 1914 bearing an American passport under the name of Charles A. Inglis. After travelling to Edinburgh, London and Dublin, Lody was arrested on 2 October. At his trial at the Middlesex Guildhall, Westminster (30 October–2 November 1914) he was found guilty of two charges under the Defence of the Realm Act of passing and attempting to pass information to the enemy dealing with defences and war preparation in Britain. His execution was the first at the Tower of London for 150 years.

18 December (Friday)

This war is becoming a popular educator in more ways than one. For instance, we are increasing our geographical knowledge and our vocabularies. Until the outbreak of war I was not aware that 'Mine' was a word for an explosive charge! There has been much talk of German 'frightfulness', officially referred to as 'atrocities', for the meaning of which I had to consult a dictionary.

19 December (Saturday)

Very few people I have met doubt the rightness of our stand against Germany, so that the war is being regarded as a righteous one. It is a war to end war. Our churches and chapels have become patriotic and war-minded. Some of our religious leaders tell us that this war is predicted in the New Testament. Often ministers and laymen read to us 'Ye shall hear of wars, and rumours of wars, and nation shall rise against nation . . . and there shall be earthquakes and famines; these are the beginnings of sorrows'. Then we are in for something. The last sentence casts a gloom over my life of a Sunday, so that I am glad when the day is over and the tasks of week-day life keep my mind occupied with healthier thoughts. One Minister of my denomination is noted for his ability to preach eligible men out of pews into platoons. In churches and chapels the Russian National Anthem, 'God Thee All Terrible', is now a popular hymn and is sung with enthusiasm. We remember our gallant seamen with Whiting's hymn, 'Eternal Father, Strong To Save', and religious services now end with the impressive singing of our own National Anthem. Music publishers are doing well with 'Songs of the Allies' and other patriotic music.

The lively 'Marseillaise' seems to be the favourite of the Allied songs. I have memorised the French words of it after hearing it recited by Edgar Ace, an office colleague who 'did' French in the County School. In our office someone reported having seen some French seamen become excited and emotional on hearing a local brass band strike up the 'Marseillaise'.

22 December (Tuesday)

The backyard space of our house had been reduced to a minimum by the erection of my grandfather's workshops where he stocks large and valuable quantities of mouldings, cardboard, backboard and crates of glass. He is a bookseller and picture-frame maker. At present the enlarged shop window is adorned with portraits of British naval and military chiefs, Jellicoe, Beatty, Kitchener and French, all with massive jaws and as handsome as their German counterparts are ugly.

1915

Failure by either side to win the war in 1914 led to reassessments of strategy, with the realisation that the goal of decisive victory would be difficult to achieve. Increasingly the belligerents began planning for a long war, where the full resources of the competing alliance blocs needed to be harnessed to the war effort. In Germany the economic effects of the war were beginning to bite as the British naval blockade became ever more effective. Bread was rationed in January, shortly followed by meat and fats. To combat the shortages, ersatz foodstuffs were manufactured to replace such commodities as butter and coffee. In Britain, the 'business as usual' attitude began giving way to government control of the purchase, supply and distribution of raw materials and some goods, such as sugar, which were increasingly scarce. Production of ammunition, especially artillery shells, was not keeping pace with rates of usage on the Western Front. This led to a 'Shell Crisis' following the Battle of Neuve Chapelle in March 1915. The result of this was the creation of the Ministry of Munitions, headed by Lloyd George. The drive was on for mass production, which would call for the employment of women in munitions factories.

Although economically things were tight for Germany, the campaigns of 1915 would see the Central Powers at the peak of their military fortunes. By early 1915, 100 German divisions were faced by 110 divisions on the Western Front fielded by the Entente and, in the east, 80 divisions from the Central Powers faced 83 Russian divisions.

Throughout the year, German focus would be in the east as they believed it easier to inflict a serious defeat on Russia rather than France. This would remove the danger of fighting a major war on two fronts and allow concentration of forces for a final reckoning with France and Britain. But, once again, a crushing victory proved illusive and, although she lost 2 million men during the year, Russia remained in the war. German successes, such as the Gorlice-Tarnow offensive, launched in May, were offset by the increasing need to support her Austro-Hungarian ally, whose own offensives during the year brought little other than a huge casualty bill. Even so, on 5 August, Warsaw fell to German forces and by September German troops were entrenched deep in Russian territory.

For the BEF, 1915 was a year of disappointments. The Battle of Neuve Chapelle (10–13 March) almost led to a breaking of the German line but failed through a combination of communication breakdowns, rigid artillery barrage timetables and an inability to deliver reinforcements at critical moments. Likewise, French attacks in the Champagne region between February and April gained little beyond casualties of 240,000 men. The pattern for the BEF was repeated during the Battle of Loos, which began on 25 September in support of another French offensive in the Champagne. The increasingly ill-considered attacks, poor handling of reserves, heavy casualties and little in the way of territorial gains paved the way for the replacement of Sir John French by Sir Douglas Haig as commander of the BEF in December. When fighting in the west petered out in November, there had been 60,000 British, 250,000 French and 140,000 German casualties. The war had also taken on a nastier face through the use of gas. The Germans got off the mark first with this new weapon on 22 April 1915 during the 2nd Battle of Ypres and the British replying during the Battle of Loos.

One notable strategic success for the Allies was having Italy join their cause on 23 May, having been promised Austro-Hungarian territory. This third front opened up against the Central Powers would primarily pit Italian troops against the Austro-Hungarians along the narrow, rugged terrain of the Isonzo River. Here the Italians began a series of offensives that brought them little but heavy casualties during 1915. The British and French also decided to fight in southern Europe in an attempt to knock the Ottoman

Empire out of the war and open a supply route to Russia through the Black Sea. The failure of British and French warships to force their way through the Dardanelles in March, in a bid to reach Constantinople, led to an escalation of the campaign, which had been planned as a purely naval operation. The initial landings of British, French and ANZAC troops on 25 April, at Cape Helles, Kum Kale and Ari Burnu, soon to be known as Anzac Cove, achieved some success but were not quickly exploited, allowing the Turks to bring in reinforcements and prevent any meaningful advance.

Trench warfare soon set in and stalemate, as on the Western Front, was the result. Attacks across the confined spaces of the Gallipoli battlefields saw casualties mount rapidly. Conditions deteriorated during the summer, with dysentery being rife among the troops. In August 25,000 men were landed at Suvla Bay in an attempt to capture the all-important high ground overlooking the Dardanelles by outflanking the main Turkish defences. However, initial successes were again not exploited and the last hope of strategic success in the campaign vanished. In October, Lord Kitchener visited the peninsula and advised that the forces be withdrawn. By late November, winter weather had set in and gales, thunderstorms, torrential rain and blizzards made life in the trenches and dug-outs a misery. Between 18–20 December, troops were withdrawn from Suvla Bay and Anzac Cove. The position at Cape Helles was retained slightly longer, but on the night of 8/9 January 1916 the last troops embarked. Only a handful of casualties were reported during the operation, confounding those who estimated that up to half the force would be lost in any withdrawal.

The year 1915 also witnessed the final defeat of Serbia, whose position astride the land route to Turkey made her a key German target as arms and ammunition were increasingly required by the Ottoman Empire. On 6 September, Bulgaria, having a territorial dispute with Serbia dating from the 2nd Balkan War of 1913, secretly joined the Central Powers. Her forces would take part in an invasion of Serbia on 7 October. In a show of force, aimed at keeping Bulgaria out of the war, the 10th (Irish) Division and French 156th Division were withdrawn from Gallipoli and sent to Salonika in Greece, where they landed between 5–10 October 1915. The gesture was a case of 'too little too late' for, by the end of November, these troops, along with the French 17th (Colonial) Division, were in the mountains of southern Serbia facing the Bulgarian 2nd Army. Here they were hit by the same appalling winter weather that affected those still at Gallipoli. This led to 23 officers and 1,663 men being evacuated, suffering from frostbite and exposure, even before the Bulgarian offensive began on 7 December. And five days later all remaining British and French troops were back on Greek soil and moving towards the relative safety of Salonika. On 14 December, the decision was taken to fortify and hold Salonika rather than withdraw troops from the Balkans. By 20 December, when the last of the 10th Division returned to the city, they found the place beginning its transformation into a huge military encampment. On the British side the 22nd, 26th, 27th and 28th Divisions were in the process of arriving, signalling a major commitment to this new theatre of war. The survivors of the Serbian Army, attacked by overwhelming numbers of Austro-Hungarian, German and Bulgarian forces, retreated across the mountains of Albania to the Adriatic coast. From here they were evacuated by British and French ships and sent to Corfu. After rest and re-equipping, the Serbs joined the Allied force at Salonika in the spring of 1916.

Further afield, increasing commitments were being made by the British Empire in Mesopotamia. Not content with securing the oil fields in the south, forces under General Sir John Nixon, spurred on by the India Office which had overall responsibility for the campaign, began to advance along the River Tigris toward Baghdad. Easy initial victories against mostly locally raised Turkish forces led to huge overconfidence on the part of the senior commanders. Major General Charles Townshend, leading the 6th (Poona) Division, supported by a flotilla of river gunboats and transports that became known as 'Townshend's Regatta', accomplished an astonishing advance, relying more on bluff and the incompetence and disarray of enemy forces, than on sound strategy and tactics. At the Battle of Ctesiphon (22–25 November 1915) the lack of troops, artillery and an overextended line of supply finally caught up with Townshend. Unable to break the Turks, he retreated to Kut-Al-Amara where, from early December, his forces were besieged.

If the war had not been going well for Britain in Europe or the Middle

East during 1915, her forces were gaining victories in Africa. The most vital of these came in February, when a determined Turkish attack on the Suez Canal was defeated. However, the forces on hand were not strong enough to pursue the defeated enemy across the Sinai Desert, leaving a potential Turkish threat to Egypt. In German South West Africa, South African forces took a lead in forcing the surrender of the colony on 9 July 1915. This freed troops for offensive operations in German East Africa, although it would be 1916 before sufficient manpower was available to challenge von Lettow-Vorbeck's Schutztruppe (Colonial security force) significantly. Until that time British forces primarily engaged themselves in trying to prevent German raids against such strategic targets as railways. The one major Allied success in East Africa was the sinking, by naval gunfire, of the German light cruiser SMS *Konigsberg* in the Rufuji River delta (11 June 1915). Elsewhere in Africa, progress of a more tangible kind was made in Cameroon, where British columns, largely composed of African troops, had, by the close of the year, brought the German defenders close to defeat.

At sea, advantage definitely swung in the Allies' favour. In March 1915, the British naval blockade on Germany and the other Central Powers became total, with foodstuffs being added to the list of contraband items. In addition, Britain began purchasing all goods carried by neutral shipping bound for Germany. In retaliation the Germans hit back with a modern version of commerce raiding, namely submarine warfare. Although merchant-shipping losses mounted, Britain was able to make excellent propaganda out of the surprise attacks by German U-boats and the inevitable killing of non-combatants. The sinking of the liner *Lusitania* on 7 May, with the loss of over 100 American lives, gave Britain a great propaganda coup and gravely damaged US–German relations. On 27 August, the German government declared that all merchant ships would be warned prior to being sunk, thus undermining the effectiveness of her U-boat campaign.

Chapter 2

I FEAR NO FOE

18 January (Monday)
Oscar Wilde's *An Ideal Husband* is to be played at the New Theatre for six nights, commencing tonight, with two performances on Saturday. The prices of admission are – Circle 1*s* 6*d*, Stalls 1*s* 0*d*, Pit 6*d*. The Lessee and Manager is Edward Furneau, a professional actor whom we have seen in melodramas at this theatre and at Vints Palace in Aberafan. In the vestibule he welcomes his patrons. He had deep seams on his cheeks, but looks immaculate in his dress suit. His heavily oiled black hair is brushed back severely over his head. (I did not have the pleasure of seeing this play.)

26 February (Friday)
Very proud to learn of the formation of the Welsh Guards.

19 May (Wednesday)
Agreement of party leaders that Asquith form a Coalition Government announced.

26 May (Wednesday)
We are pitted against a most formidable foe, who leaves us wondering what will be the next surprise he'll shock us with. His employment of chlorine gas towards the end of last month has left the civilian population gasping, in addition to the wretched victims on the Western Front.

We are naturally proud of our vigorous countryman, Lloyd George, who is now Minister of Munitions, and feel sure our troops will soon have a plentiful supply of guns and ammunition. The formation of the Coalition

Government gives us fresh confidence, for nothing can be lost by pooling the best brains of all political parties. To have Italy join us makes ultimate victory for the Allies more of a probability. Will the USA cast her lot in with us after the outrageous sinking of the SS *Lusitania* on the 7th. 1,195 people were drowned, including many American citizens. What possible excuse can the Germans have for so dastardly a crime?[1]

29 May (Saturday)
Abram and I met on the General railway station J.E. Rogers, the theological student who is to preach at our church tomorrow. He is studying at Trefecca College. When we reached 7 High Street, my home, the doors were locked as my parents and grandfather were down in Loughor burying an aged relative. I managed to prize open the top half of our middle-room window and entered that way to the amusement of Abram and Rogers, who seems to have a very ready laugh. Supper time he and I could not look at each other without bursting into laughter.

30 June (Wednesday)
In the magazine of the annual exhibition of the Royal Academy there is a reproduction of a painting entitled *Bringing in the Wounded Lion*, Beatty's flagship, which the enemy almost sank in the Dogger Bank naval battle. She is portrayed lying on her port side.

After this battle the newspapers reproduced a wonderful photograph of the German battlecruiser, *Blucher*[2] sinking with its keel uppermost and the surviving sailors swimming towards our ships.

30 July (Friday)
At Port Talbot Steelworks we have been given the brass badges issued to

---

1. The *Lusitania* was torpedoed by *U-20* commanded by Kapitanleutnant Walther Schwieger. The liner sank in just 20 minutes. It is thought that 1,201 passengers and crew lost their lives. Justification later given for the sinking was that the ship was carrying a consignment of arms and munitions. In 2008 dives on the wreck of the *Lusitania* resulted in the discovery of US-made .303in calibre bullets, of which the dive team estimated totalled some 4 million rounds.

2. SMS *Blucher* was a large armoured cruiser. She was constructed following reports that the Royal Navy was developing improved armoured cruisers. In fact British reports were false and the Admiralty was actually preparing to build fast, 12in-gunned battlecruisers. *Blucher*, with her maximum speed of 24.5 knots and 12 x 8.3in guns was no match for these ships. Unfortunately, in 1914, she was attached to the 1st Scouting Group of the High Seas Fleet. This consisted of Germany's own battlecrusiers. At the Battle of Dogger Bank the shortcomings of the *Blucher* were fully exposed.

munition workers. I suspected that Head Stocktaker Charles Routledge wasn't enthusiastic when handling me one, for his manner conveyed the question very popular nowadays, 'Why aren't you in the Forces?' Surely he should know that I am only 16 years of age. I felt the slight keenly.

15 September (Wednesday)

Abram Marienberg is now goalkeeper for St Agnes' Church (Anglican) Association Football team. It seems odd having a Jewish boy playing for the team of a Christian church, but no one appears to object. In fact Curate Dredge thinks the world of him.

Sometimes Abram accompanies me to the services at our church (Presbyterian) on Sundays, usually in the evenings, unknown to his parents of course. Sitting with me in the back row he listens intently to the sermons, especially if he has met the preachers, some of the theological students now being among his best friends. One Sunday evening, after the audience had sung Lyte's famous hymn, 'Abide With Me', he said, 'Ivor, I was tremendously impressed with the words of that hymn. Will you write it out for me?' At home, after the service, I wrote it out for him, and fascinated, he read it again, then placed the copy carefully in his wallet, after he had memorised the verse:

> *I fear no foe, with Thee at hand to bless;*
> *Ills have no weight, and tears no bitterness:*
> *Where is death's sting? Where grave thy victory?*
> *I triumph still if Thou abide with me.*

10 October (Sunday)

It doesn't now look as if the war will be over by Christmas. In fact we are becoming resigned to the view that it is going to last for years.

My maternal grandfather, Daniel Harries, has pinned on the wall of our kitchen a map of the Western Front, with small flagged pins to indicate the battle lines. These lines do not appear to alter much, so that the boast, 'Off to Berlin', chalked on troop trains has now lost most of its bravado humour. One of my father's younger brothers, Will, a Private in the 5th Welsh

Regiment, called at our house to say goodbye, on his way to Neyland in Pembrokeshire, he and others belonging to the Volunteer Training Corps having been called up. He is a big man, is tall, weighs about 15 stone and looks fine in uniform. Admiringly my grandfather said to him, 'The sight of you will frighten away the Germans.' But Uncle Will's contribution to the war was to guard bridges on the Home Front.

26 November (Friday)

To my modest little library have been added Jack London's *Valley of the Moon*; and *The Land of my Fathers*, the latter being a Welsh gift-book, sale profits of which are being given to the National Fund for Welsh Troops, a fund which provides comforts for Welsh regiments at home and abroad. I bought the novel in Swansea market, after a conversation in a train with an admirer of Jack London who considered *Valley of the Moon* its author's masterpiece. It is a vigorous and manly tale, and a good argument for the back-to-the-land movement. I enjoyed reading it immensely. The Welsh gift-book was presented to me today on my seventeenth birthday. It is a work of art and an embellishment to my small but expanding library. It is an anthology of Welsh prose and verse, with beautiful illustrations and reproductions of paintings, some in gorgeous colours by living Welsh artists, including Frank Brangwyn and Augustus John. Abram was at our house to tea, and as usual, Jock, our fox-terrier, made a great fuss of him when he arrived. As soon as he sees Abram's face he goes hysterical with joy, running around the kitchen and leaping into the air. When Abram manages to sit Jock leaps on his knees, licks his face and covers his suit with white hairs. Abram, rendered powerless by laughter, is unable to do anything to stop him.

Twelve students from Aberystwyth Theological College have offered themselves for military service, one being rejected because of varicose veins. Among those who have enlisted are our friends J.E. Rogers and W.T. Davies. Suitably, they have been posted to the Royal Army Medical Corps, and are now being trained at Flowerdown Camp, Winchester. One lady admirer refers to them as the flowers of Flowerdown Camp.

14 December (Tuesday)

Among the magazines my father brings home is *Review of Reviews*, founded by W.T. Stead, who was drowned on the SS *Titanic* in 1912. I am especially interested in its cartoons, which being cosmopolitan show us the war as seen by foreigners including our enemies.

By now we are no longer shocked to see HM King George V so shamefully caricatured. Yet can we wonder when we observe what asses our cartoonists make of the Kaiser and his son, 'Little Willie'. This kind of propaganda is so successful that we have come to look at the Kaiser as a demon and his son as an idiot, although I have read somewhere that the Crown Prince is a competent army commander.[3]

Among these cartoons Kitchener is usually represented as an ugly monster; and one depicting a squad of British soldiers was laughable. They were drawn as an odd lot, some tall, long legged, skinny and weedy and others short and stunted and all with tall pith helmets and big mustachios.

Port Talbot now has a prisoner of war camp in the brick buildings of the idle celluloid factory up in the Dyffryn. One of the prisoners acts as an interpreter, and it is rumoured that among them are artists, musicians and scientists. Some of them are employed helping farmers and others are engaged in the erection of the new Margam Iron and Steelworks.

They march to and from the works under guards with fixed bayonets. At first they did the journey by train, but this treatment was considered by local inhabitants to be too indulgent and was stopped.

---

3. Nicknamed 'The Clown Prince' in British newspapers, Crown Prince Wilhelm served with some success as both an Army and Army Group commander on the Western Front.

1916

In 1916 the strains of war were increasingly apparent as the scale of the conflict, especially on the Western Front, grew again. A strategy of attrition took hold and the ability of each nation to sustain the demands of total war was put to the test. This was the year of those defining battles, Verdun and the Somme. The former offensive was planned by German Chief of General Staff, von Falkenhayn, to 'Bleed the French Army white' by attacking a point that the French would never willingly abandon. The plan failed in that the Germans too were dragged into the attritional fight. Between 21 February and 15 December the French lost 542,000 men at Verdun and German casualties stood at 434,000. For his failure in this battle, von Falkenhayn was replaced by the Hindenburg–Ludendorff command team, which would lead Germany until the end of the war.

On top of fighting at Verdun, the German Army went through the Somme offensive. This operation was one of a number of coordinated Allied efforts across the Western, Eastern, Italian and Salonika Fronts in an attempt to weaken greatly the Central Powers by preventing Germany, and to a lesser extent Austria-Hungary, from concentrating their forces. The Somme battle, which was to have included a major contribution by French forces, became primarily a British operation once the scale of the German effort at Verdun was realised. The battle witnessed the blooding of a large part of 'Kitchener's Army' of volunteers. By the time Haig called off operations on 19 November, the Somme had claimed 419,654 British and Dominion casualties, 204,253 Frenchmen and 600,000 Germans. The first day of the battle, 1 July 1916, was the bloodiest day of the British Army, with some 57,470 casualties. The offensive also witnessed the first major operation by ANZACS on the Western Front, namely the taking of Pozieres (25 July–5 August). There were also innovations such as the first use of tanks (15 September), improvements in infantry–artillery co-operation and a growth of tactical knowledge across the vastly expanded British Army.

In the Balkans too, Allied forces were advancing into contact with the enemy. The direct Bulgarian threat to Salonika had passed by May 1916 and troops under the French General Sarrail moved north from their defensive lines towards the Greek–Serbian frontier along which the Bulgarians were entrenched. In August, when Sarrail launched his first offensive, spearheaded by French and Serbian troops, the British Salonika Force (BSF), under Lieutenant General George Milne, was holding a 90-mile front that included the wide, flat Struma Valley, which during summer was one of Europe's malarial blackspots, and the tangle of hills and ravines beside Lake Doiran, a position that German and Bulgarian military engineers had turned in to a veritable fortress. Later advances by French, Russian and Serbian forces placed the latter back on home soil with the liberation of Monastir on 19 November, the last major action before worsening winter weather conditions intervened.

The round of coordinated Allied offensives was kept up by the Italians in August when they launched the 6th Battle of the Isonzo. Unlike earlier attacks over the same ground, this brought a measure of success. Much of this was due to the Austro-Hungarians needing to rush units to the Eastern Front to counter the Brussilov Offensive begun by the Russians on 5 June. By the end of July, the Russians had taken 380,000 prisoners, scoring their greatest success of the war. However, with German units stiffening the Austro-Hungarian defences, the Russians were eventually halted. This failure had a devastating effect on military and civilian morale in Russia from which it was never to recover. However, while it lasted, Brussilov's success proved a real morale booster to the Allied cause. Indeed, the offensive was the reason for Rumania joining the conflict in August with a declaration of war against Austria-Hungary. Unfortunately, she had left her move too late to coordinate with the Russians and once the latter were halted it proved easy for the combined forces of the Central Powers to deal with this new enemy in the Balkans. Entering Rumania on 1 September, the invasion force all but concluded the campaign on 6 December by entering Bucharest. Like the Belgians, the Rumanians were left holding just a small corner of their homeland.

In the Middle East the early months of 1916 witnessed increasingly desperate attempts to relieve Townshend's besieged garrison at Kut-al-Amara. Forces under Major General Sir Fenton Aylmer and later Lieutenant General Sir George Gorringe attempted to batter their way through strong entrenched Turkish positions along the Tigris. Although the Turks lost some ground, the relief force suffered around 23,000 casualties as it fought its way over open ground in the face of heavy machine-gun and rifle fire. This and the inability to move reinforcements quickly to the front sealed the fate of Kut, which surrendered on 29 April. Turkish success here, coming just four months after the final evacuations at Gallipoli, was a severe blow to British prestige and many feared it would trigger an Islamic uprising against the British in the Middle East and even parts of India. However, by December such fears had receded and in Mesopotamia the British poured in men and materiel ready for a major offensive that was launched on 13 December under the command of Major General Sir Stanley Maude.

While Maude gathered his forces on the Tigris, further pressure was being brought to bear on the Turks by a British advance across the Sinai Desert. By the end of 1916, General Sir Archibald Murray's force had established a strong defensive position 100 miles east of the Suez Canal, so ending the Turkish threat to this vital Imperial artery. Once established in this position, Murray began to assess whether it would be feasible in the new year to advance into Palestine and inflict a decisive defeat on the Turks. One of the key settlements occupied in Sinai was the town of El Arish on the coastal plain. This soon became the main advanced camp for the Egyptian Expeditionary Force (EEF) where men and materiel began to concentrate for the coming offensive. During this time the British received assistance from Arab forces under Hussein, Sherif of Mecca. In June, Hussein's forces, led by his son Feisal and British Captain T.E. Lawrence, expelled the Turks from the holy city of Mecca and moved on Medina. They also attacked the Hejaz railway, which offered the Turks their only reliable supply route in Arabia. Such romantic escapades made good press back in Britain and the myth of Lawrence of Arabia was born.

Even further afield and probably unknown to most members of the British public, final victory against German forces in Cameroon came in February 1916, when Colonel Zimmermann's forces, numbering some 1,000 Germans, 6,000 Askaris and 7,000 civilians, crossed into Spanish Guinea. The survivors remained a force in being as the Spanish authorities were too weak to intern them. Zimmermann's plan was to await German victory in the war after which his troops would move to re-establish German rule in Cameroon. Defeat in West Africa left the Kaiser with just one colonial possession, German East Africa. Here, General Jan Smuts was given command in the spring of 1916. His first offensive saw the taking of Tanga (7 July) and Dar es Salaam (3 September), but attempts to surround and destroy von Lettow-Vorbeck's Schutztruppe proved a failure owing to the greater mobility of the German force, its knowledge of the terrain and acclimatisation to local conditions; by May 1916, half the South African troops were down with disease. Smuts regrouped his forces ready for a second offensive in 1917. The high sick rates led to a decision to 'Africanise' the campaign bringing the Gold Coast and Nigeria Regiments to East Africa.

At sea, the long-awaited clash of the British Grand Fleet and German High Seas Fleet took place between 31 May and 1 June, in what became known as the Battle of Jutland. An attempt by the Germans to lure out elements of the Grand Fleet looked to have succeeded when battlecruisers under Admiral Sir David Beatty ran into Admiral Scheer's main German fleet. However, the British had broken German naval codes and Admiral Sir John Jellicoe was following Beatty with the bulk of the Grand Fleet. Those hoping for a decisive battle in the mould of Trafalgar were disappointed. Although Jellicoe lost 14 ships against Scheer's 11, with a much higher number of casualties, this was but a tactical victory for Germany. Strategically nothing changed. The naval blockade of Germany continued and Britannia continued to 'rule the waves'. Another German attempt to undermine British control of the seas through a second and this time unrestricted U-boat campaign failed. Again this was due to the reaction of the US government after American citizens lost their lives when *UB-29* torpedoed the cross-channel steamer *Sussex* on 24 March. A threat by President Woodrow Wilson to sever diplomatic relations with Germany was enough to see the campaign called off on 24 April.

With all the news from the fighting fronts reaching them in newspapers and cinema newsreels, the British public were reasonably well informed. However, equally notable events were happening much closer to home in 1916. Conscription was introduced for all men aged between 18 and 45 years of age under a Military Service Bill of 25 January 1916. The following month, to increase government access to funds for the increasingly expensive war effort, a National Savings scheme was introduced. In May, daylight saving was brought in with the introduction of British summertime. Through this measure it was hoped to increase production in factories and munitions works. The year had also brought armed conflict to the British Isles when on 24 April members of the Irish Republican Brotherhood seized the General Post Office in Dublin and declared an Irish Republic. British forces put down the uprising within a week as it lacked popular support, with less than 2,000 people taking part. However, the execution of Irish rebel leaders won much sympathy for the republican cause, forcing the British government to maintain a sizable garrison in Ireland for the remainder of the war, and leading to civil war and ultimately independence in 1922. But, by Christmas 1916, the situation on the British home front appeared calm, Ireland was quiet, the Royal Navy's 'victory' at the Battle of Jutland (31 May–1 June) seemed to underline British dominance of the seas and military training camps were full of men preparing to take their places in the front line for what were hoped to be the decisive battles of the coming year.

Chapter 3

RAILWAYMAN

21 January (Friday)

These are my last days in Port Talbot Steelworks, for I shall soon be a railwayman, like my father, and my father's elder brother, George, who is the station-master at Cockett, a few miles west of Swansea. Uncle George visited us recently, informed me that his goods checker had been called up for military service, and offered me the job. It did not take me long to accept the offer as I shall be assured permanence and shall have good chances of promotion. Also I shall have a commencing wage higher than that paid me in the steelworks. Today the Head Stocktaker, Charles Routledge, and others on the staff wrote suitable things in my autograph album, and, I understand, they intend presenting me with something.

22 January (Saturday)

In Mr Routledge's room the whole of the stocktaking staff crowded. Feeling rather sheepish I listened to eulogies by Routledge, his senior assistant, James Dick, and several others. George Battersby, an outside stocktaker, who possesses a fine baritone voice, sang 'I am the Bandolero'. They presented me with a Gladstone bag and a shiny imitation-leather wallet. I felt very proud of being held in such high esteem. Afterwards Mr Routledge presented me with a personal gift which I treasure highly. It is *Browning as a Philosophical and Religious Teacher*, by Henry Jones, Professor of Philosophy at the University of Glasgow.

24 January (Monday)

At the office of the Chief Inspector of the Swansea Division of the Great Western Railway I proved my colour sight sound by pairing different strands of coloured wool. All the staff there knew my father and Uncle George. A soft-voiced Inspector who measured me for a uniform decided that I was 'a bit thin around the loins'. Lastly I was ushered into Chief Inspector Dalton's room. Dalton, a dark, serious man, sat at a desk, with our intimate friend Inspector Harry Bowen sitting at another. Dalton surprised me by asking, 'D'you think you'll agree with your uncle?' But it may have been asked as a kindly warning. I replied, 'I ought to.' I caught Inspector Bowen grinning. Dalton hastened to say, reassuringly, 'Yes, you ought to.' I proceeded to Cockett by train with my huge parcel of railway clothes done up in brown paper, and a book of rules, and was met by Uncle George, who, after attending to some business at the booking office, took me to Prospect House, his home, where I am to stay, except for weekends which I shall spend at home. My aunt, who is a second wife, did everything to make me feel at home. After lunch Uncle George took me to the goods yard of which I am to take charge, and we walked via the village of Fforestfach. The road was very muddy and near the Police Station a motor lorry liberally splashed my new uniform with mud. The goods depot is quite a new, model yard, fenced with iron railings and situated about ¾ mile from the main line and railway station.

There is a well-built red brick goods shed and an office with a weighbridge attached to match. There is a gleaming, white-limed cattle pen, a steel crane, and I observed, sets of red buckets, filled with water, with FIRE painted on each of them. Uncle George introduced me to Wright, the present goods checker, whose manner towards me was rather cold. Anyway, it is not my fault that he has been called up for the forces.

1 February (Tuesday)
We shudder at the news that Germany has declared unrestricted submarine warfare from now on.[1] Yet we are still confident of ultimate victory, chiefly because we believe our cause to be in the right.

1. The actual order for unrestricted submarine warfare was issued on 12 February. In April, sinking rose to 183,000 gross tons as against an average of 120,000 gross tons between September 1915 and January 1916. The submarine campaign floundered amidst threats by the US Government to break off diplomatic relations with Germany. (Figures from G. Hardach, *The First World War 1914–1918*, London, Pelican Books, 1987).

6 February (Sunday)

Visited Abram's house, 32 Crown Street. His parents speak gutturally and always pronounce Ws as Vs. When he caught me studying the benign photograph of Dr Hertz on the parlour wall, Abram told me that his name was Dr Joseph Herman Hertz, that he had been born in Hungary and that he was the Chief Rabbi of the United Congregations of the British Empire.

28 March (Tuesday)

Last night's blizzard is the worst in living memory and the whole district is covered with snowdrifts. This was a bitter winter and lasted long, snow surviving until April.

21 April (Good Friday)

Tonight the choir of Cockett church rendered Stainer's 'Crucifixion', a beautiful, haunting cantata which I enjoyed in the company of Uncle George and Aunt Fanny. Our ticket collector, Sidney James, was among the tenors and through him I had an added interest in the event, having accompanied him to two of the rehearsals. Uncle, Aunt and I sat in a pew in line with the door, and each time someone came in we could see the Roll of Honour that I had recently taken hours to design and letter, and which had been attached to the swing door by drawing pins. My relations were disgusted and so was I when I came to realise it fully. I had charged nothing for doing it and I agreed with my uncle when he protested, 'At least they could have put it in a more dignified position and even framed it.' Sidney James is always looking for ways of exploiting my talent for drawing. It might be to my advantage if I developed the business side of it myself. After the Roll of Honour incident – and no doubt my uncle had complained to him, since it was Sidney who had sparked off the church to ask me to do it – he must have now thought that the artist was also worthy of his hire, for he suggested that I design for him a poster which he is submitting to the Great Western Railway suggestions department for advertising purposes. He composed the rhyme and if any payment is made we shall divide it between us.

Some people travel by aeroplane,
Some go by motor-car.
But to travel with ease and comfort,
You must go G.W.R.

Sidney hasn't a bad voice but when we were working together his favourite song appears to be:

Why do you keep laughing at me
With those big blue eyes?
Why do you keep laughing at me
When I want you to sympathise?
Take, oh take those eyes away,
How can I say what I want to say
When you keep on laughing at me
With those big blue eyes?

2 June (Friday)

The Battle of Jutland has completely disillusioned me as to the vaunted superiority of the British Navy. Whatever the newspapers tell us, the facts speak for themselves and point to a victory for Germany, who lost one battleship, one battlecruiser, four light cruisers and five destroyers, whereas we lost three battlecruisers, three cruisers and eight destroyers. British casualties at least doubled those of the enemy and our tonnage sunk far exceeded theirs. The *Invincible* and *Indefatigable*, whose pictures we admired so much in a set of cigarette cards a few years ago, are among the fine ships lost.[2]

13 July (Thursday)

Ditfil, my uncle's elder daughter has been here (Prospect House) for a holiday. She and her sister Connie are away in domestic service since their father's second marriage, but they are on the best of terms with their father

2. The British Grand Fleet lost 14 ships in the battle: 3 battlecruisers (*Indefatigable, Invincible, Queen Mary*), 3 armoured cruisers (*Black Prince, Defence, Warrior*) and 8 destroyers (*Ardent, Fortune, Nestor, Nomad, Shark, Sparrowhawk, Tipperary, Turbulent*). Losses in the German High Seas Fleet totalled 11 ships: 1 battlecruiser (*Lützow*), 1 pre-dreadnought battleship (*Pommern*), 4 light cruisers (*Elbing, Frauenlob, Rostock, Wiesbaden*) and 5 destroyers (*S35, V4, V27, V29, V48*). Total British casualties were 6,945 and for the Germans 3,058. (Figures from J. Campbell, *Jutland an Analysis of the Fighting*, London, Conway Maritime Press, 1986).

and stepmother, who regularly cleans and places flowers on their mother's grave, an act which I think very beautiful. Hitherto I have never heard the name Ditfil and can't say I find it attractive. They told me that she was named after a maternal aunt. I wonder if it is a mutated version of Merthy Tydfil (Tydfil the Martyr). Ditfil is tall and ladylike, has nice kind eyes, full lips, and a slightly receding chin.

A little goods train shunts into my yard every day. There is usually a truck or van or two of miscellaneous goods and a few wagons of house coal and road stones. Sometimes the guard is an ashen-faced consumptive with a weak, tenor voice. He delights in teasing me. A shunter from the station usually comes up with the train. This afternoon it was Garahan, a short fellow who is married and has children. Unsolicited, he told me some astonishing things about sex, explaining some of the intimate details of married life. He treated the subject respectfully and I appreciated it for I might have learned the same information in a far less respectful way. My uninitiated mind is being continually subjected to such mild shocks which unsettle me at first, but later make me feel that I understand life a little better. Recently a bearded old man, who must be between 60 and 70, and who drives a grocer's cart, came to the shed for his master's goods. When I complimented him on the agility he displayed in shifting some sacks of flour, he amazed me by confessing that he still enjoyed sexual intercourse. When I said, 'Are you trying to tell me that you can perform the sexual act at your age?', he replied very definitely, 'Yes.'[3] On the same subject I had a very informative discussion with a signalman who is a bachelor. When I asked him why he had never married, he said that he hadn't the right temperament for it, but that occasionally he enjoyed sex outside it. At the time this seemed shocking to my nonconformist upbringing. Sex (more especially then) meant children and children were so constituted – maturing so many years after birth – that they required parents. He did not believe in promiscuous sex, but saw nothing wrong in sex relations outside marriage if both parties agreed to it happily. This certainly set me thinking, but I still had my doubts, for such conduct was fraught with dangers. Marriage had not been invented for nothing.

3. The original diary at this point read 'Like the piston of a steam engine'. This has been crossed out and replaced by the single word 'Yes'.

17 August (Thursday)

Cockett railway station is a mass of flowers just now. During the ticket inspection on the up trains, the next stop – Swansea – being an open station, passengers lean out from their compartments or alight on the platform to admire the beauty, to congratulate my uncle, or to ask him for tips or information. Prior to joining the railway he was a junior gardener at Miss Emily Charlotte Talbot's Margam Park. He is an expert flower and vegetable gardener and his station wins regularly the annual prize offered by the Great Western Railway for the prettiest, cleanest and best-kept station in the Swansea Division. The extra work this makes for his staff and the exacting demands he makes on them makes him unpopular with most of them. Once after studying the many blooms in the flower beds, I asked him which was his favourite. 'Begonia,' he answered definitely. To anyone who imperilled his beloved flowers in any way, even inadvertently, his bluntness could be savage, even to me, for on one occasion when I slipped on a banked flower bed and nearly trod on some geraniums, he said to me acidly, 'Be careful. I think more of them than you.' He didn't of course, but that was his way of putting it.

Abram and I are determined to enlist as early as possible. To ensure that no physical defect shall prevent this happening, we have both had our teeth attended to, and a few teeth decayed beyond the possibilities of filling, extracted. I went to a Swansea dentist, a young, dark, handsome fellow, clinically immaculate in his white overalls. When he completed the job I asked him to recommend me a good toothpaste, and without having to think he said 'Euthymol'.

20 September (Wednesday)

My father's youngest brother, James, has been discharged from the Army because of slight lung trouble. His military life has been short, for it is only about a month ago that he enlisted in the 2nd Monmouthshire Regiment, stationed at Bedford. His Corporal reckoned he was 'a lucky bugger' to get out of the Army so quickly. Uncle Jim agreed with him entirely.

27 October (Friday)

Arriving this evening by train Abram and I are at Builth Wells for a few days. Both of us have spent previous holidays here, though not together. Abram has a girlfriend here, a beautiful though rather fragile young lady named Mabel. They seem very devoted to each other, but as she is a Gentile, I often wonder how the relationship will develop. I know that Abram would not hesitate to defy racial views on such matters, and I foresee trouble ahead. This morning Abram and I strolled along the bank of the River Wye, as far as the Pump Room, where out of curiosity, we sampled the saline waters. Returning, near the large, stone, arched bridge, we met Dilys, Abram's friend's elder sister, who works in a photographer's shop here.

She is pleasant, prim, and her eyes twinkle when she smiles. She has a firm, though feminine chin and she wore a broad-brimmed hat, formerly a soldier's, for afterwards Abram told me that it had been given her by an Australian. She produced a little pocket camera with which she took a snap of Abram and one of me. We had tea at their home, a quiet, snug cottage, among the trees, well out of the town. Proceeding there this afternoon we were astonished at the unusually rich range of autumn tints of the trees, from various greens to all kinds of yellows, browns and reds. I am preserving a sycamore leaf which I picked up on the road, and remarkable for its colour and size. It is a livid vermilion and as large as a dinner plate.

At their home I came to like immensely the two girls and their angel-faced widowed mother. What a happy, hospitable trio they are. We discussed the war, our home and ambitions, and after tea sang some popular songs with Mabel at the piano. Mabel sang a song, 'The Rose, Sunflower and Chrysanthemum', which charmed Abram especially. When we left the girls came to send us off, Abram and Mabel soon losing us. Dilys led me to a seat alongside the river where for the first time I kissed a girl and discovered how exquisite it was. Tonight in our bedroom Abram told me much about the two girls.

On a previous trip he had met a visiting cellist, a man of easy morals, who admitted having been repulsed by Dilys when he had attempted to take a liberty with her. It appeared that the effect of that was to make the musician admire the girl more than ever.

28 October (Saturday)

Arrived at Builth railway station this afternoon to find that the last passenger train for the day had left. Abram had made a mistake about the time. As we were railwaymen, a porter prevailed upon a goods guard to give us a lift in the guards van, a chance we seized in spite of the fact that the train was not going farther than Llangattock. At Llangattock we walked to the town and knocked at the inn. It was late and the proprietor, who had retired to bed, leaned out of his bedroom window, listened to our plea, but regretted that he could not help us. We returned to the railway station, hoping to spend the night in the waiting room, but it was locked and the only light in view was that of the signal-box at the end of the platform. The signalman took pity on us and allowed us to sleep on his table which was wide enough for the two of us. We were almost mortified when the signalman told us that there was no train for Llanelli until 4 pm on the following day (Sunday 29 October). In the morning we arose from our hard bed and feeling grubby asked the railwayman where we might shave and wash. He told us that there was a pump on the station platform. The upper glass portion of the waiting room door provided our mirror. The noise of the station pump in action aroused the curiosity of the station master whose house adjoined the station, and he sauntered along to see what was taking place. He received our tale of woe charitably enough to invite us into his house for breakfast. Between Llangattock and Llanelli Abram enjoyed reading a novel by his countryman, Maxim Gorki. Later we were joined by two privates of the Lincolnshire Regiment with whom we quickly got into conversation to learn that they had been wounded at Festubert.[4] How we both envied them and their wounds.

20 November (Monday)

Accompanied by my uncle, who had some business to transact in the town, went to Swansea Recruiting Office for the purpose of Attesting,

4. Battle of Festubert, 15–27 May 1915. This was the second attack by the British Expeditionary Force in support of a French offensive in Artois. Initial strikes saw British units take significant areas of German front line. Subsequent attacks on 18 May failed to take any further ground, as did those launched by two Canadian brigades on 24 May. The battle ended with German attempts to retake the ground lost. British and Canadian casualties for the battle totalled 16,000 men.

the present method of registering for service used by volunteers under the Derby Scheme of 1915. My uncle knew the Sergeant Major who was obliging, but unable to deal with me because I had not thought it necessary to take my birth certificate. For this carelessness, which means another delay in my progress towards enlistment, I was furious with myself.

22 November (Wednesday)

Took my birth certificate to Swansea Recruiting Office and was Attested. In other words I am now a soldier on the Reserve and have received my first Army pay, which amounted to 2s 8d.

The military staff were polite and addressed each of us as Mr. A 'horsey' looking Captain 'swore us in' in batches, and while waiting in the queue I was interested in a vigorous Corporal, with an arm missing, and wearing the ribbon of the Distinguished Conduct Medal, who, documents in hand, bustled importantly to and fro. I wondered how he won his medal and guessed the loss of a limb was part of the price. Had it been possible I think I would have gladly changed places with him. We shall be medically inspected another day.

26 November (Sunday)

Today I am 18 years of age and among the gifts I have received are two nice books which I am impatient to read. They are *Adam Bede* by George Eliot, from Uncle and Aunt at Cockett; and *Katerfelto* by Whyte Melville, from Abram. *Adam Bede* is beautifully bound in soft, red leather. I am not due for service with one of the forces until I am 18 and 8 months old, but I shall not wait to be called up. Abram and I have decided to enlist as volunteers and are impatient to go. My father will back me whatever I do, but my mother will be non-committal and will worry herself ill over it, but Abram and I feel that our first duty is to our country. By leaving them I feel a little guilty towards my uncle and aunt who have been so kind to me, for Prospect House has been a second home. Among the pleasant outings they have treated me to during my year at Cockett are trips into Swansea to see a captivating play at the

Grand Theatre called *Romance*; a visit to a cinema to see a fine American motion picture, *Birth of a Nation*; and to the annual prize-giving ceremony of Gregg's College.

7 December (Thursday)
As Welsh people we are exceedingly proud to hear of the elevation of our countryman, David Lloyd George, to the Premiership.

12 December (Tuesday)
Today I was examined by the Swansea Medical Board, housed in the Old Training College, Nelson Street. It was my third attempt to get examined. The first time I journeyed there the recruits awaiting examination were too numerous for the Board to deal with, and I was one of the unfortunate ones told to come again. My second attempt failed because for some reason or other the doctors were all absent. Feeling so impatient and so determined to enlist, I proceeded to Cardiff Recruiting Office only to find that the depot had been closed for the day. Today, however, I succeeded, and the result has made me supremely happy. The first doctor examined my teeth and I guess I scored full dental marks, for some weeks ago I purposely had some decayed teeth extracted. A doctor tested my heart and lungs and on one memorable occasion asked me to cough. I was A1 in all those respects too. Eventually each candidate was perfectly nude and while waiting for my examiner to make entries on my documents I saw some of the sights of my lifetime, for the final test was a march by each candidate in the nude, up and down the room before Major Lucas, Chief of the Medical Board. Short and tall, lean and fat, and some pot-bellied, all did their unique parade proving for me conclusively that clothes add to the appearance and dignity of most men nowadays. The next doctor tested my eyes by setting me to read various letters and figures at a distance. Rapidly and with perfect ease I read the letters and figures on the cards hung before me, the doctor stopping me in the middle of the last and saying, 'All right, that'll do.' Finally I did my nude parade in front of Major Lucas who studied me and asked, 'How do you feel?' to which I replied truthfully, 'I feel quite well.' He then proceeded to make

entries on my card, and eagerly I twisted myself round to be thrilled to
see him enter against my medical category the sign A1. Happy and
confident, I marched into Prospect House to inform them proudly that I
had passed A1, but the impression I had was that in spite of their
approving smiles my uncle and aunt were disappointed with the result.

23 December (Saturday)

Having received no reply to the two applications, made to Chief Inspector
Dalton of the Swansea Division of the Great Western Railway, for permission
to enlist in HM Forces, I tendered to him my resignation.[5]

---

5. Sometime in 1925 Ivor's uncle confessed to him that wishing to discourage or delay his enlistment, he had intercepted Inspector Dalton's replies to the two applications.

1917

A s 1917 progressed the Allies were in a position of strength despite the collapse of Russia into revolution during November. The Germans' launch of unrestricted submarine warfare and withdrawal to the Hindenburg Line (March–April 1917) were admissions that the fighting on the Somme and at Verdun in 1916 could not be sustained for another year. The U-boat campaign, designed to starve Britain into submission, only worked to draw the USA into the war against Germany (6 April). This gave a huge advantage in terms of raw materials, manufacturing power and manpower to the Allies. To make matters worse for Germany, by late 1917, the U-boats had failed, defeated by the Royal Navy's anti-submarine measures, including the introduction of a convoy system for merchant shipping. Overall the war had now become increasingly brutal. Propaganda inflamed hatreds, creating stereotypes and dehumanising the enemy. At the same time each of the belligerents was increasingly war weary through the ever increasing demands of the battlefield and home front.

On the Western Front pressure was maintained on the Germans. On 9 April the British opened the Battle of Arras, in support of the French 'Nivelle Offensive'. The opening day of the battle saw the Canadian Corps take Vimy Ridge and during the initial fighting the British Third Army also made inroads into the Hindenburg line. However, stalemate returned as fighting dragged on until mid-May, and General Nivelle's much-vaunted offensive on the Chemin des Dames, which opened on 16 April, was a total failure costing 135,000 casualties. This proved to be a disaster for France as a massive propaganda campaign had made the whole country expectant of decisive victory. The defeat broke the morale of the French Army and led to widespread mutinies that lasted until the autumn. From this time Haig's BEF became the main Allied offensive force on the Western Front.

In the summer of 1917, Haig launched an offensive in Flanders. Heralded by the explosion of 19 large mines under German positions on Messines Ridge (7 June), the offensive, known as the 3rd Battle of Ypres, or more popularly Passchendaele, got underway on 31 July. However, with over 4 million shells being fired in the preparatory artillery bombardments, the ground over which the infantry was expected to advance was badly torn up. Added to this, Flanders experienced its heaviest rains for 30 years and the battlefield turned into a quagmire. After four weeks many of the initial objectives were not taken as the troops struggled forward through mud. A change in tactics, bringing in 'bite and hold' operations to win limited objectives met with some success. But, with increasingly poor weather conditions, the battle degenerated into a slogging match with both sides losing in the region of 250,000 men by the time Haig halted operations in November following the capture of Passchendaele Ridge.

If the Germans believed this to be the end of major operations for 1917, they reckoned without Haig's willingness to employ novel tactics in a final attempt to pierce the Hindenburg Line before the new year. On 20 November, over hard, chalky, open fields near Cambrai, tanks, used in large numbers for the first time, led six British divisions forward. Surprise was achieved and early gains were made. But the loss of 179 tanks on the first day, with few reserves available, slowed the advance as German resistance stiffened. Nine days after the attack began, Haig called a halt to the battle. The British had created a vulnerable salient, which they were preparing to evacuate when German troops counterattacked on 30 November. When fighting ended on 7 December, the Front Line was back in a similar position to where it had been prior to the British attack in November.

Alongside fighting his three major offensives in 1917, Haig also had to agree to six of his divisions (5th, 7th, 21st, 23rd, 41st and 48th) being deployed to Italy. They were sent, along with six French divisions, to help shore up the Italian Army, which had been severely shaken by the Austro-German attack at Caporetto (24 October 1917). In the following month,

Italian forces were pushed back 80 miles to the River Piave, during which time the Italian 2nd Army ceased to exist as a fighting force. Throughout 1917, the Italian Army's morale was increasingly shaky. They had suffered huge casualties for little gain since entering the war and the spreading of socialist anti-war propaganda was rife among the troops. One casualty of the offensive was Italian commander General Luigi Cadorna, who ceased to have any credibility with his troops. His replacement, General Armando Diaz, worked hard to reorganise the army and improve general service conditions for the men. By the time the Front stabilised in mid-November, the first British and French troops were arriving on Italian soil. First into the Line were the British 23rd and 41st Divisions, which relieved Italian troops along the Piave between 30 November and 4 December. They were to find northern Italy a pleasant change from France and Flanders. Views of dramatic snow-capped mountains, wooded slopes and wide rivers combined with a lower intensity war. This was especially true after the Austro-German offensive ceased in early December and German units were withdrawn for service on the Western Front.

Across the Adriatic, men of the British Salonika Force had seen their first major action, namely the 1st Battle of Doiran (24–25 April and 8–9 May 1917). This operation was in support of a Franco-Serbian offensive west of the River Vardar in which the Allied commander, General Sarrail, hoped to break decisively the Bulgarian line. For their part the British XII Corps were to pin Bulgarian units to the maze of trenches in the hills around the town of Doiran, thus preventing them moving west of the Vardar. This aim was achieved at a price of 5,024 casualties, although ultimately it proved a wasted effort as Sarrail's offensive failed to achieve anything close to a breakthrough. Failure led to the removal, during the summer, of the 10th (Irish) and 60th (London) Divisions to Palestine, where forces were being built up for a major offensive against the Turks. One point in favour of the Allies in the Balkans was the entry of Greece into the war on 29 June, following the abdication of King Constantine. The availability of Greek troops went some way to offsetting Allied manpower shortages in the Balkans and made it possible to consider offensive operations for 1918. However, it would not be Sarrail who would be in charge as his military failures and meddling in Greek political affairs led to his replacement by General Guillaumat in December 1917.

In the Middle East British forces were on the offensive during the year. The new Prime Minister, Lloyd George, wanted a significant advance in Palestine to achieve the kind of victory he believed to be impossible on the Western Front. Although General Murray requested additional troops for the undertaking, he was told to make do with what he had to hand. On 26 March, Murray attacked the main Turkish Line at Gaza and almost succeeded in breaking through. He tried again on 17 April and a second failure saw him replaced as commander of the Egyptian Expeditionary Force (EEF) by General Sir Edmund Allenby. After building up his forces, which included the addition of the 10th and 60th Divisions from Salonika, Allenby launched the 3rd Battle of Gaza (31 October–7 November). This proved a complete success and steady progress was maintained towards Jerusalem despite tough Turkish resistance. The surrender of Jerusalem on 9 December and Allenby's formal entry into the city two days later fulfilled Lloyd George's request that the city be delivered as a Christmas present for the British people, who had had little in the way of striking victories to celebrate that year.

Jerusalem was not the only famous city of the Middle East to be captured by British forces during 1917, as on 11 March, troops under Major General Maude had entered Baghdad in Mesopotamia. The capture of this fabled city was a great morale boost to the Allied cause, being the first major victory, in any theatre of war, after the very tough and generally inconclusive fighting of 1916. In just three months Maude had steadily advanced his force up the River Tigris, prizing the Turks out of a number of tough positions and taking Kut-al-Amara on 24 February. Although offensive operations continued after the fall of Baghdad, there was to be no decisive end to the campaign in 1917. Indeed, the gloss was rather taken off the year's successes by the death of Maude from cholera on 18 November. Operations were then halted for the winter by his successor, Lieutenant General Sir William Marshall.

In East Africa, German forces under von Lettow-Vorbeck slipped into Portuguese territory on 25 November. Although this left German East Africa in British hands, another chance to destroy the German force and thus end the campaign had been missed. The Schutztruppe now numbered only some 300 Germans and 1,700 Askaris. But these were the fittest men von Lettow-Vorbeck had and for the remainder of the campaign he would rely on mobility rather than fighting strength as his chief weapon. During December the Germans re-equipped with weapons and ammunition by raiding Portuguese garrisons, the latter's forces being too weak and disorganised to prevent this activity. At the same time British forces did little to assist their ally and were content to patrol the frontier, increase their hold on German East Africa and ready their forces for a new campaigning season.

Politically, the most momentous event of 1917 was the collapse of Russia into revolution. On 23 February, riots and demonstrations broke out in Petrograd (St Petersburg), the Tsarist regime fell and a Provisional Government was formed. This new administration pledged to remain in the war and in July launched an offensive in Galicia. After making initial gains a major Austro-German counterattack began on 19 July, leading quickly to the complete collapse of the Russian Army. Most soldiers no longer recognised the authority of their officers and formed soldiers' committees (soviets) that took direction from the central soviet in the Russian capital Petrograd. Failure of the military offensive led to Bolshevik-inspired demonstrations against the Provisional Government. In a move to push Russia out of the war by fermenting the chaos, Germany took the decision to allow exiled Bolshevik leaders, headed by Lenin, to travel from Switzerland across German territory to Finland, from where they quickly moved to Petrograd. By 31 August, the Bolsheviks had seized control of the Petrograd Soviet and on 25 October they took political power. By this point, Russia was in a state of internal chaos with hunger and poverty rife, a collapsed transport system, reactionary 'White' forces building for civil war and no organised army of any kind. On 12 December, an armistice was agreed between the Bolshevik government and the Central Powers. This led to the Brest-Litovsk peace negotiations. Although no formal settlement had been reached by the end of the year, Germany had all but rid herself of the strategic burden of a war on two fronts.

Chapter 4

BETTISFIELD PARK CAMP

6 January (Saturday)

Today my fourteen days' notice ended, and having received no reply from the Divisional Office, I left the Great Western Railway and bade goodbye to my uncle and aunt and many of my Fforestfach friends.

13 January (Saturday)

At Taibach Post Office, Mrs Price of Gallipoli Row said to me, 'I hear you've been called up, Mr Hanson.' Proudly, but rather curtly I informed her, 'That's not true, for I shall not be of military age until about nine months time, but I am enlisting as a volunteer.'

15 January (Monday)

After receiving documents from Swansea Recruiting Office, a squad of us were sent to Cardiff Recruiting Office, situated in the former premises of Thomas Cook, near Duke Street arcade.

Abram Marienberg met me at Port Talbot railway station and accompanied me to Cardiff. He intends following me into the Army when he receives from the Port Talbot Railway and Docks Co. permission to join HM Forces.

His reason for coming to Cardiff was to seek an interview with the Adjutant of the Recruiting Office to ascertain if, when he enlists in a week or two, they will send him to my camp. For two friends volunteering for active service, this we consider a reasonable request. In those congested rooms he succeeded in obtaining an interview, but the officer, though promising to do his best, did not commit himself. Abram and I would be mortified if the war ended before we got into the Army.

A courteous Private dealt with my papers and fixed the rate of the financial allowance (allotment) my mother will receive, an amount towards which I shall have to subscribe a small weekly subscription from my Army pay. I then joined a long queue that slowly melted into the Sergeant Major's room. This important NCO was a fat individual with a face like a brigand, and the cap perched on his black pall was adorned with red, white and blue ribbons. He scanned each man's papers, cast a swift, ferocious glance at their owner, then bawled out the regiment to which the recruit would be allocated. Thus the queue was divided into infantrymen, artillerymen, airmen, engineers, etc., and as the different regiments were named one wondered what one's fate would be. To me he said, 'Gunner, Royal Field Artillery', and I felt perfectly satisfied and not a little proud. The clerk who wrote out my railway voucher which was to Bettisfield (Salop) dated it for the following day as it was too late to catch today's railway connections. We were to spend the night at the Depot, but my request was granted to spend the night at home in Port Talbot, provided I paid the railfare, which I willingly did. In the train I imagined the Royal Field Artillery would be similar to the Royal Horse Artillery, a Battery of which was formed at Port Talbot before the war, and for which a riding school was built at Port Talbot. I also imagined Bettisfield Park Camp to be similar to the local barracks. At home I wrested from my mother the admission that I might have been put in worst regiments.

16 January (Tuesday)

I did not bid any of my neighbours goodbye, due to shyness, and I unobtrusively slipped away, having the company of my grandfather as far as the first house in Maesycwrt Terrace, where he just shook my hand, too emotionally upset to speak, and he left me with rather a heartbroken expression. I left Port Talbot with the 9 am train, and with five other artillery recruits left Cardiff for Bettisfield.

It was a fresh morning and the sunlight streamed pleasantly into our compartment. One of the original party from Swansea goes to the RFA Depot at Preston, and as we had already become good pals we were sorry to part. One of the party was a loquacious Londoner who has been employed in the grocery trade in Swansea for some years. He waxed eloquent on the glories of the RFA. I told him that I was delighted with the regiment, but that my friend Abram and I had meant to join the Royal Navy, but when we finally reached the Royal Naval Recruiting Office in Cardiff, it was closed for the day. However, I now seemed to think that I was glad it was closed when we called. Another member of the group, a burly, robust man, surprised us by complaining of periodical bouts of depression, describing to us the morbid thoughts that came to his mind, for instance, at the sight of a razor. The sun retired early and the afternoon sky was dull. Herefordshire fields were covered with snow, a dreary landscape with the sepia-coloured earth showing here and there.

On Whitchurch (Salop) railway station, where we had to change trains, we conversed with some men returning to Bettisfield from leave. Their dialect and their brass shoulder titles revealed them to be Lancashire men.

They looked smart and spruce and from them we learned much about the life at Bettisfield Park Camp. As we neared Bettisfield railway station about 7 pm we were thrilled to hear bugles sounding. The camp was about a mile from the railway station and we followed the 'leave' men along frozen slippery roads, between tall, dark hedgerows. As we neared the camp lights appeared, and in the park one of the first huts we passed had a snorting gas engine. 'That's the camp cinema', someone explained. We, the recruits, reported to the Brigade Office, outside which a slim sentry, with gleaming equipment and rifle, paced faultlessly to and fro. From there we were escorted to 'C' Battery, where, in a hut, deserted except by one of its occupants, we were each given a basin of hot and rather gritty soup which they called gippo.[1] After drinking this welcome stimulant I asked the occupant how he liked being at Bettisfield. He grinned and in a tired and fed-up way replied, 'Oh, it's not so bad – for the Army.' We were then taken to Hut 15 which housed about 30 men who were all trying to outdo each other in making a noise, the result being pandemonium. A little North Walian, doubtless feeling that I needed sympathy, assured me that the 'noisy blighters were quite harmless', and advised me not to notice the language.

1. Used here as a slang term for a meat and vegetable stew, rather than its usual meaning in the First World War, which was as a derogatory term for an Egyptian 'gippo' or 'gyppo'.

My bed consisted of three boards placed on two trestles, and four blankets. While making his bed I overheard one of the new recruits mutter, 'How the hell does the missus do this?'

17 January (Wednesday)

For breakfast we had bread and margarine and a rissole. We were told that they get jam, bacon, porridge, sausages and cold ham in daily rotation. Hut orderlies carry the meals from the cookhouse to the huts. The tea arrived in an urn, and as the tap was clogged with tea leaves a practical fellow put his mouth beneath it and blew through.

There are no cups supplied, but pudding basins, and each man places his basin beneath the tap and takes what he wants. Bread and margarine are plentiful, and as the hut orderlies are cute enough to draw rations for men who are absent for various reasons, a cupboard fixed at the end of the hut is full of surplus margarine and slices of bread, which look like thin books in a bookcase. From this larder we may help ourselves when we care to. After breakfast, at the Battery Office, our particulars were taken, and then we were marched to a hut where we received our uniforms and small kit, all of which we stuffed into white kit bags and deposited in Hut 15. Next, under the direction of a Corporal who was a regular, we each filled a palliasse with straw for our beds. When one tired fellow-recruit sat on his palliasse the Corporal shouted mischievously at him, 'Don't sit there on your palli-asse', to which general laughter came easily.

Before dinner, at the stables, I groomed a horse for the first time in my life, a memorable achievement, for it seemed to me that half of the animals are untamed. Great spirited beasts they are, tigerish-looking animals that greet our entry into the stalls with bared teeth, ears thrown back, swishing tails and dancing hind legs. Old hands were not encouraging when they recounted the number of deaths and injuries caused by horse kicks.

However, we survived the ordeal by skilfully avoiding teeth and hind legs and by grooming in the safer middle parts whenever possible. While grooming we were ordered to doff tunic and waistcoat, and during my absence with a broncho at the water troughs, someone relieved my waistcoat of my three-and-sixpenny fountain pen. I should have known better. For dinner we had gippo, sepia in colour, followed by rice pudding. I have never seen such queer-looking meat and have even suspected it was horseflesh, but having a healthy appetite I ate it and also the rice pudding in spite of its paraffin-oil flavour. Despite these criticisms I must say that the food has exceeded my expectations. This evening I examined the small kit issued with our uniforms and felt the Army had been generous, although I did not voice that opinion as I already notice that it is not fashionable to praise anything connected with the Army. We were each given two pairs of strong, substantial boots, two complete sets of underclothing, knife, fork and spoon, and a little cloth hold-all containing khaki cotton, needles and buttons.[2] Old sweats advise us to buy bachelor buttons[3] for our breeches.

Our cap badge has the design of an old-fashioned cannon surrounded by scrolls bearing the motto *'Ubique quo vas et gloria ducunt'* ('Everywhere where duty and glory lead'). My address is:

203348, Gunner J.I. Hanson,
Hut 15, 'C' Battery, RFA
Bettisfield Park Camp,
Near Whitchurch (Salop)

Bit by bit we pick up fragments of information about the camp. Bettisfield is 6 miles from Whitchurch, the nearest town. Our camp contains four Training Batteries and a Brigade Ammunition Column. About 6,000 men are being trained here. In addition to a cinema serving the whole camp, each Battery has a Dry Canteen, with one Wet Canteen to serve the camp.

There is also a Salvation Army recreation and refreshment hut and a large YMCA hut which has a concert hall attached. The YMCA has a library, writing table, refreshment bar and billiard tables. We hear that the Wet Canteen does a roaring trade. This evening at the YMCA hut I wrote home and to Fforestfach, letters that were generous in their praise of the RFA.

2. The sewing kit was known as a 'Housewife' or 'Hussive'.
3. A 'bachelor button' is a form of button that can be secured to a garment without sewing using a snap-together mechanism.

Reveille is blown so that we are on parade at 6.15 am. The trumpeters are experts in it by repetition and as the blasts ring across the camp the old hands sing words of their own composition: 'Come to the stables. Get out of your beds and water the horses.'

The following is a list of parades:

On	Off
6.15 am	7.30 am Breakfast
8.30 am	11 am Break
11.30 am	12.30 pm Dinner
1.45 pm	3.30 pm Break
4 pm	5 pm

18 January (Thursday)

This morning on parade I was reprimanded by a drill instructor for not having polished my cap badge, and I now understand clearly that brass polishing will have to be a daily task. Copying our seniors, we apply the polish, suitably named 'Soldier's Friend', to the brass with a toothbrush and shine with a larger brush. The old soldiers consider the first few weeks of foot drill on the 'square' the hardest of our training. I should have enjoyed it perfectly up until now had it not been that my stout boots gave me a pair of skinned heels, until I was forced to revert to my light civilian pair. One of the drill instructors, Corporal Meredith, is an exceptionally smart soldier, wearing his cap strictly to regulation – peak 1in from the tip of his nose, which turns slightly upwards as if to oblige. His eyes are thus nearly out of sight. Though he has been twice stripped for overstaying leave, we hear that the Major thinks highly of him as a drill instructor and thus has reinstated him on the two occasions. This afternoon, in the Dry Canteen, we had our first Army lesson in semaphore signalling. Having learned the alphabet as a Boy Scout, I had a fairly good start on most of the squad.

A Stafford laundry sends a lorry weekly for our washing. Some of the fellows tuck into their underwear frivolous notes for the amusement of the laundry girls, and when the clean laundry arrives, notes tucked in them by some of the laundry girls are equally frivolous. Each Battery has a bath house accommodating about 20 men at a time, a hot bath being available any evening except Saturday or Sunday.

In Hut 15 there are about ten Welshmen, one of whom hails from Anglesey. This islander is a fat, smiling, inoffensive fellow, liked by everyone.

The remainder of the occupants represent a number of places, but chiefly Lancashire. This evening, sitting around the hut stove the Lancastrians sang 'She's a Lassie from Lancashire', which the others accompanied with catcalls. One of the Lancashire men is Gunner Grail, who has small, dark, beady eyes, and closely cut jet-black hair which sprouts from his head like wire. I learn that he has spent most of his Army life of several months in the Guard Room or 'clink' as he calls it. He was transferred from the infantry as an unmanageable case, yet one day Grail offered to go to France instead of a father of seven children.

27 January (Saturday)

The first morning parade at 6.15 is a freezer. Within a few minutes of the bugle call we are out from a rough but warm bed and on the square answering the roll call read out by an NCO, aided in his check by an electric torch or hurricane lamp. Standing waiting for this procedure to end I think I would have frozen to the marrow were it not for the deep breathing that I assiduously practise in the open, especially on occasions such as this or when out walking, a life-saving habit I learned from an article that appeared in one of the monthly shilling magazines some time ago. Deep breathing is not only an antidote to chills, but a wonderful aid to good general health. After the roll call has been called we 'double' to the stables, and in the darkness a few leadswingers, unseen by the NCO's, slink back to their huts. The ground is covered with white frost and on the roads the thin ice cracks beneath our formidable Army boots. The weather is so extremely cold that much of our training consists of indoor talks, flatteringly called lectures, and usually given by a Corporal or Bombardier. We are now getting accustomed to our uniforms and have learned that this khaki cloth is very serviceable. From it mud, if left to dry, can easily be scraped and brushed off. Puttees tire the legs and when unwound leave our calves cold, but relieved, especially after a long march.

We wind on puttees opposite from the infantry way, that is, we commence under the knee, wind downwards and secure the tapes around the ankles where they are less likely to loosen when riding a horse. The uniforms of the commissioned officers are immaculate, giving them a smart, distinguished yet comfortable appearance.

28 January (Sunday)

This morning the wash-house water pipes were frozen and to wash and shave we had to make use of water left by others in the wash pans, after breaking a layer of ice on the surface, take our turn in the queue and wash in unpleasantly thick, dirty and soapy liquid.

Morning church parade is compulsory, and we may choose from Roman Catholic, Church of England or Free Church. The 'C of E' parade is the largest, the band heading it playing Sousa's 'Washington Post' to the YMCA hut from the parade ground. The other services are held in dry canteens, one of which has been allotted to each Battery. Falling in with the Free Church men I was marched by some youthful 2nd Lieutenant, who badly bungled the words of command, to 'B' Battery Dry Canteen where we sang 'Fight the good fight with all they might' to the accompaniment of a honky-tonk piano, after which we listened to a superficial sermon based on a most unusual text, the first line of the popular war song 'There's a long, long trail awinding' and delivered by a thin, ashen-grey Wesleyan chaplain. After the service some of us strolled outside the camp to Hanmer, the first sight of whose beauty strikes one with awe. The now frozen mere looks like a crystal, embellishing the green mantle of the scenery. I guess the mere to be about ½ a mile long and about 300yd wide. At the farther end a grey church tower guards the pretty, sleeping village of Hanmer. At the village end of the mere we watched with enjoyment some graceful skating. Once I had had a game of ice hockey on it, during which I was more horizontal than vertical. Remained in the hut for the rest of the day suspecting a slight touch of influenza.

29 January (Monday)

It is extremely cold, but much preferable to rain which is rare here. This evening I heard from Abram who has not yet been allowed to leave Prees

Heath camp, but when it is granted he is coming to see me here. I hope he succeeds soon. I did not bring my International Bible Reading Association card with me, but have read a chapter of the Bible every evening so far, in an attempt to keep up my old custom.

We are still doing a great deal of foot and Swedish drill[4] and have had four lessons on the rifle, and have had several marches carrying a rifle, and after a time it feels more like a hundredweight than nearly 9lb. There are occasional lectures, and we have had one short route march through a small, picturesque village called Welshampton. When we got clear of the camp the officer in charge gave us the order 'march at ease' and songs broke out. Not exactly angelic songs are swelling, but what was sung gave an easy swing to the marching, and that, combined with the delightful scenery on all sides, made of it a very pleasant outing. In the camp supply store bought a cap badge and sent it to Aunt Fanny and Uncle George. Have been inoculated twice against fevers. It is not very painful and we are given 48 hours off each time.

30 January (Tuesday)

This evening at the YMCA hut enjoyed a lantern lecture entitled 'The Great War', given by a gentleman who had served with the YMCA in France and Egypt. After the show the lecturer presented to each man who promised to read it daily, a neat, khaki-coloured pocket New Testament. Behind the refreshment counter are a beaming old man who makes me hope that I'll be as jolly as he at his age; a serious individual, very conscious of the important service he performs; a businesslike RFA orderly; and a most beautiful girl, whose strong, clean, frank face suggests the best type of English girlhood. By a little manoeuvring I avoided the male servers and was graciously supplied by her with a cup of tea, a pastry and a charming smile.

31 January (Wednesday)

Becoming acquainted with rifle drill, having been taught how to slope, order, reverse and present arms. We recruits can now tell an officer's rank from a 2nd Lieutenant to a Field Marshal, and when on guard we have to

---

4. A form of physical exercise needing no specialist equipment. In an open space a single instructor could drill large numbers of men as they simply copied whatever exercise he was demonstrating. Rather like an old-fashioned form of aerobics class but on a much larger scale.

salute all officers and present arms from Majors up. Our Battery Sergeant Major is named Bonser, a grave man of medium height, with sweeping moustachios, massive chin and small feet. His head and roar are leonine. 'Attention' bawled by him becomes 'Shown'. On one occasion when some men shuffled on parade he shouted, 'Lookatum, lookatum. They're like the ingels of Mons flying abaht.' Today in 'C' Battery Dry Canteen he addressed our squad in a frank and encouraging way. Part of his speech was as follows: 'If you do your best, I'll do my best for you. If anyone thinks an injustice 'as been done 'im, advise me, and I'll investigate matters. We're all in the mess, but it's up to you and me to do our utmost, and by so-doing end the war as quickly as possible.'

For dinner we had fish of doubtful species, and afterwards we (new recruits) were inoculated at the camp hospital. The doctor pinched up the flesh on my bicep and plunged into it his needle in no uncertain manner, but for 48 hours our duties were excused. The effects of it make me feel sick and miserable, and I cannot raise my arm which is stiff and too painful to touch. Over the hospital door a wit had pencilled Dante's forlorn phrase, 'All hope abandon, ye who enter here.' Anyone requiring medical aid must report to the orderly NCO at night, and parade, if he is able, at 8 on the following morning. This is unsympathetically known as the parade of the sick, lame and lazy. It is said that the medical restoratives at the hospital are very limited in kind and that pills called 'Number nines', gargles and bandages are all a sick person may expect whatever his ailments are. One of the doctors, a thin, irascible fellow has served in the Indian Army for about 20 years and is said to suffer from ague.[5] Such a place and period of service has fitted him admirably to deal with most 'old soldier' tricks.

2 February (Friday)

Every Friday evening we are paid at the Battery Office, usually by a Lieutenant assisted by a clerk. They sit at a small table at one of the doorways. Everyone whistles or sings. From our pay a small amount is deducted for the Battery

5. A fever that is marked by paroxysms of chills, fever and sweating recurring at regular intervals; also a fit of shivering, a chill. Hence, ague can refer to both chills and fevers.

Fund, and another amount is deducted towards the allotment received by our relatives, leaving us to draw weekly the princely sum of 6s. Our names are called out in alphabetical order, and we have to salute before and after receiving the money. If ever I have to enlist again I should delete the H from my surname. Though we all receive the same amount, we are already split into two classes – borrowers and lenders. Some will have lost the whole of their pay by midnight through gambling. Those of us who have to provide ourselves with stationery have to share such necessities with those who haven't any money left to buy it. Some of us even manage to place a small deposit in the Post Office Savings Bank towards our leave expenses.

This evening I went to the camp cinema. The seats at the rear of the hall are reserved for officers. At present a serial is being screened in which the stars, Pearl White and Eddie Polo, have some miraculous escapes from death, and each part usually ends with the muscular hero emerging either without his shirt, or with it torn to shreds, after he has victoriously fought single-handed about 20 men.

4 February (Sunday)

This afternoon attended a Bible Class in the library of the YMCA. An elderly Gunner named Taylor, from Hut 15, persuaded me to go with him. Taylor is fat, waddles along, wears pince-nez and has a walrus moustache. He has left behind a wife and a business of some sort and it is nearly breaking his heart. Sitting around the hut stove one night I was conscious of him studying me intently. Then he placed his fingers on my head and felt my 'bumps'. It appeared that he is an amateur phrenologist,[6] and when I asked him what he had found, with some surprise, and rather grudgingly I thought, admitted that he found on my head a bump that denoted pluck. Having joined the Army voluntarily, with genuine hope of engaging in active service abroad in the near future I did not find this flattering, but he only smiled when I told him so.

This afternoon I borrowed from the YMCA library, *When Valmond Came to Pontiac*, by Gilbert Parker, but did not very much care for it.

---

6. Phrenology was the study of the shape and protuberances of the skull, based on the now discredited belief that they reveal character traits and mental capacity.

7 February (Wednesday)

Received a delayed postcard from Abram Marienberg written at Cardiff. It read:

> *I failed to get along with you and am joining infantry, being posted to Training Reserve Brigade, Prees Heath. I am already equipped. Prees Heath is 8 or 9 miles from Bettisfield, so in spite of the fact that they have not been generous enough to put two volunteer friends together, we shall be able to see each other occasionally.*

Chapter 5

GUNNERY

8 February (Thursday)

We have commenced gun drill, using obsolete pieces that probably served in previous wars. Our first gunnery instructor was Bombardier Sinclair, a sour-faced, bow-legged individual with an exaggerated opinion of his own importance. I dislike him very much because he called me a shirker during one of the gun drills.

We were practising a drill called 'action front', at which order a man goes to each gun wheel, and by forcing the spokes in the opposite direction to his neighbour, the direction of the muzzle is reversed. The Gunner on the opposite wheel, a strong, hefty, 15-stoner, forced his wheel around before I had shifted mine out of its rut, with the result that I was subjected to an ill-tempered criticism. It was the word 'shirker' that made me wince, and I should have liked to have called him a liar, but knew that would have meant further humiliations and the Guard Room.

Afterwards someone told me that Sinclair held the opinion that all recruits arriving these days were conscripts.

I have just completed my first experience on guard. The squad consisted of an NCO, six guards and a waiting man. The smartest man on parade is selected by the inspecting officer as waiting man, but the officer last evening was unorthodox and chose the eldest man, whose sole duties were bringing our meals, running errands and temporarily relieving us when necessary. The period lasted 24 hours, each of the guards having to do 2 hours on and 4 off in rotation throughout the period. Two guards were out at a time, one outside the office, and on the roadside, not far from and known as 'The Main Gate Guard'. We tossed up for turns and my first beat was at the Main Gate from 9 pm until 11 pm.

Felt very proud and important pacing to and fro with my shouldered rifle. An officer and a NCO came to inspect me here, and the officer cunningly asked me if he could examine my rifle, but having been well prepared by the instructors for this and other possible traps, I refused definitely, experiencing the rare thrill of refusing to obey the request of an officer.

He seemed satisfied and he and the NCO marched away. After 10 pm everyone had to be challenged, and I enjoyed the experience of abruptly stopping all comers with a loud and imperious 'Halt! Who comes there?', and to the invariable reply, 'Friend', a less-stern command, 'Pass friend, all's well.' After a 4-hour sleep, fully dressed in the Guard Room, dimly lit by an evil-smelling hurricane lamp (the electric power is switched off at 11 pm), I did my second beat from 3 am to 5 am. Here I realised how much an 8lb rifle can make the shoulder ache. Reluctantly, for I hate to criticise the Army, I began to think what a farce this guard business was. Here was I marching to and fro with an unloaded rifle, drilling with as much precision and discipline as I would had a drill sergeant been watching me. There was not a soul to witness whether I did it or not. Was it just a stupid perpetuation of tradition, or was it an important lesson in military discipline? I forced myself to think it was. In the dark woods behind me, hooting owls disturbed the otherwise perfect stillness of the early morning. Rabbits and rats crept up softly, in pairs to my feet, when I kept motionless, but bounced and streaked away when the cold morning air made me commence another period of brisk marching.

12 February (Monday)

The Brigade brass band, numbering about 50, gave us a rousing concert at the 'YM'. The conductor looked both unmusical and unmilitary-like, but those were trivial defects when under his able baton the band played delightful selections from 'The Bing-Boys', and a lively medley of American tunes from a suite called 'Americana', by Thurban. In the rear an energetic and overworked drummer boomed, smashed and crashed at about six percussion instruments, so that at times we expected the noise and vibration to cave in the roof. In the front row, with legs crossed were several sturdy clarinet players and I decided that were I a musician capable of playing in such a band, a clarinet would be the instrument of my choice. In between the band selections a chivalrous-looking flautist, wearing a long-service medal ribbon, played some solos, and a Welshman, Gunner Lewis, sang 'My Dreams'. I was proud of this fellow countryman, standing there, raven haired, short and sturdy, a typical Celt, and singing with an uncommonly beautiful lyrical tenor voice, so faultlessly this moving song of Tosti's. With the rest of the audience I revelled in all of it and experienced emotions of a thawing kind, and I know that I shall be straining my musical memory until I have pieced together some of tonight's lovely music.

13 February (Tuesday)

The food here is very satisfactory and at times attempts are made to vary it. This morning for breakfast we had porridge and bacon. For dinner we had meat, potatoes and carrots, with duff as the sweet. These days, for tea, we get either tinned salmon, loaf cake, cold meat or cheese. Very occasionally we get a supper of gippo and biscuits. At farms in the vicinity six eggs may be bought for a shilling.

The camp is kept very clean and orderly at all times by 'category' men. One of these men walks around every morning with a canvas bag and a spiked pole, picking up every scrap of paper and litter. Lately extra cleaning and polishing has been done, and the camp was spic and span for the inspection by a General which took place today. When he arrived our class was doing physical drill. His large, shining car flashed in the sunlight, and a bugler heralded his approach to the Brigade Officer. First he inspected our mounted parade and as the detachment came nearer us I noticed that one of the General's Aides-de-Camp wore a kilt. On their way to the gun park the detachment stopped in front of our squad, I being one of several in it to whom the General spoke. Placing his hand on my shoulder in a fatherly way he asked me confidentially where I was from and if we were being treated all right. Very definitely I replied in the affirmative. This incident has bucked me so much that I have resolved to make soldiering my career. He was quite an orthodox General, portly, florid-faced, a large white moustache and rows of medal ribbons. This evening, from the Order Sheet posted up in the Salvation Army hut, I learned that he was Major General Sir W.R. Pitcairn-Campbell of the Western Command.[1]

16 February (Friday)

The people of Fforestfach continue to be very kind to me. They have sent me a beautifully knitted khaki scarf. Aunt Nannie has been appointed assistant church organist.

Gradually I become acquainted with gun drill, and the angle of incidence, the trajectory, the axis of the piece, the trunnions and the other language of gunner is less like Greek to us than it was a week ago. The guns, camouflaged in jigsaw-puzzle-pattern style, with green and brown paints, prove that artillery cannot exist without art. Among the instructors, some of the officers and NCOs have returned after active service, and especially those from the Western Front have a strained look, but this may be only my imagination. One of the Sergeants has a homely way of speaking, and when explaining the use of a dial sight he bids us look through the 'lickle owl'.

At times, on the exposed gun park we feel cold, and recently we were given a race to warm us. The distance was about 150yd, about 50 men took part and Palmer, my Swansea friend, smiling broadly, romped in an easy first. Palmer, whose place in the hut is next to mine, is as talkative as ever. He reckons that I look better every day, due to the fresh air and physical drill. Palmer has a complexion like a peach, protruding eyes and thinning hair, parted in the middle to look its maximum. He is excitable, has a puckish laugh, and bony legs – the same thickness from ankle to knee, which are not improved by the way he winds on his puttees. He should reserve more of the cloth for his calves, but I don't like to tell him about it.

When I congratulated him on winning today's race, he grinned, chuckled and said, 'I'm like the champion walker. I gave them a run for their money.'

He then surprised me by informing me that he had been a sprinter, and

---

1. Lieutenant General Sir William Pitcairn-Campbell, KCB (1856–1933). Commissioned in the King's Royal Rifle Corps in 1875 and holding the rank of Colonel by 1900, Pitcairn-Campbell served in the Sudan (1884–85) with the Mounted Infantry Camel Corps. During the Second Boer War (1899–1902) he commanded the 1st Battalion, King's Royal Rifle Corps and a Column in the Eastern Transvaal. In South Africa, Pitcairn-Campbell was three times mentioned in despatches. He also served as an ADC to King Edward VII. Back in England he was General Officer Commanding (GOC) 3 Brigade, Aldershot Command (1904–8), GOC 5th Division in Irish Command (1909–13). During the First World War Pitcairn-Campbell served as GOC Southern Command (4 August 1914–7 March 1916) and GOC Western Command (8 March 1916–4 August 1918).

he gave me a useful tip. 'Except in short distances,' he advised, 'always run the first half of the distance without strain, especially if the first half is up hill as it was today. By so doing you reserve your strength and wind for the second half.' One night Palmer took me to the Wet Canteen where we sat around a small table and supped beer from thick heavy glasses. The room was fogged by tobacco smoke, and shiny faced Gunners talked loudly in order to be heard in the awful din.

19 February (Monday)

Today our NCO paired us for semaphore signalling practice. The messages we flagged across to each other were in military terms and the urgency of some of them was amusing. Tonight we enjoyed a fine concert at the YMCA, the principal entertainers being Gunner Jepson and his wife, ex-music-hall artistes, who, it was rumoured, had appeared at the London Coliseum. Jepson and his wife sang one or two captivating duets which brought the house down. The YMCA was packed, the front rows being occupied by impeccably groomed officers. Jepson possesses a surpassing baritone voice, is a consummate entertainer, playing as finely as he sang a grand piano, accompanying himself and also for the duets. Among the songs he sang were 'Pearl of Sweet Ceylon', 'Rosebuds in My Lady's Hair', a cute little lovely ditty which ended with the words, 'And the little maid said Amen', and a mischievous song of which Jepson rapidly taught us the chorus. We enjoyed it and sang it enthusiastically, the words being:

I try to be good, but the girls won't let me,
The girls won't let me be. Oh! Those glad eyes beaming everywhere.
How they make me feel – well, I don't care.
I do not get home 'til the morning early,
One, two three – or four.
I try to be good but the girls won't let me,
So I'm not trying any more.

The Battery postman followed with two violin solos – Raff's 'Cavatina' and 'Phantom Melody', played faultlessly and with wonderful artistic feeling. This musician has a most sensitive face, is innately shy, speaks quietly and when walking sags slightly at the knees. He seems a real artist and his playing elevates me into moods of aspiration. A roguish-looking elocutionist gave a humorous rendering of Longfellow's 'Village Blacksmith' in which he impersonated the singing of the famous poem by a crude rustic who is made to accompany his singing with exaggerated but significant gestures. For instance, the word 'chestnut' was accompanied by a vigorous smack on the performer's chest and head. The audience, rocking with laughter, demanded an encore, and we were treated to a complete change, with a very touching impersonation of an old soldier reciting a poem called 'I Forget'. The fragments I remember went as follows:

T'was out in South Africa we captured De Wet.
Or did he capture us? I forget. I forget.

And ended impressively with the old soldier hoping that when for him the last trump should call, his Maker would mercifully FORGET.

There followed a flute solo, a tenor solo and then a 'C' Battery star sang with gusto a rollicking shanty, the chorus of which the audience delighted in and sang again with abandon:

I love to be a sailor, a sailor, a sailor,
I love to sail across the ocean blue,
Yes I do – oo – oo.
I love to be a sailor, a sailor, a sailor,
Sailing on the good ship Kangaroo.

20 February (Tuesday)

Mud is ankle deep in the camp so that one may have two kinds of baths here now – the usual kind or a mud bath. It has rained all day, so we have had indoor lectures on range finding, the dial sight and aiming posts. It is pleasant to imagine that one is back in school. The range finder was jointly invented by two professors, Archibald Barr and William Stroud. The dial sight, fixed on the gun, is focused on an aiming post positioned in front of the gun. As the gun jumps off target after firing, it can be brought back to it by manipulating an instrument which brings it in alignment with the aiming post. Aiming posts can be illuminated at night time. The scarf from Fforestfach is so warm that it will need very cold weather to penetrate through it.

Assembled in 'C' Battery Canteen, we were given a lecture on venereal disease by the camp medical officer who holds the rank of Captain. He urged the necessity of immediate notification should anyone contract it, and described the symptoms so realistically – for instance, he used the words 'like pissing fish hooks' – that Gunner B, a pale-faced, large-headed individual, fainted and had to be assisted out of the room.

22 February (Thursday)

Some of Hut 15 men are ready to go abroad. The older men are going either to Egypt or India. Salonika too claims many of our comrades, a draft of about 40 leaving twice weekly. Some of these men have been trained here from four to six months and we look upon them as veterans. Palmer still insists that I look better every day. In fact since being here I have increased my weight from 8 stone 13 pounds to 9 stone 5 pounds. Palmer has applied for a few days' leave in order to do work of national importance – attending to his garden.

Received letter from Abram, written on notepaper bearing the stamp of Whitchurch Soldier's Home. His address is:

Private A.G. Marienberg, 3/9113,
Hut 14, E Company, 50th Training Reserve Brigade,
No. 7 Camp, Prees Heath,
WHITCHURCH, Salop

He writes stating that he has been in hospital, very ill with flu, but that things are looking brighter now. He adds:

I think the first fortnight the worst. To be candid, I hate writing about the military side of our life so many times, though I will say this, that if the Army has its disadvantages, so also has its advantages. It teaches you adaptability to probable conditions, repose and mates. It does away with false pride and domesticates you. The obvious danger of Army Life is that it tends to destroy individuality, unless you are very alert... Today I had a game of football, in goal, and our hut won 2-1.

27 February (Tuesday)

Received letter from W.T. Davies, our theological student friend. The letter comes from France where he is serving as a Private in the 45th Field Ambulance. He writes: 'Since you told me your intention was to join the Navy, I was somewhat surprised to find that you are in the RFA.' When I reply I shall have to explain that a temporarily closed Royal Navy Recruiting Office was the means of Abram and I becoming soldiers instead of sailors. I shall add that I am perfectly satisfied with the RFA.

A cousin of mine, Harold Hanson, of Scrutari Row, Taibach, has been killed by a sniper in France. Volunteering for service when he could have been exempted, he became a Signaller in the Royal Welsh Fusiliers.

2 March (Friday)

The Gunners are divided into four classes. Last Wednesday, with seven other fellows, I was promoted from Class 4 to Class 2. I wrote home rather proudly about it, but have since then been thinking that my mother won't be as pleased as I about it, as in her view it is a step nearer active service. At the gun park we are sometimes visited by the O/C of 'C' Battery, Major Bertram Ford.[2] Immaculately uniformed, he sits on a satin-coated charger, wears pince-nez and has a sprouting moustache. The men dread his censure and during his presence officers and NCOs shout louder their commands and we load into the breeches with increased speed dummy projectiles made of wood. If the Major's scrutiny reveals any defect in the drill, in a rasping voice he chastises the offender with the peculiar phrase, 'Oh! You horrible man.' Today we were again inspected by a General. When

2. Son of Major William Henry Ford, he was born at Wolverhampton in 1869. After leaving Wolverhampton Grammar School he qualified as an accountant and became a Fellow of the Institute of Chartered Accountants. During the First World War, as a Territorial officer, he took his battery to France, only to be invalided home before going into action, and was relegated to home service for the rest of the war. His professional engagements included auditing the accounts of the *Birmingham Post* and the *Birmingham Evening Mail*. Under Lord Illife, Ford became managing director of the two newspapers. He died in 1955.

he arrived on the gun park, our class, wearing gas helmets, were doing gun drill. The guns are camouflaged with crazy patches of brown and green paints, so far the only art I have seen in the Army.

3 March (Saturday)

This afternoon a few of us strolled out to a hamlet called Welshampton, about 3 miles distant from the camp.

The countryside surrounding us is charming and we shall have plenty of time and opportunities to study and enjoy its loveliness. In modest beauty short-stemmed daisies dotted the hedgerow bases, and also celandine of shining varnished yellow. The fields were manured, and feathered creatures were very active.

At our approach numerous thrushes and a wren retreated passively, but blackbirds fled with agitated protests. Furry catkins trembled on their parent boughs, and bushes of gorse with pure chrome yellow bloom lit up the scene. Then we arrived at Welshampton, a pretty village, composed of a cluster of sleeping cottages, spotless, with leaded-light windows and generous gardens. All this we had reluctantly to leave, as we were due back at the camp stables by 4 pm to water and feed the horses. I am getting used to the horses and now fear them much less, though recently, during the exercising of them I was kicked above the knee. We were in a field and were each leading two horses. When crossing a narrow ditch, one of my beasts suddenly made a bid for freedom, darting off and letting out viciously with his hind legs. One of his hoofs caught me, and although it only glanced off my leg, it lamed me for a few minutes and I was forced to let go the reins of one of the mounts. I got told off vigorously by the cadaverous-looking Lieutenant in charge.

Today I received from Swansea Recruiting Office my 'Calling Up' notice, which had been posted to my former address at Fforestfach. What an insult. How I enjoyed enlightening them. When I enlisted the minimum age for military service was 18 and 8 months, so I actually volunteered underage. Now the minimum age has been reduced to 18 years. The oldest recruit here is about 38 years of age and in a letter home I described them as elderly men. I have read that the age of enlistment for Roman soldiers ranged from 17 to 46 years.

7 March (Wednesday)

On guard at the Brigade Office. It is called the main guard, being more important and busier than the other guard. Here we were inspected by the Regimental Sergeant Major, a frigid disciplinarian with a voice that freezes us. He has nearly completed his Army service. He has a daughter, who we hear, revealed her knowledge of ju-jitsu on an occasion when a man tried to take liberties with her. The weather is fine but cold. Tuesday night we had a snowstorm and tonight the prisoners, seven or eight of them, begged our NCO to be allowed to come around our stove. When everything became quiet the NCO risked it and the prisoners filed in from the cell that is part of the Guard Room, and settled down appreciatively around the stove to recount details of the offences that had earned them their ignominious isolation. One small, wiry fellow named Davies had deserted, known in the Army as 'jumping it', and had enjoyed three months in civvy life until an in-law, with whom he was on bad terms, reported him to the police. For that he had served a sentence in Bedford Jail. I seized the opportunity of inspecting the cells, and read the elaborate pornographic prose and poetry on the grey walls. They were profusely illustrated and were legacies of a legion of former defaulters. From that abominable accumulation of filth which I found debasing and disturbing but alluring, one might obtain a depraved, distorted, yet complete knowledge of sexual intercourse.

Theoretically my sexual education was greatly extended tonight. Some time ago a prisoner escaped from this Guard Room. After being giving permission to go to the lavatory, the guards who thought he was taking a long time, found that he had escaped by burrowing under the lavatory wall, This wall of this lavatory has also been used by the 'scribes', but mostly for humorous observations such as 'Always carry your gas mask'.

9 March (Friday)

Last night there was a heavy snowfall, and today, as it is still falling, we were kept indoors listening to lectures. In the camp gardens are being cultivated, the chief intention being to augment our potato supply. Recently potatoes have been so scarce that we have been given rice as a substitute.

10 March (Saturday)

Bob Palmer has a beautiful boy and girl. A coloured photograph of them hangs above his bed. He has been on a musketry course, and at the ranges had done very well. After securing passes last night Bob and I went by train via Whitchurch to Prees Heath Camp where 20,000 men are being trained. One of them mistook our bandoliers for Sam Brown belts and saluted us. We acknowledged the salute with as much dignity as we could muster. An infantry platoon marched by and they seemed to have been perfectly drilled. Had no difficulty in finding Abram Marienberg's hut, and after waiting there a few minutes, he arrived all smiles, and looking very fit, in spite of the fact that he had again been in hospital, this time with a sore throat, and also he had been inoculated. Very closely cropped hair did not improve his appearance, but we understand that is the regulation style here. While Abram had tea in his hut Bob and I had some light refreshments in the Dry Canteen, after which the three of us were photographed together. Owing to his inoculation Abram was not allowed out of the camp, so we entered the camp cinema and saw the film of *The Battle of the Ancre*,[3] Bob and I being particularly interested in the 18-pounder guns which in real action seemed so spiteful and savage.

---

3. The full title of this British official film is *The Battle of the Ancre and the Advance of the Tanks*.

Chapter 6

SIGNALLING

15 March (Thursday)

For some time I have been interested in the signal section of the camp. A large number of men are being trained as Signallers here, and are drawn from each of the four Batteries. There is one Signaller in this hut, O'Reilly, and I have watched him and others trailing their flags back and forth to the Signal School. I like the look of these fellows somehow, and am sure signalling must be very interesting work. The section is named by the others as 'The Intelligence Department', and by those who have returned from France, 'The Suicide Club', which was why Palmer chuckled and replied 'Nothing Doing', when I suggested that we join the Signallers. However, I was quietly convinced that danger or no danger, it was the job for me, and when I read a notice outside the Battery Office asking for volunteers for the Signal Section, I applied yesterday for a transfer. My request was granted, and today I commenced at the Signal School where a Sergeant said, 'You've made a good move, for among other things you'll be taught a trade – telegraphy. What use will a knowledge of gunnery be to you after the war?' Corporal Webster praised the merits of former 'C' Battery men, being one himself. The Signal School is up on the hillside, near the gun park. From 'C' Battery our shortest cut is around a pond on which a snow-white swan glides gracefully. The weather is now very fine, in fact, it has been so summer-like during the last few days that we were instructed to discard greatcoats.

24 March (Saturday)

We have done a considerable amount of flag drill, learning after the alphabet and numerals many abbreviations. Flag drill tires the arms to a surprising extent and is certainly a harder job than it looks. Frequent arm rests are necessary. We practise in a dell and as we go through the alphabet the instructor keeps us in time by shouting 'Iddy umpty, Umpty iddy iddy iddy, Umpty iddy umpty iddy', the iddy corresponding to a dot and the umpty to a dash in the Morse code.

At this stage in our progress we are frequently stopped as a squad because our flag drill is 'Like washing on a clothesline'. I am now able to read fairly well Morse by flag and buzzer. Signallers are exempted from 'fatigues' such as grooming and orderly work. We finish our duties at 5 every evening and at 11 am on a Saturday, and there is a half-holiday every Wednesday to compensate for occasional night signalling we shall have to do.

29 March (Thursday)

Apart from our duties, life in the camp would be boring were it not for the hospitable recreational rooms of the YMCA and the Salvation Army. At the YMCA I occasionally borrow a book, and one evening I played a game of billiards with Wheeler Pritchard who hails from Risca. Pritchard has three brothers in the Army, one an officer in a kilted regiment. My friendships are now becoming matters of choice rather than chance. Palmer and I are still on the best of terms, but we are inevitably drifting from each other. Neither of us mention it, but we are both aware of it. Pritchard and I get on together splendidly, becoming friends in an effortless manner, simply because we like the same things and frequent the same places. Tonight at the YMCA we heard speak Dr Bruce and Canon Hicks. Dr Bruce delivered a very fine lecture entitled 'Birds, Beasts and Padres', amplifying his talk with lantern slides. Canon Hicks, who has done great work among the soldiers, tonight gave us a very candid talking-to and afterwards shook hands with us all. The Salvation Army hut is controlled by a Salvation Army officer and his wife, who has the face of a madonna.

He has skin like alabaster and soft black flowing hair. I was there last night writing a letter, as the bedlam in Hut 15 sometimes makes such an act impossible. On the orders posted up on the notice board there I read that our Commandant is Sir Godfrey Thomas DSO.[1] He is a handsome old gentleman and his tunic breast has several rows of medal ribbons. Last evening in this Salvation Army hut a fellow played 'Annie Laurie' on the piano; and a military policeman, returned from the Front sang Fletcher's 'The Holy City'.

Hundreds of men who were here when we joined the camp have gone abroad, their places filled by recruits. Three weeks ago a number of C1 category men, employed in the camp as hut orderlies, etc., were drafted to the Labour Corps. They were led away by the band.

1 April (Sunday)

Walked with Wheeler Pritchard and Gunner J.R. Evans to Bronington, a hamlet about four miles away. Evans comes from Carmarthen, is a schoolmaster, a BSc and a wit. He is a burly chap with closely cropped hair beginning to grey. He confessed to me that he owed his entry into the RFA by giving a recruiting sergeant a 2s 6d tip and by asking him if there were any vacancies in the Camel Corps. The woods we skirted were draped in gentle shades of green. A thrush alighted on a boundary wall and stood motionless for us to admire her immaculate fawn coat.

An old lady cordially invited us to tea in a cottage that was so clean that we might safely have eaten off the floor if necessary.

2 April (Monday)

All those under 19 years of age will soon be drafted to another camp. A week ago about 40 left for the Artillery Reserve, Norfolk. Being underage, I expect every moment to receive orders.

It will be a change living on the East Coast, probably at some seaside resort, but I shall regret leaving dear old Bettisfield. Where could you find a nicer, quieter camp? Besides, on the whole, there are rather a fine lot of men training here now. Recently we have had much snow and at present it

1. Brigadier General Sir Godfrey Vinnoles Thomas, 9th Baronet Thomas of Wenvoe in Glamorgan. He saw service with the Royal Artillery in Afghanistan (1878–80), the Egyptian Campaign of 1882, the Sudan (1884) and the Second Boer War (1899–1902). In South Africa Thomas was twice mentioned in despatches and awarded the Distinguished Service Order. Between 1909 and 1911 he commanded 3rd Division artillery and held the same position for the 24th Division between 1914 and 1915. During 1916 and 1917 Thomas commanded No. 2 Reserve Brigade, RFA (TF). He was a Companion of the Order of the Bath (CB) and Commander of the Order of the British Empire (CBE). He died on 17 February 1919 aged 62.

is knee deep in camp. In Hut 15 there is a nightly argument over the opening of windows, the fresh-air enthusiasts, of which I am sensible enough to be one, usually winning. This morning some of us awoke to find ourselves nearly snowbound in our beds and we were subjected to a good many 'I told you so' from our opponents. This afternoon the weather was so bad that Lieutenant Ince,[2] officer in charge of the Signal School, gave us an indoor general lecture on signalling. Ince is a very decent officer and has an athletic body, although I always think his appearance is spoiled by the absence from his cap of a spring for lifting up the front of the crown which, without it, lies too flat on the rim.

6 April (Good Friday)

We are elated at having duties excused until Tuesday. After lunch walked with Pritchard and J.R. Evans to Sarn, a picturesque village 6 miles from the camp. Having been before, Pritchard acted as guide, and on the way he pointed out the distant snow-capped mountains of Wales. At Sarn we knocked on the door of an inn and a head emerged inquiringly from a latticed window above. We were welcomed and ushered into a well-furnished room which had in it a cheery fire burning in its low grate.

On the piano Evans played several pieces from the Star Folio which I discovered amid a pile of music. Several of the Star Folios were among my sister's collection of music. Oh, the luxury of that tea. Bread and butter beautifully cut and tasting deliciously; home-made cakes and jam, and tea served not in pudding basins but in exquisite porcelain; refinements I had almost forgotten existed after three months of military camp fare. After tea our hostess carried in a gramophone and a pile of records. As we returned a new moon appeared and Pritchard timed us to reach the camp just in time to catch the 'Selly Ack' (Salvation Army) hut open for a cup of tea before retiring. We are all heartened by the recent news that the USA has declared war on Germany.

2. Later Sir Godfrey Ince GCB, KBE, BSc. In 1955 Ivor received Christmas greetings from Cyril Bunker, then Manager of an Employment Exchange in Staffordshire, in which he wrote: 'You will be interested to know that I had the pleasure of meeting Sir Godfrey Ince, our Permanent Secretary (Ministry of Labour) who is retiring shortly. This was at a meeting of Midland Region officers. He was delighted to meet one of his old 'boys'. He told me that Sergeant Morrison was at Denton (Lancs)'. In 1957 Bunker wrote informing Ivor that Sir Godfrey was then Chairman of Cable and Wireless Ltd. The Royal Academy exhibition of 1958 included a portrait of Sir Godfrey by Harold Knight RA.

9 April (Easter Monday)

Walked with Pritchard to Whitchurch, passing through pretty lanes and quaint villages. One village had a pump on its square and some of the buildings were timbered and looked Elizabethan.

On entering Whitchurch we were forced to shelter from a violent hail storm. At the Soldier's Rest we scanned a few magazines, then at the Soldier's Club we had for 1s 5d each a good tea of bread and butter, eggs and pastries.

The club contained a piano, library, periodicals and games. By the yellow band across their shoulder straps, recognised two of Abram's Company, and inquiring, learned from them that my friend had that morning gone home on leave.

Afterwards we went to the local cinema and enjoyed seeing Sir John Hare in Goldsmith's classic, *The Vicar of Wakefield*.

10 April (Tuesday)

The weather is still wintry and there is still plenty of snow about. This afternoon we practised signalling with lamps of two kinds, the electric kind and the oil type named Begbie.

After this our class had a buzzer reading test, having to read at a speed of 30 letters or 6 words per minute. A friend named Cyril Bunker and I had 'R Don', which is the signalling abbreviation for read correctly.

I am now looking forward to my first weekend leave at home. The application I made last Saturday was unsuccessful, but I understand that every week about 15 Signallers are granted weekends, so my turn to apply will come soon.

13 April (Friday)

One of our number became insane, and was recently removed from the camp. His name was Blackett. I saw him chase imaginary rats around Hut 15 one day. He flogged them with a huge stick. It was after he marched onto the parade ground and ordered the assembly to dismiss that they sent him away.

16 April (Monday)

'C' Battery provides two huts for its Signallers, Huts 22 and 23. Yesterday, with the other Hut 15 Signallers, I was instructed by Bombardier Walton to move into Hut 22. At first I disliked the idea of a change, feeling sorry to leave Hut 15, but already I am beginning to realise the advantages of having all the Signallers together, and what a fine lot of fellows my new hutmates are. The senior NCO at the Signal School is Sergeant Major Garvey, an old-timer, wearing the Rooty Medal ribbon.[3] He is a large, ungainly individual, with a short temper, but a heart of gold, they say. This afternoon he gave us a lesson in knot tying.

I already knew the reef, sheepshank, clove hitch and bowline, and tied them all correctly, thanks again to the training in the Boy Scouts years ago.

18 April (Wednesday)

Our camp has again been inspected on two occasions, last Friday by Brigadier General Fox, and today by Major General Sir Pitcairn-Campbell.

19 April (Thursday)

The YMCA continues to stage excellent features for our amusement and edification. Last Friday evening we heard an address by the Rev'd R.J. Paterson, who has gained some renown as the founder of the 'Catch-My-Pal' movement.[4] In the camp there is a detachment of the Royal Garrison Artillery, physically bigger men on the average than the RFA men, very disciplined and very fine marchers. Tuesday night they gave us a first-rate concert, one of the best numbers being given by a Scot who sang with vigorous abandon the Harry Lauder songs, 'I Love a Lassie' and 'Romain' in the Gloamin''. Tonight Bombardier Jepson, who is now a musketry instructor, gave another of his superlative entertainments.

22 April (Sunday)

This afternoon Gunner Thompson gave an organ recital at Hanmer church. Even with the addition of desks from the schoolroom, the seating accommodation was inadequate. The church is illuminated with oil lamps.

---

3. Army slang for the Long Service and Good Conduct Medal. It comes from an old Army term from bread, which comes from Urdu: 'Roti'. The derivation comes from the idea that as the holder has spent many years eating Army rations he probably deserves a medal.
4. Paterson was known as 'Catch-My-Pal' after the Presbyterian-backed temperance organisation he founded in 1909. The movement met with much success in Northern Ireland and England. It was one of many temperance groups popular from the mid-nineteenth century that attempted to tackle the problems caused by alcohol through a call for abstinence.

Thompson is a 'C' Battery Signaller and lives in Hut 23. This afternoon he played in a masterly way, but I admit I was rather bored, because a pipe organ is not one of my favourite instruments and the music was beyond me. In between, several artists of note sang solos.

26 April (Thursday)
At the YMCA a lantern lecture was given on Mexico by a gentleman who had lived there. It was very interesting and instructive.

27 April (Friday)
Today our class completed its first telephony course which has lasted a fortnight. It commenced with a simple general lecture, which I had to force myself to be interested in. However, the practical part was more interesting and we worked in pairs with a portable 'Don 3' telephone each. The way the earth conducts the electric current was a revelation to those of us who were new to the subject. One day, under the supervision of Sergeant Major Garvey, whose short temper was strained to breaking point, most of the time, we laid a cable for a long distance.

In places we had to climb trees to hang the cable, and we crossed roads by erecting tall, slight poles, if no trees were available.

28 April (Saturday)
The weather is glorious and I am becoming bronzed. This morning we Signallers had a roundabout route march to Horseman's Green. Patches of lace-like May blossoms enlivened the hedges at whose bases celandine shone brightly, while pink and white daisies and seeded dandelions adorned the meadows.

Gunner Benison is the Beau Brummell of Hut 22. He spends more than the average time over his toilet and causes much amusement when he stands on a form in order to wind on his puttees, aided by the mirror fixed on the hut wall. He commissioned the tailor to alter his tunic and breeches, and with cap at a rakish angle, leather-pleated lanyard, fancy flags (for which he has not yet qualified) on his sleeve, jingling spurs and riding whip, he marches up and down the hut a few times whistling 'Stars and

Stripes', then marches out of the hut and proceeds to Wem where we tease him he has a girl. When new clothes are coveted, say previous to a leave, it is not unusual to see someone carefully sandpapering a hole in the knee of his breeches or the elbow of his tunic, or some other conspicuous place, then going to the Quarter Master with a tale of woe. So many of us are dressed alike that it is refreshing to meet with a difference, a cap badge of another regiment for instance.

About tea time Abram and a friend arrived, having walked from Prees Heath. As it has been a fine day they enjoyed the walk and the scenery.

On Saturdays so many leave the camp that rations are plentiful, so Abram and his friend had tea with us in Hut 22. As the walk from Prees Heath had tired them we only went as far as Hanmer Mere, which I showed them with a measure of pride. They were charmed by it, and I shall not be surprised if Abram is inspired to write an ode to it. We sat among the daisies on the green carpeted bank. On the opposite side of the mere were brilliant splashes of rhododendrons. Gnats danced in swarms before us and swallows made rapid swoops and dives at them. Afterwards I took my friends around our camp and they were very interested in an 18-pounder gun, which to them looked so smart, so neat and so deadly. They thought our RFA uniforms very smart. I pointed out that the difference was due to the riding breeches which accentuates the figure more than the footsoldier's slacks. It was our common experience that we could always tell a new recruit. However carefully dressed, there is always something indefinable about a recruit that gives him away. From the gun park we watched the sun, like a ripe orange, slide down behind a bar of pale-mauve cloud, then we watched pictures of another sort at the camp cinema, but we had so much to tell each other that little notice was taken of the films. After coffee at the YMCA we walked to the railway station where our friends had a train at about 10 pm.

29 April (Sunday)

After tea walked with Pritchard and Evans to Horseman's Green, and for the first time this year we heard the cuckoo, but a long way off. The country is a feast of colour now, bushes of may enlivening the hedges, patches of chrome gorse, dark olive-green fir plantations, relieved by clumps of livid crimson rhododendrons. Bullfinches, yellow-beaked blackbirds and fawn thrushes disappeared at our approach, and young rabbits, caught off their beat, ran stupidly hither and thither, until they mustered themselves for a bound to safety. Outside a villa named 'The Poplars' we paused for some time to admire a wonderful garden ablaze with spring flowers. An elderly woman came out and graciously invited us into her garden.

She said her gardener was 80 years of age and that consequently she had to do a considerable amount of gardening herself. The house took its name from the eight tall, graceful poplars that screened one side of the garden. It was her intention to have the trees photographed in moonlight.

I have just finished reading a touching Western yarn, *The Sky Pilot*, by Ralph Connor. The slow, drawling speech of the ranchmen is perfectly presented, and in one of the early chapters there is this fine description of a sunset: 'The sun had taken his plunge, but he had left behind his robes of saffron and gold.' In a later chapter, the parson, a lovable individual, makes this criticism of his raw audience: 'You all do just what pleases you regardless of any other, and so help one another down.'

30 April (Monday)

Hut orderly for the first time. Now that the 'category' men have been drafted away we each shall have to take a daily turn at it. Secretly I dreaded the approach of my turn, but after tackling it, I thought it easy, and I found the complete change of work restful. For dinner we had herrings which the men decided tasted badly and they asked Corporal Walton to make a complaint. When the Orderly Officer arrived and his Orderly NCO shouted, 'Any Complaints?', Walton stood and very courteously replied, 'Yes Sir. The men complain that the fish is tainted.' The officer stepped forward, bravely tasted a piece of fish said, 'I find nothing wrong with it' and marched out followed by the NCO. Some went dinnerless, others were more persevering, and all had some caustic things to say about the Orderly Officer.

This evening had a long talk with Walton who has recently been promoted to Corporal. He complimented me on the way I had cleaned and tidied up the hut during the day. He told me of one of the Signallers, that he actually liked being in the Army, a state of mind that amazes the majority whose chief ambition seems to be to get 'demobbed'. Though I share that Signaller's feelings, I was ashamed to admit it to Walton. Walton comes from Chester.

Early in the war he was drafted East with the Cheshires and he told me the following story of an experience in Egypt:

One day we were entrained at a railway station and a small native boy carried over to us a pitcher of very welcome drinking water. As our train steamed away an ANZAC soldier teased the child by holding the pitcher just out of his reach.

Breathlessly the little fellow ran alongside the accelerating train, and when it seemed he must daunt, the soldier released the vessel which the boy missed so that it crashed in pieces on the track. That kid, hunched up and weeping on the track was about the most pathetic sight I ever saw, and had that ANZAC been alone I'd have punched his bloody head for him.

4 May (Friday)
Among the drafts that have left the camp recently was one for Mesopotamia last Sunday night, equipped with khaki drill suits and pith helmets; and that of the Wheelers (wheelwrights) which left today for the RFA Depot at Winchester. With the latter went Pritchard, whose companionship some of us shall greatly miss. He had fine physique, shapely calves and looked a picture in uniform. He had soft, slightly wavy black hair and his pale handsome face emphasised his dark eyes. Perfectly mannered and poised, he seldom spoke, but always kindly and with a quiet firmness.

He was a perfect listener and while other people talked, he smoked a pipe, gave the speaker his complete attention and the bright twinkle that occasionally illuminated his eyes was more eloquent than words.

5 May (Saturday)
This morning Lieutenant Ince led the Signallers on a route march and it looked as though our athletic chief had mustered everybody for a livening

up. Burly Sergeant Morrison lumbered up and smiling wickedly said, 'You wait 'til Ince gets into his stride. He'll move your stumps for you.' Outside the camp boundaries we marched 'at ease' and some enthusiastic singing took place, 'Hey Ho, Totty will you go' seeming to be the favourite. A stupid fellow behind me kept stepping on my heels until I bawled at him, 'Keep your three pace distance man.' Then Ince began to step it out, the singing became less lively, died out and marching for most became a serious business. Tunics and shirts were torn open at the neck and the stouter marchers mopped their brows with sodden handkerchiefs. We returned via Hanmer where we had a welcome half-hour break. Morrison looked serious and as though he had had a Turkish bath. 'What did I tell you,' he stammered as he mopped his neck. We were dismissed in the centre of the village, near Copnall's store, and that worthy establishment must have sold its record number of oranges this morning.

7 May (Monday)

At present we have night signalling twice weekly and are on from 8.15 pm until 11 pm. In the Signal School there are four divisions or classes, each numbering about 40 men and named A, B, C and D, these letters called by Signallers Ack, Beer, C and Don, these and other letters whose sounds might be confused with those of other letters being given special names. On Tuesday last each of the divisions was photographed by Signaller Sharples of Hut 22. Officers and NCOs were included in the groups and a heliograph was placed in front of each. During the last week we had our general signalling tests and as a result I passed up today from Don to C Division.

19 May (Saturday)

Feeling extremely happy and excited proceeded home for my first weekend leave. My pass was routed 'London and North Western Railway'. After four months of constant polishing my brass and leather work is now easy to shine, but of course leave stimulates extra care so that my bandolier has come up to a fine condition. For it I use a mahogany coloured paste which, with plenty of elbow grease, has toned it so nicely that already two men have borrowed it to wear on their weekend leaves home. The lending is not so nice for me as I am usually left with a poor, colourless specimen of a bandolier. Benjamin Haycock, a corpulent and loveable old neighbour who amuses himself in his leisure by playing hymns, especially 'The mistakes of my life have been many', on a concertina, was one of the first to welcome me. He looked me up and down and said admiringly, 'My word you do look spruce', which this not too commonly used word helped to make unusually flattering. Almost everyone I meet says the following: 'When did you come home? You look well. When do you return?' and finally, 'See you again before you go back.' My sister, Nellie, discovered in my speech a slight brogue of which I was completely unaware.

13 May (Sunday)

Nellie took me for a walk up to the Goytre, where at the prison camp the prisoners were playing soccer. One or two of them returned my stare. I am told that some of them are naval men from the sunken armoured cruiser *Blucher*. Nellie told me that when they marched to Margam Steelworks, where they are engaged on its erection, she had noticed that one of them bore a striking resemblance to me. She added that it had upset my mother to see him. We met Major Llewellyn David of the local Battery of Royal Horse Artillery. He stopped us and after asking me a number of questions he eyed me up and down and flattered me by saying, 'Hanson, you're the smartest soldier in the British Army.'

14 May (Monday)

This morning I walked to the end of the South Breakwater which Taibach people call 'The Stone Pier'. German prisoners were labouring in Margam Steelworks, guarded by lazy looking sentries with fixed bayonets. I thought it must be a dull life aboard the gloomy looking ships coaling in the docks. One sailor played a concertina and another shouted to an errand boy on the quay, 'Wot time do the pubs open?' On the pier leading to the breakwater the timber footboards were wet and as slippery as ice, making walking perilous until I learned to tread on the large nailheads. Grey and white gulls matched a grey and white sea. Patches of mist hung over the shore and on the brows of the hills in the background, and a thin silver gleam of sunlight denoted the southern horizon. The waves thundered against the large concrete blocks at the breakwater's head and were cast high into fountains of white spray. Returning, I called to make a small purchase in Dangerfield's little sweet and newspaper shop. Lilian Haycock, Mrs Dangerfield's granddaughter, a buxom girl, about four years my senior, in a moment of patriotic zeal, flung her arms around my neck and kissed me audibly. After answering a few questions, I was about to leave, when to my astonishment, I was subjected to a repetition of the embrace, and feeling rather shaken and rather foolish, I bade her a hasty goodbye.

Left Port Talbot this evening, awaking after a refreshing nap at Shrewsbury, where Bettisfield men were informed that they would have to proceed via Crewe, where we arrived at 11.30 pm. At this important railway centre, with its many shining railroads and signal lights, hundreds of sailors and soldiers thronged the platforms. On an automatic weighing machine I learned that I was 9 stone 6 pounds, the heaviest yet for me. I was lucky in having one of my Bettisfield pals as a travelling companion on the outward and return journey. Near the railway station was a Soldier's and Sailor's Rest, congested with representatives of many regiments and ships. Here we passed the time trying to stimulate the veterans to talk, having tea and sandwiches or adding our names and observations to a ponderous visitor's book.

15 May (Tuesday)

We left Crewe at 2 am after some mischievous eavesdropping at the railway station. Our train was in a bay with a platform on one side only and hoardings on the other, and leaning out of our carriage window to enjoy the sights of platform activities, we saw enter into the first-class compartment adjoining ours two officers and two girls. Of that we thought nothing until we noticed that the blinds had been drawn. We retreated to the hoarding side to find the blinds carelessly undrawn, and to see a susceptible porter peeping over the base of the window. As he was breathing heavily we speedily joined him, arriving at that stage when one officer had removed a garter from his girl's leg. It was all very foolish to look at. Then someone over eager to see exposed himself too much, thus attracting the attention of one of the subalterns, who, extricating himself from his lover's arms, made for the carriage door, to find no one there, as we had swiftly re-entered our compartment while the porter hid beneath the coach.

By that time it was 2 am when we were due to leave. We arrived at Bettisfield about 3 am and after depositing our passes with the NCO in charge of the guard, laid down to a welcome sleep.

Later in the day Corporal Walton had news for me. Had I not been on leave, I should have been drafted with all the other underage lads to an infantry battalion at Frinton-on-Sea in Essex. Walton added that Lieutenant Ince and the Adjutant had 'squared' it. Discussing the Adjutant, Walton told me that as a ranker the Adjutant was offered a Commission or a decoration for distinguished conduct on the battlefield and that he chose a Commission.

16 May (Wednesday)

Leave is a tonic and from a distance one's home town can be seen in truer perspective. I return to my training with a new zest, though, after a re-taste of the comforts of home life, universal kindness, a soft bed and delicious food in variety, bare tables, tea basins and margarine are repulsive.

22 May (Tuesday)

This evening a party from the Royal Garrison Artillery, a Battery of which is stationed at Bettisfield Park Camp, gave us a grand Pierrot concert, which everyone enjoyed, especially the humorous items.

Each week the signalling work brings something fresh and interesting. Lately we have been doing much transmitting station work. This takes us far out into the country from which we return with enormous appetites.

23 May (Wednesday)

At present the weather is glorious, enabling outdoor sports to be added to our activities. The Signallers have raised a fairly good cricket team, composed of officers and men, and in their first match this evening they just managed to beat the team from Don Battery.

26 May (Saturday)

Anxious to discuss my leave with Abram, I went this afternoon to Whitchurch, and had a bus to the camp gates at Prees Heath. It was sunny and the doors of Abram's hut being open, I saw him lying on a form reading the Bible and on nearer examination discovered the book to be that of Job. His reply to my question whether he was trying to find the secret of Job's patience was lost in the hearty greeting he gave me. After a long chat we welcomed the arrival of tea which I shared with him in the hut. This over, Abram, with the assistance of a few friends, one of whom was named Pat, gave me an exhibition of bayonet fighting, which included a thrust at the junction of the neck and chin and what to do with the rifle butt if you missed. The side of the hut suffered some severe jabbing. Pat is a born humorist and Abram had quoted some of his witty sayings in his letters to Nellie. Nellie therefore asked Abram to share with Pat the contents of a parcel she sent him, Pat's comment on this being, 'Oi can see, O'ive been mentioned in despatches again.' Afterwards Abram and I bussed back to Whitchurch, sat and talked in a little park, went to the pictures, and then I returned with the 9.35 pm train.

28 May (Whit Monday)

Half-holiday. Spent the afternoon watching the Signallers eleven beat Don Battery at cricket by 17 runs. The match was played on the neatly trimmed lawn in front of Lord Kenyon's stately residence, Greddington Hall, an ivy clad mansion with a four-pillared porch entrance. Our band played popular pieces and among the spectators were many civilians. Our new Commandant, a Colonel, who has succeeded Sir Godfrey Thomas, and the Adjutant sat under a cedar tree. Lieutenant Ince was bowled for a duck. After tea I went to the pictures with a hut mate, Don J. Jones, a slim, boyish fellow from Aberystwyth, Don J. talked of his father, a member of a lifeboat crew who has saved many lives and received many honours and decorations. He also told me about the regimental rivalries existing between the Welsh and the Cheshires camping at Aberystwyth. In the end the quarrelling reached a serious state when one of the Cheshire men was flung through a pork butcher's window.

30 May (Wednesday)

This afternoon being a half-holiday, a cricket match was played between two teams of Signallers, one Welsh and the other composed of Cheshire and Lancashire men, but having some letters to write, I stayed in the hut to learn later that the English team won by a few runs.

1 June (Friday)

The YMCA continues staging a variety of features for our edification and amusement. Tonight we enjoyed a miscellaneous concert. The tenor Gunner Lewis again thrilled us with 'Songs of Araby', words by William Gorman Wills and 'My Dreams'; an elocutionist followed with 'The Whitest Man I Know', and a fellow played 'The Lost Chord' on a banjo. Previously I had heard Sullivan's popular tune played on a coronet, sung by a contralto, played on a pipe organ, and once at Vint's Palace in Aberafan I heard four girl trumpeters play it on very long instruments. The girls, dressed in white classical costumes, looked like angels, the turn sending shivers down my spine. But 'The Lost Chord' played on a banjo was certainly original.

2 June (Saturday)

Every Saturday the huts get a special cleaning and the floor is scrubbed or 'swabbed' as they call it here. The hut orderly is assisted by three men equipped with brushes, squeegees, mops and pails, and eventually the floor dries up beautifully clean and white.

My immediate neighbour in the hut on my right and next to the wall is Signaller Hyde and the man on my right is Signaller O'Reilly. Coincidentally Hyde comes from a town in Cheshire called Hyde. He is a curly headed man with small features and a gentle, tired voice. He is respectable, straightforward and has the look of a man slightly disgusted with most things. When speaking he hesitates very much. His chief aversions are brass and its daily cleaning. 'Why can't they issue leather buttons?' is his frequent grouse. 'T'would save time, energy and Soldier's Friend (Polish), and besides polished brass is too conspicuous on active service.' Hyde is invariably late on parade and sometimes too late for his pay, as he never proceeds to the Battery Office on Fridays until I arrive at the hut with mine.

Then he knows that they have started calling the Hs.

J.P. O'Reilly is a man of the world, well read – he devours a book four times as fast as I – was on the staff of a Liverpool newspaper and is an enthusiastic cyclist. He had cycled through many parts of England and Wales and remembers the Swansea region. He advocates the fixed wheel and says, 'These free-wheelers tire themselves out by peddling and resting. Down hills they whizz past me, but by steady, constant peddling I generally overtake them on the climbs.' His hair is crisp and greying, his eyes peer through powerful spectacles and twinkle during his witty moments. Occasionally he surprises and antagonises me with an uncalled for and withering insult, but his predominant mood is sanguine. Arising in the morning, he addresses his bed thus: 'Ah well, the best of friends must part.'

Then he usually exclaims once or twice in between yawns, 'Fresh as a daisy' and proceeds to awaken those still asleep by bawling loudly in their ears, 'Ahoy, Ahoy. Come on my hearties.' He borrows a new mirror, studies his chin carefully and decides, 'Aye, it's a good mirror. I can see tomorrow's growth coming up.' He mimics cleverly and his memory is so retentive that one hearing of a song is often sufficient for him to know the words and tune. He often sings 'Burlington Bertie' and 'Oh I wonder what it feels like to be poor' in an amusing way, as his singing voice is so funny.

When I asked him ironically if he came from a musical family, he replied, 'No. The only singer in our family is a machine.' One of his impersonations is that of a boy bereft of his marbles. Dancing about the hut like a frenzied child he cries, 'Mamma, Mamma, my marbles have gone down the grating.' Very occasionally he imbibes too freely and very late one night he swayed into the hut. Correctly foreseeing the situation I had made his bed for him.

When he arrived everyone was asleep, but he woke a few of us up by fumbling with the door latch. In he rolled, stumbling over a few beds, whose occupants uttered dreamy curses, and in the chaos he put between his lips the lighted end of his cigarette, that causing pandemonium. I was told that when he lived in Hut 15, O'Reilly one night sprawled in 'paralytic' drunk and so helpless that he had to be undressed and put to bed like a baby. When after much difficulty two or three men got him under his blankets, he sat up, perfectly sober and very politely thanked his helpers for saving him the trouble of undressing. He had not been drinking at all.

3 June (Sunday)

The surrounding country is a series of pictures of summer beauty, recent showers having freshened the verdant scenes.

Every nook and hedge is gay with wild flowers and everywhere there are vigorous, sprouting shrubs. Some of the men, returned from a ramble, brought with them bunches of wild flowers which now fill two vases on the hut tables.

On Sundays quietness rules the camp. All the hustle and bustle of GS (General Service) wagons, horses, squads drilling and marching ceases and instead friends may be seen walking leisurely into the country to enjoy its panorama, or are making their way to some quiet sanctuary. Others take advantage of the quietness by enjoying a peaceful read or sleep. Others spend Sunday as they spend nearly all their leisure, playing pontoon or brag. This feverish gaming goes on incessantly and often after 'Lights Out' at 11 pm, for the players procure a supply of candles for the purpose. Frequently the game ends with a violent quarrel.

7 June (Thursday)

Today it was a pleasant surprise to receive a letter from Mr T.W. Lewis MA, Head of my former school, Port Talbot Higher Grade. His nickname of 'Tom Bull' came with him to the school. From this letter I learned that Mr A.J. Richards MA, a former master at the school and now an infantry captain, is at Pembroke Dock recuperating from a bad attack of trench fever which has affected his heart. For an historical thesis he gained his MA degree at the early age of 23. One of the most popular teachers I have ever known, Richards was noted for his patience and good humour and for the personal interest he took in his pupils. To encourage me in my sketching activities, Richards was one of the few people who were ever interested enough in me to give me a commission for a painting of a castle, which he paid me for.

In our hut now boxing is the chief pastime. We remove all tables and forms to the hut sides and spar in turns. This evening I was matched against Maxwell, a tall, rosy faced fellow of about my own age who is one of a butcher family in business at Abergavenny. We pounded each other until we were almost too exhausted to stand, and though stripped bare to the waist we perspired so freely that we looked as if we had been dipped in a pond. Maxwell is slightly heavier than I, but the result was given as a draw. Stripped we were both in the featherweight class.

9 June (Saturday)

Abram Marienberg and a friend, Lance Corporal Wooley, arrived about tea time for the weekend. I had arranged for them to stay at Hanmer, but the occupants of Hut 22 insisted on them staying with us, and they were given the two beds vacated by men on leave.

Everybody was nice to them except Jolliffe, who slept opposite and whom I heard discuss Abram rather snobbishly with his neighbour. I certainly overheard him remark, 'I believe he's a bloody sheeny', and I knew by Abram's clouded face that he had heard it too. I also knew that such a remark was enough to darken Abram's life for weeks. This antipathy to his race disclosed by certain Gentiles has always been the bane of Abram's life.

However, Bombardier Michael, a dissipated looking little fellow, started telling yarns, and Abram was soon laughing with the rest of us. Michael, during an intimate disclosure, had everyone laughing when he confessed, 'It's the preliminaries I like best.'

Jolliffe is a big fellow, approaching middle age. He has blonde hair and moustache. If he had his way he would shoot every German over the age of 14 and every Jew. His chief regret is that he did not enlist in the Royal Flying Corps instead of 'this grovelling, mundane mob', and his chief ambition is to have sexual intercourse in an aeroplane.

10 June (Sunday)

This morning while I attended church parade, Abram and Wooley strolled around the camp. Meeting afterwards, we walked to Hanmer. They had watched our parade and told me that they considered the response of the Artillery to the command 'Shun' inferior to that of the Infantry at Prees

Heath. I argued that much of our drill was done mounted, that all Infantry drill was done on foot and that therefore they had more practice. From whatever angle you view it Hanmer Mere is always a picture of loveliness. Today it was a sheet of shimmering silver. Its banks are rich with buttercups and marguerites – tall and slender, also red clover, while there are fragile wild roses of shell-pink bloom in the bushes. We watched a thrush impatiently hammer a snail shell against a stone. A military policeman was jotting down the names of a few men who had broken a rule by bathing in the mere on a Sunday. We discovered that one of the offenders was a schoolmate of Abram and mine named Len Jones. Joining the Port Talbot RHA he had been in France for two years and four months from whence he had recently returned. The RHA and RFA are very similar regiments and often RHA men come to Bettisfield Park Camp from Command Depots. Abram and Wooley confessed this to be the best weekend they had enjoyed since donning khaki. They walked back to Prees Heath this evening.

13 June (Wednesday)
A letter arrived from Abram written in his usual neat, firm, office-clerk handwriting:

> After leaving you last night we walked at an easy pace and so did not arrive back in camp until 12.30 am.
> Five hours sound sleep were not so bad, though I awoke feeling rather stiff. It was fine last night, walking along the canal bank in the varying shades of light, daylight changing into twilight and then twilight into darkness. Everything was so quiet, save the occasional hoot of an owl, so that there was hardly anything to disturb our thoughts of gratitude for such a happy weekend. Please remember us to and thank the Corporal (Walton), Bombardier, (Michael), Mr O'Reilly and all the others for being so hospitable and entertaining. This evening and that of tomorrow we shall be getting ready for Fenn's Bank where I now understand we may fire our full musketry course.

Hanmer Mere is ideal for bathing. We may bathe in the evenings and on Saturday afternoons. During swimming hours a picket of competent swimmers is in attendance. Even on the hottest days the water is always soothingly cool and, near the centre of the lake where the diving board is, the bottom slopes gradually.

14 June (Thursday)

Today, among other things, we learned heliograph aligning. The helio is a very neat and exacting instrument and though its manipulation is very simple, it has to be continually reset as the revolving Earth keeps putting it out of perfect alignment with the sun. We were informed that it may be read at a distance of thirty miles in the British Isles on a clear day, and in Africa and India where the atmosphere is clearer, 80 miles. One of the Signallers in Hut 23 is a Frenchman, who is the proprietor of a restaurant in this country. His name is Bonnet and he speaks English well, but with a conspicuous French accent. Hut 23 had a hired piano, due chiefly, I imagine, to the influence of the organist, Signaller Thompson, who often plays it. Corporal Webster amuses himself for hours playing it with one finger.

Like nearly everyone in the camp, I have had a rash of tiny red irritating pimples all over my body. They call it scabies or common itch and they say it comes from the blankets we use. A bath of a strong solution of flower of sulphur was provided us at the hospital, a remedy that kills it completely in a day or so. We learned that the rash is caused by a parasite which burrows under the skin. I heard one wit say, 'Don't worry. Napoleon had it. That's why he put his hand under his tunic.'

15 June (Friday)

Spent the day well out in the country on long-distance station work with heliographs. It was a gorgeous day and the trees were masses of shimmering green and silver. The tilled earth was a rich reddish-brown and the large prosperous-looking red-bricked farmhouses were more reminiscent of Western ranches than English farms. Fragile, livid, red poppies were sprinkled here and there. Each station had about ten men, a few to receive, a few to send to the next station, one to keep records and one in charge. I was detailed in charge of the station near Three Fingers, and I felt quietly bucked at the honour, though I have known all along that my progress has given the staff satisfaction. For instance, Cyril Bunker and I nearly always head the list in visual signalling. We both have excellent eyesight and have a perfect understanding when paired off for reading practice. We never muddle each other by asking such questions as 'What did you say?' during a flag-reading test. The messages are made up of words of five jumbled letters so that you cannot guess what the word is going to be when you are halfway through it. The station sending to us was comparatively near and the flashes were so blinding that we had to read the messages through our flags. Ravenously hungry, we were taken to the kitchen of a large farm and ate numerous slices of wholemeal bread and fresh butter carved from huge oval loaves. This simple bread and butter meal was about the most enjoyable I ever had and it cost us nothing as the NCOs paid the bill.

16 June (Saturday)

Commenced map reading which I know is going to be absorbingly interesting to me. It is considered a very important subject and includes scales, contours, field sketching and the conventional signs to be used and also the practical use of the compass. I have become very friendly with Cyril Bunker who comes from Stafford. He is pale, has rather full lips and sandy hair, which is thick and plentiful and parted in the centre. This afternoon we went together to Whitchurch and enjoyed ourselves immensely, for it is such a change to see trains, shops and civilians. We had tea and scanned a few magazines and newspapers at the Soldier's Institute. Met an infantryman who hailed from Aberafan and after discussing the old borough for some time, he accompanied us to the pictures.

Abram of course is at Fenn's Bank on musketry. The infantry course includes night firing and we hear the racket of it at Bettisfield Park. Our train left Whitchurch at 9.30 pm.

17 June (Sunday)

At 3 am we were all aroused by a terrific thunderstorm, the worst some of us had ever known. Lightning came in long, flickering flashes, illuminating the whole place. After breakfast, during church service, the storm had not quite abated.

19 June (Tuesday)

Since Sunday's storm the weather has been cold and wet. Twice weekly we have night signalling schemes which are usually successful because of the keen interest taken in them. Tonight we had central station work with signalling lamps.

20 June (Wednesday)

The huts look spotlessly clean after recent special cleaning. Every table and form was scrubbed and each man had to scrub that portion of the hut nearest his place. All blankets were to have been fumigated, but the weather was too bad. A Llanelli man, wounded in France, has come to our hut. I have had several chats with him and he has given me a small photograph of himself. He has a two-year service stripe and a wound stripe which I silently envy. His eyes have that strained look so often seen in men who return from the battlefields. This afternoon was our half-holiday and stretched out on a form, he fell asleep and rolled off with a thud, but was unhurt. He said that he had dreamed that he was back in France and that the shock caused him to tumble off the seat.

23 June (Saturday)

The Day of Judgement has arrived, for in addition to our ordinary work, signalling examinations have made the week a very busy one. Corporal Walton detailed me as hut orderly again today, giving me two assistants, as every Saturday morning the huts undergo a very keen inspection. I told Walton that I was fed up with the job but he laughed it off by the flattery – 'Why, you're the best hut orderly in dear old Bettisfield', adding, 'Besides, you're so well forward in your signalling that we can spare you.' We worked hard on the hut and were rewarded by hearing the Orderly Officer say to his accompanying NCO – 'A very nice hut.' Walton was tremendously bucked.

My parents intend coming here for a holiday and I have arranged for them to stay with the Copnalls who keep a butcher's and greengrocer's shop in the centre of Hanmer and who also accommodate visitors regularly. At present Bombardier Chivers and his wife are staying there. Chivers is a physical drill instructor, a genial, excitable, rapid-speaking Cardiffian, who told me that the Copnalls were excellent hosts.

4 July (Wednesday)
Much excitement here today, for we had sports at Bettisfield Hall grounds. There were refreshment stalls, bowling matches, while the band was in attendance and also played for the dancing on the green which took place this evening. Sergeant Major Bonser looked well dancing around with a lady.

6 July (Friday)
Called at the Copnalls to ascertain if they had received this morning from my parents the time of their arrival. Miss Copnall, a good-looking brunette, told me that they had not only heard that morning, but that her father had already taken the tub-cart to meet the train. She added that my parents might be bringing a Mrs Marienberg. This latest news was a surprise to me as they had not mentioned anything about Mrs Marienberg's coming in the recent letters. Of course they know that I am not agreeable to it because I know better than they that her traditional domestic habits and customs are going to cause complications at the Copnalls. Miss Copnall kindly offered me her bicycle for the purpose of proceeding to meet my folk at Bettisfield railway station, but I had not ridden far when the tub-cart appeared round a bend in the road. Mr Copnall pulled up and I tried to look as pleased as possible when I saw Mrs Marienberg grinning like a Cheshire cat in the overladen tub-cart. Last Saturday, when I met Abram at Prees Heath, he told me that he expects to be drafted to the East Coast soon, so Mrs Marienberg should be able to see him before he goes, and I have to try to believe that it's an ill wind that blows nobody any good.

7 July (Saturday)
After lunch Ma and Pa proceeded to Prees Heath to see Abram, whose mother refused to travel further than Bettisfield railway station as the rest of the journey would entail travelling by rail on the Jewish Sabbath. She handed her purse to my mother with instructions that Abram should take

from it what money he required and she loitered about the quiet, little railway station until my parents returned that night.

10 July (Tuesday)
Passed signalling classification tests and am now considered a first-class Signaller and entitled to wear on my sleeve crossed flags. On Saturday last, Corporal Walton told me unofficially that I had done very well in the tests. During the next two or three months I shall be instructed in anti-gas drill, riding and musketry.

12 July (Thursday)
Spent the evening helping Mr Copnall in one of his hay fields. Copnall is a corpulent, prosperous yeoman and an ex-member of the Volunteers or Yeomanry in which he was a champion swordsman. Yesterday he drove my parents and Mrs Marienberg to Ellesmere, a beauty spot about 6 or 7 miles away from here. During the drive he drew their attention to the sky and informed them that whenever clouds looked like a flock of sheep, rain wasn't far off. So here in the hayfield we were tonight, Ma, Pa and myself, augmenting Copnall's 'hands' in an endeavour to harvest the hay before the rain came. Prominently displaying her false teeth, Mrs Marienberg sat and grinned at the proceedings. Tea was brought out to us.

15 July (Sunday)
This evening accompanied my parents to the Wesleyan chapel, a prim little red-bricked building at Horseman's Green. We walked through the fields whose hedges were decked with pink bramble blossom and immaculate convolvulus, with vigorous purple thistles, crimson campion and marguerites at the bases. The mown hay looked mauve in the evening light. In spite of the number of stiles we had to cross Ma enjoyed this lovely walk. The chapel was packed, for it was an anniversary service and the singing was very hearty.

This morning my visitors inspected the camp and Pa, especially, was thrilled at the march past after church parade, the service this morning taking place in a coppice-fringed dell where signalling classes do their flag drills.

Pa presented Hut 22 with a framed, tinted reproduction of Bernard Partridge's famous *Punch* cartoon in which King Albert and the Kaiser stand amid the debris of Belgium, and the Kaiser says, 'See, you have lost everything', to which King Albert replies, 'Not my Soul.' Ma recognised Trevor Davies, a Port Talbot 'boy', on Guard at the Brigade Office and oblivious of all rules, and in spite of my discouragement, was determined to go up to and have a few words with him. Ma is charmed with Hanmer which she says is just the place she'd like to live in. The only thing that has marred her holiday is the night firing at Fenn's Bank which has kept her awake for nights. The Copnalls told them that the camp now had a particularly fine type of recruits, but that previously there had been a rough crowd there.

16 July (Monday)
Supped at the Copnalls. Mrs Marienberg could not pronounce Copnall, her nearest essay being 'Cockerel', which amused herself and the rest of us immensely. Inadvertently, the maid washed her dishes and cutlery, which renders them now unclean to her and she has bought a new set of each at the stores nearby, a little shop that supplies nearly every article a visitor might need. Mrs Marienberg called this little emporium 'Benevns' after Ben Evans & Co., the large Swansea store.

20 July (Friday)
This week we have been doing telephone exchange work in the offices, dug-outs and trenches in the vicinity of the Signal School. One of the offices possessed an efficient exchange worked by switches. Startling messages like 'SOS' came through at times, and when 'GAS' was signalled, we worked with respirators on until the message 'GAS Off' was received. Yesterday our School was inspected by a Royal Engineer captain, and on Wednesday the camp was again inspected by Brigadier General Fox.

21 July (Saturday)
Sergeant Major Garvey has finished his time and we have presented him with a handsome smoking cabinet. Thawed of his usual austerity, he

beamed upon everybody and we are now genuinely sorry to lose him, but he is well represented with us, for his son, an exact, youngish replica of him, is one of our Signallers. Tonight, two of us Signallers commenced a 12-hour duty (8 pm to 8 am) at the Brigade Office telephone exchange. We had very few calls and it was exceptionally quiet during the early morning. We sat up in turns and heard the incessant pacing to and fro of the sentry outside and his occasional bold challenge to anyone approaching.

23 July (Monday)
Ma and Mrs Marienberg returned home today after a splendid three-week holiday. Pa also enjoyed the week he stayed and he was greatly impressed with our camp. They went all round the camp even into the trenches and dug-outs and were also present at an outdoor religious service. We learned that Abram was drafted with his Battalion to Suffolk on the day after his mother refused to travel to see him, which was rather a pity.

26 July (Thursday)
For a few hours tonight from 9 pm lamp-signalling practice.

Chapter 7

ANTI-GAS DRILL AND THE
RIDING SCHOOL

27 July (Friday)

During the week we did some long-distance signalling station work for which we used large flags and telescopes. Also we have finished our anti-gas course. Our squad were assembled in a circle from the centre of which either an officer or NCO explained and demonstrated the use of a gas helmet and respirator. When the alarm was given we had to don either of these protectors in a given time. The alarm consisted of a gong, a racket or a revolver fired unexpectedly by an officer prowling behind us. The PH helmet, a grey cloth bag, redolent of some strong anti-gas chemical, is fitted with eye-glasses and an exhaling valve, inhaling being done through the cloth.[1] The helmet had to be thrown over the head, the ends tucked in beneath the tunic, the tunic buttoned and the whole operation completely performed within 20 seconds. The box respirator had to be adjusted from the alert to the complete within 6 seconds; and changing from box respirator to helmet had to be done within 10 seconds. We walked through dug-outs and chambers containing asphyxiating and tear gas, the neighbourhood surrounding the gas chambers having a faint smell like that of pineapple. The tear gas made us weep so copiously that for a time we were blinded with tears. Our brass has been tarnished to a greenish grey and we learn from our predecessors in the gas course that it takes days of polishing to restore the brass to its former brightness. The gas instructors are granted frequent leaves as their job is very unhealthy.

1. PH stands for phosgene and hexamine, with which the helmet was impregnated. When goggles were incorporated it was known as the PHG helmet.

28 July (Saturday)

During the last week of very warm weather the only comfortable place to be in was Hanmer Mere. I had four invigorating bathes, swimming with a comfortable side-stroke well out to the colder, deeper places and feeling immensely superior to the novices who exhausted themselves by too rapid movements in the shallows. Then, as the heat of the sinking sun diminished, we dried ourselves and revelled in that tingling vitality which bathing more than all other exercises gives.

10 August (Friday)

I am one of the next on the rota for a weekend leave, but have been baulked by Port Talbot being added to those places 'out of bounds' on account of outbreaks there of epidemics and fevers. By this present weekend I had fully expected to hear that the ban had been removed and had written home telling them to expect me, but I learned that today I was to commence at the Riding School. I telegraphed home an explanation, and resigned myself to the miserable fact that I shall have to wait at least another fortnight. Two other men were similarly disappointed. Knowing the riding course to be rough and dangerous, we view the next fortnight's proceedings with a mixture of humour and apprehension. I had assisted in shouldering to a hospital a stretcher bearing a Hut 22 victim of the Riding School, and had observed the wreck it had made of my neighbour, O'Reilly, yet I realised that the men who fared worst were my seniors and on the whole felt quite confident of not letting the Riding School beat me. My sole experience of riding is having shared with another lad the broad back of a farm horse returning from the harvest fields during a holiday I spent in Gower.

When O'Reilly had recovered sufficiently for the return of his sense of humour he told me the following incident concerning Signaller Hyde, one of his contemporaries in the Riding School. During the jumping exercises, Hyde had on that particular occasion failed to urge his mount into the preliminary canter leading to the hurdle. The horse persisted in walking to the jumps, which it crossed one leg at a time, then it turned round and started eating the foliage on the hurdle sides. Not having witnessed a sight such as that in all his experience, the Riding Sergeant gazed for a few seconds in speechless horror, then he collected himself, gave Hyde the cursing of his life and striding forward lashed the animal with his riding whip. The horse, frightened into animation, bolted furiously and contemptuous of Hyde's tugs and 'whoas' never stopped until he reached the stables ¼ mile away. The sight was so comic that it actually thawed the crimson and disgusted looking face of the Sergeant into a grudging grin.

15 August (Wednesday)
Last Friday, when we commenced this course, we filed into the stables and took a horse each. I had a black mare with a silver tail, and afterwards learned from a stableman that her name was actually 'Silver Tail'. A short distance from the stables we halted and retightened the saddle girths, the explanation given being that horses habitually puff out their bellies during the initial saddling. Riding drill takes place in a large field between the camp and Bettisfield railway station. At the portion of the field farthest from the road the Drivers practice their six-horse teams and vehicles. Surreptitiously we watch them trotting through improvised gates, their instructor controlling them sometimes with arm or whistle signals. So far the course has been very strenuous. We have had to ride around a ring, exactly like a circus, and without saddles, first walking, then trotting at the command 'Turrr-ot', with arms folded, outward or upward stretched, this bumping procedure being considered necessary to teach us the value of the all important knee-gripping. After a few days of this our legs became skinned, stiff and sore. There was a much-appreciated rest from this particular experience when we were given a lesson in saddling. The saddle blanket has to be folded exactingly, and with the open end and side facing the rear and off side respectively. The stirrups should hang your arms length and your legs should be as straight as possible, just as though you were standing on the stirrups rather than sitting on a saddle.

20 August (Monday)
We have progressed so far in our riding as to reach that stage when we can ride in safety on the highways. This morning we had a mounted march over the roads and fancied ourselves considerably.

At given commands we had to do various drills such as 'Circle Right', when in turn we wheeled from the column and walked to the rear, a procedure not so simple as it would seem because the horses have an instinctive aversion to walking in the opposite direction from the others. On the canal that runs through Bettisfield we saw a gaily painted barge drawn by a pony. Occasionally we enjoyed an exhilarating trot.

24 August (Friday)

Qualified at the Riding School, feel very sore, but very happy. I have not tumbled off once and that's saying something, though Silver Tail, whom I have ridden for the fortnight, proved a good, steady and intelligent friend. I am now able to ride any way or any shape and henceforth shall not fear any horse or mule. The Riding School staff from the Major down are a fearful lot, with vile tempers. The Major, a handsome old devil, possesses the minimum of patience and those who cause him to explode may let themselves in for another fortnight in the circus.

The Sergeant at times goes purple and speechless with rage. In one of those fits of temper we saw him beat his horse about the head unmercifully with the handle of his riding crop. I was told that one Corporal, a coarse-skinned fellow, threatened to knock one beginner off his horse. The beginner coolly reined in his mount into the ring centre and challenged the Corporal to try it, but the cowed NCO knew the rules and regulations as well as the novice, so he just ordered him back to his place and proceeded with the drill. One of our instructors is a famous jockey, a little fellow who looks like a boy on his very big horse. I was too indifferent to horse racing to be interested enough to ascertain his name. All the Riding School staff have a spur above their chevrons and they all ride magnificently, sitting in their saddles like cavalrymen. During the last few days we did our jumping. The thought of it gave us mixed feelings for the hurdles looked the most likely places for breaking one's neck, but when it was all over, it seemed to me to be the best part of the course. The first hurdle bars were placed very low and gradually raised. We jumped singly and when one's turn neared our horse became impatient to be off. It pulled and reared and it was difficult to hold it in. When our turn came we broke into a canter, bent forward when the animal leaped up and backwards when it was across, and we were almost over before we knew it, taking our places at the rear of the file ready for the next jump. Approaching the hurdle we kept the reins tight in order to keep the horse's head up.

Several were thrown but unhurt, because horses dislike treading on a fallen rider as we dislike treading on a banana skin. Of course it is impossible for them to do so always, but they have been known to fall themselves in attempting to avoid a fallen rider. Finally we were leaping over with arms folded and feet withdrawn from the stirrups. We were just allowed to guide our mount towards the hurdle then we folded arms, withdrew our feet from the stirrups, gripped like grim death with our knees and hoped for the best. The correct mounted posture, being unnatural, was for us beginners painful. We had to sit perfectly erect, with elbows pressed to our sides and 'not flapping about like a pair of wings', as the instructors described it, and with toes pointing inwards, so as to point the spurs outwards. I rocked about a bit in some of the highest jumps but did not get thrown once.

This evening Corporal Walton strolled over to me. He is a handsome fellow with crisp, wavy hair, and a pleasant smile is almost his normal expression. Studying the cigarette he smoked he made the following fastidious remark: 'D'you know, I can judge a man by the way he holds a cigarette. I never like a man who points the lighted end towards his palm.' Then he came down to business and afterwards it seemed to me that he had previously discussed the subject with Lieutenant Ince. 'Well,' he commenced, 'you've qualified at riding. How did you like it?' 'I'm glad it's over,' I replied, 'but I thought it was thrilling – at least the latter part.' 'Good lad', he said encouragingly. Then he paused, smoked his cigarette elegantly for a few seconds, then asked, 'How would you like me to recommend you to Ince for a stripe?' I felt flattered and as I had secretly toyed with the possibility, I was not quite unprepared for the question. 'No thank you Corporal,' I replied definitely. 'I'm keen on going to France. I should like to see the real thing.' This truthfully, for were the war to end now, I should be genuinely disappointed. I hope I shall be drafted to France too, for I should prefer that to any other front. Walton never betrays any emotion. He showed no surprise whatever, but added, 'Just think it over. Of course you realise that it would mean you going to Dunstable for a NCO's signalling course and then returning here to be a permanent instructor, probably for "duration" and it could lead to a commission' – 'I appreciate your offer, shall certainly think it over, but know my answer will be the same.'

31 August (Friday)

Proceeded on my second weekend leave at Port Talbot, which, during eight months of absence I have idealised together with its people. I have come to love Shropshire and Herefordshire too, and have enjoyed the panorama of their richness today from the train. In the fields I could often spot foxgloves, while the rail-side gardens were ablaze with roses, hollyhocks, lupins, sweet peas and marguerites. It was very hot and cows stood up to their middle in the cool ditch water or lay beneath shady trees, while horses scratched each other in those regions beyond their personal reach.

1 September (Saturday)

The staff at Cockett railway station, together with some other friends, have presented me with a silver wrist-watch. It is a little gem, Swiss-made, illuminated, while its back has my rank, name, regiment and the name of the donors engraved on it. I am very proud of this useful gift and deeply appreciate the people of Cockett and the Fforestfach district who have treated me with more kindness than those of my home town.

3 September (Monday)

My leave was one of those delightful breaks that we all live for. Pa accompanied me to the railway station where I met an infantryman returning to Prees Heath. At Cardiff, having to wait some time, we descended into the YMCA canteen, just outside the station and had some refreshments. On returning to the station I found four Bettisfield Signallers returning from leave and we shared a compartment with a South Wales Borderer and an acquaintance of his, a member of the

WAAC[2] and a King's Liverpool man. For a party returning from leave we were unusually hilarious, singing and joking until one by one we fell asleep. At one time I awoke momentarily to see the sleeping girl's head lying on the breast of the Borderer, whose arm affectionately encircled her. We awoke with a jolt at Crewe about 11.30 pm, and having another long wait, made for the Soldier's and Sailor's Rest, conveniently situated outside the station, its large red lamp beckoning a hearty welcome. It is open all night, provides refreshments and a bed if you desire one, the attendant waking you at any time requested.

4 September (Tuesday)

Leaving Crewe at 2.30 pm we reached Bettisfield about 3.30 am. Wearily and silently we trudged into the camp, handed our passes to the NCO in charge of the gloomily lit Guard Room and dispersed to our respective huts. O'Reilly had remembered to make my bed. When I awoke I was informed that I was hut orderly for the day, which will suit me, for after dinner I can have a much-needed rest. It has been a happy weekend and everyone has been exceedingly kind. I have been presented with so many cigarettes that I shall have to give some away, as I am a very moderate smoker, who for long periods abstains altogether from it.

Received a letter from Abram, who gives his address as Henham-on-Mud. He writes:

We have been getting ready for France and have had several inspections by Generals. Last Thursday we went for a route march to a place called Walderswick and had to fight our way back to Blythburgh in full marching order. Waves of about 250 strong going over the top and in and out of trenches, through barbed wire, made a fine picture. We have been doing a great deal of wire-laying, field engineering and also much practice with rifle grenades. Our draft is 200 strong and will leave here on the 10th inst; that is, a week tomorrow and shall probably be played away by the Royal Welsh band. Next

2. The Women's Auxiliary Army Corps was established in January 1917 to allow soldiers to be released from administrative duties in Britain and France following the heavy losses suffered in 1916. Members of the WAAC were not given full military status and its 'rank' system reflected this with its officers being call Officials, its NCOs Forewomen and Assistant Forewomen and its privates named Workers. In total 57,000 women served in the WAAC during the First World War in such roles as drivers, clerks, telephonists, waitresses and cooks.

week a few of us in this tent are going to have a farewell supper and a good sober 'bust up'. We also intend playing a few pranks on some 'stay-at-home' NCOs. I have had a decent feed nearly every night this week at Wangford and hope for the same next week.

8 September (Saturday)

During the week I have been out with the cable cart, a four-wheeler, specially designed for carrying drums of wire and drawn by four horses. On each of the near horses was mounted a Driver. Sergeant Jones, who was in charge, and I were mounted on outriders.

On the outward journey I rode behind with a crook stick, a pole with a hooked head. Leaving the camp main gates we turned right and proceeded in the direction of Welshampton, a quiet road where meeting a civilian is an important event. We had not ridden far when Jones ordered the cable to be dealt out and he gave me a brief demonstration of what I was expected to do – ride behind the cart and fling the wire on to the hedges. This procedure being done at a brisk trot, I soon found that it looked easier than it was, for besides swinging the swaying cable up on to the branches, there was the horse to manage. Boldly he plunged through the road gulley which was deep with fallen leaves and decayed vegetation. The distance between the cable-cart and myself increased rapidly and Jones on one occasion halted and rode back to my assistance. He seemed to do it with such perfect ease, the result of constant practice I expect. After the first drum was unreeled we turned to the right into the hamlet of Braden Heath. Here Bunker and I occasionally attend the Sunday evening service at the little chapel. We sit in the back seat listening to a worthy layman expounding the Word, although my attention is usually divided between the preacher and the demure brunette who plays the harmonium. Nearly every country chapel I visit has an attractive female organist and though this one is not even aware of my existence, she is more responsible than the desire to worship for my presence in those pews. Although I hardly alluded to her, even to Bunker, I was recently astonished to find my name associated with hers. An elderly hut mate called Aldous had introduced me to Mrs Crosby, who during a holiday here had been brought by her husband to see our hut. Aldous embarrassed me considerably by informing the good lady that I was the best lad in the hut. A few minutes later Aldous said to me, 'I know of a girl who'd be just the match for you.'

'Where does she live?' I asked, feeling rather amused. 'She's the organist at Braden Heath chapel', he replied to my great surprise and I wondered for a moment if he were a thought-reader. Intensely interested, but pretending to be unconcerned I got him talking about her. Also a frequenter at the chapel, Aldous had become acquainted with the young lady's family and to my envy had had tea at their home. Aldous thought her a very fine girl. We saw her today for a few seconds and she smiled at us, one of those generous greetings with which patriotic girls delight the troops and which will cause me to dream about her from now on.

Then we dealt out the second cable, which I handled much better, and on the return journey, riding in front, I pulled down the cable from the hedges, a much simpler task than throwing it up. After we reached the end of the wire we rode leisurely back to camp and there was time to observe that the greens of the landscape were slowly dissolving into browns, russets and reds.

Wild flowers were still plentiful, dandelion, convolvulus, bramble blossom, campion and shaggy thistles, while in places there were brilliant clusters of vermilion hips and haws.

9 September (Sunday)

Arriving at the hut after church parade I found awaiting me on my blankets a letter from Abram who says he is quite well, in good spirits and expecting to go to France tomorrow. He is now in the Cheshire Regiment of which he has enclosed a cap badge and also a photograph of himself and a group of hut mates armed with brushes, mops, buckets and pans. I am glad to have the cap badge, partly because it is that of his regiment and also because I am collecting badges. Among the specimens adorning my leather belt are a 10th Lancers' badge, and an Australian badge.

13 September (Thursday)

Last night's concert, given by the Signallers' party who call themselves 'The

Salvoes', and which was presented in Hanmer Hall Riding School, was eclipsed by the one that delighted us tonight at the YMCA. Tonight's party came from Wrexham and each member was a competent entertainer, the brightest being the lady member, who during her vivacious singing winked naughtily at the lucky subalterns sitting in the front rows. The programme consisted of items ranging from the sublime to the ridiculous, and therefore suited all tastes. Among the humorous songs was a parody on 'Cock Robin', fragments of which ran: -

Who saw him die?
I, said the Daily Mail,
With my little eye,
I saw him die.

Chorus: *For our paper taught you how to win the war,*
You can't deny it.
We'll teach you everything on earth
If you will only buy it.
When they heard of the death
Of poor Bill Kaiser.

Another chorus ran: *Then the man up in the moon said*
No more zeppelins to try us,
And Satan softly murmured
Here's a pal for Ananias,
When he heard of the death of poor Bill Kaiser.

14 September (Friday)
My father has received from Abram a strange letter written at Folkestone on the 11th inst. Abram writes:

It is about 9 am, and before falling in at 9.30 am, I am at a dry canteen doing my best to send you a message before embarking for France. When I heard about the order for proceeding overseas I danced with delight, but when the lads returned to our tent I suggested that one of the company, a Roman Catholic lad, should offer up a prayer on our behalf, but they all insisted on me doing it. I asked them to give me a few moments for thought, then I had them, seven in number, kneeling with bared and bowed heads, around the pole of the tent which was illuminated by the faint glimmer of a flickering candle. That night a few of the draft were the worst for beer, but not so one of us, and in a trembling voice I prayed for God's blessing and protection. Next day from 6 am until 4.15 pm we never had a moment's rest, being paraded for so many things.

One of the parades was for a medical inspection and I could have got off the draft if I chose by telling one thing. At three o'clock we had tea, and would you believe it, we only had syrup with the bread and margarine for our last meal in the battalion. At 3.45 pm we fell in for moving off. Oh, the excitement was intense for the whole battalion turned out to see us off. There was a speech by the General and by the Colonel. We cheered them all and they cheered us as we marched away in fours without even the gift of a bar of chocolate or a cigarette each. Not that we needed anything, but because we wanted to see the right spirit displayed. We marched to Blythburgh, trained to Halesworth and thence to London. Oh! Three years ago I never thought that I would some day march thro' London in full marching order and singing like a lark. That was about 10 pm. At the Free Buffet on Victoria Station we had a bit of supper, left there at 12.45 am, arriving at Shorncliff, marched to Folkestone which we reached at 3 am and were put up at the Kenworth Hotel. Ten of us slept in a small room, on the bare boards and without blankets, but the rest was welcome. This morning we had an excellent breakfast. Somehow tho', I think something is going to happen to our ship, for I dreamed of it a few months ago and also three of my tent mates dreamed the same dream and told me of it separately. It is consoling to be able to say that we left Henham in better spirits than we had on arriving there. I am alright and if I can stick the march from Boulogne to Etaples (17 miles), I shall not worry.

P.S. Please take care of the enclosed and put it safely away from all.

The 'enclosed' was a packet on which was written, 'To be opened in the event of my death.'

For years I have had the conviction that Abram Marienberg has an important mission to fulfil in life and therefore neither the dreams, which are very strangely coincidental, nor the fact of him making a will can ever convince me that he will not come through the war safely. I also have a presentiment that I shall survive unscathed and for that reason shall leave blank the leaf in my pay book that is headed, 'Last Will and Testament'.

15 September (Saturday)

Bunker and I secured half-fare travelling vouchers and proceeded to Chester. Delivering us into Chester railway station about 4 pm, the train groaned as if in travail. After tea we walked along the Roman Wall, which has a circumference of 2 miles. Near the Cathedral a resident pointed out to us parts of the Roman Wall still exposed, but said that the present wall dates from Saxon times, say the thirteenth or fourteenth century. Presently we came to a decaying tower, bearing a sign informing that from it Charles I stood and saw his army defeated at Rowton Moor in 1645. Millions of feet had worn to smooth concavity the steps leading up to it. The Cathedral and Wall are built of warm, red-tinted stone and even the gravestones in the Cathedral yard have been hewn from the same stone and because of that look less grave. Bunker called my attention to the purple hills flung across the horizon, guessing them to be the mountains of Wales. Chester, home of so many of our Bettisfield comrades, seethes with historical interest. What an exhibit of England. Many of the half-timbered buildings were dated and most of them belonged to the seventeenth century. We thought unique The Rows with their exquisite shops where shoppers are independent of all weather. Later we sat under a chestnut tree, near the bandstand on the bank of the Dee, a Venetian scene. On the gently flowing river launches plied and rowing skiffs and canoes skimmed. Glowed by the stimulating music provided by the band of the Cheshire Regiment, playing Suppe's popular overture, 'Poet and Peasant', Bunker invited me to his home in Stafford next Saturday.

16 September (Sunday)

This morning, after church parade, a few of us went for a walk in the direction of Hanmer. Recognising Aldous, one of our number, an elderly cottager invited us all in and presented each of us with some delicious pears from her trees. The hedges are heavily hung with fruit too, sparkling haws and luscious blackberries which we plucked from the most fruitful branches. Growth everywhere is thick and congested, with the conspicuous white of marguerites and tissue-like convolvulus here and there. This evening a friend and I went to Horseman's Green chapel, where we arrived late to find the little building packed. We were ushered to front seats facing the audience. Feeling foolishly self-conscious I found some relief in admiring the harvest thanksgiving fruit and large, gorgeous dahlias that almost obliterated the more modest but not less-colourful sweet peas arrayed before the pulpit. Then I completely forgot myself in listening to a layman's very homely and sincere message.

17 September (Monday)

Out all day with the Brigade on manoeuvres which they called a 'G Scheme'. The signal section of 'C' Battery staff consisted of four Signallers, including myself, riding at the head of the column with horseholders ready to take charge of our mounts when we went into action, this proudly reminding us of our importance. Before moving off we had a hectic few moments in 'C' Battery when Maxwell's reel of wire unrolled and became entangled in the mules' feet. We had already mounted, but Maxwell quickly dismounted and for a few seconds had an impossible task as the mules insisted in complicating the tangle by stepping all through it. Unnoticed, and risking death from mule kicks, I slipped down in what looked like a forest of horse and mule legs and after a frantic struggle we managed to gather up the coils and remount just about a second before the command 'Walk-March' was bawled out. How we escaped the notice of so many eyes was a mystery. All the Signallers were mounted on mules and it was my first ride on one and I was impressed by the difference in the ride. They are tall beasts with long, flapping ears and with tails closely cropped except at the end on which is left a brush-like mass of hair. Lacking the magnificent contours of a horse, they are the subject of endless jokes, but trotting with short, steady, almost dainty steps, they are surprisingly comfortable to ride and there is less tendency to jolt.

Near Fenn's Bank our Battery split into sections – Headquarters, Observation Post and Battery, which we quickly linked up with our cables and were immediately sending and receiving messages. After an interval for lunch, which consisted of hefty culfs of dry bread and cold meat, we resumed the mock battle which absorbed the afternoon, our duties being occasionally enlivened by a mule ride with a despatch when our wires were said to be 'Dis' (severed), presumably by an imaginary projectile. How I revelled in those thrilling gallops, which the mule seemed to enjoy as much as I, judging by his enthusiasm.

Returning, the reeling in of our cables gave the Brigade a good start on us. With the thought of Bettisfield stables awaiting them, and their companions so much nearer the oats and hay of the stalls, the mules were impatient to be off, so my companion suggested that we race for it. We did, the animals looking a rare sight, galloping to their limit with ears thrown back and tails sticking out horizontally. Swerving to a bridge that led to the main road and galloping at top speed, I left my challenger behind, but I give the credit to my mount which was an excellent specimen.

Villagers laughed aloud at this unusual race. We found the column halted and we dismounted before the final ride into camp and retightened the girths. In the stables I felt very guilty in having slightly galled my mule. He must have puffed himself out more than usual. We ended up by feeling that we had been given a very good idea of what the real thing must be like, minus of course any danger.

20 September (Thursday)

Dated last Sunday, Abram's first letter to me from France arrived. Headed 'Somewhere in France', this letter gave me a slight feeling of envy at his being overseas before me. He writes:

> *During the days when we thought of enlisting, I expected we would have been out here together. I wish in a way we were together, but for your sake I am glad you are not. . . . Our ship carrying about 2,000 was escorted by three torpedo-boat destroyers. Cheerful though I felt the whole of the time, I felt a bit queer when I saw the grey cliffs becoming fainter and fainter.*

We landed in France about 7 pm after a pleasant voyage, marched to a rest camp on top of some big hill and stayed there for the night. Next morning we started off on our famous 20-mile march to our base and arrived there tired and footsore at 4.15 pm. At the base we go each day from 7 am until 5 pm to the 'Bull Ring', 4 miles away. Each day is spent at a different kind of training. Friday we did trench work and Saturday we had gas drill. Saturday is an ordinary day here, but today we had a rest and this afternoon I went to a Jewish service. If I could tell you all the humorous and pathetic sides of life here I could make this letter really interesting. As it is, this will be censored. Believe me, I have been slogging at it since last Sunday and have had only a few hours rest each night. There is no such thing as leisure. You come back from the 'Bull Ring' exhausted. All you want is a wash, food and rest. I don't complain, could have got off the draft at Henham and can stop here for a while if I desire, but I am going thro' to the end. We go up the Line probably next Saturday or Sunday and all I can tell you is to watch the newspapers just about that time. Think of what this means. I am glad you are not with me. Think. I am quite cheerful and look forward to getting up the Line with the zeal not of bravado, but of self-vindication... May God be with us 'til we meet again.

22 September (Saturday)

If any soldier will do his bit bravely and with a consciousness of idealism, I'm sure Abram will. To no other friend have I yet been able to think aloud as I could with him. His companionship has been impossible to replace adequately and though I have the honour to possess many fine friends here, I am not really intimate with one.

My best friend here now is Cyril Bunker, whose rearing seems to have been similar to mine. Slightly my senior, he addresses me as 'Kid'. 'What d'you think of this kid?' He is rather flabbily built, has a vigorous mop of sandy hair, a pale face, full lips, a roughish smile and an easy going manner. He has arranged for our visit to his home in Stafford, and being always glad to escape from the monotony of camp life at weekends, I accompanied him there today. In the train Cyril expressed some misgivings about his spurs, which were of the heavy steel pattern issued. He has not yet bought a pair of neat, nickelled ones as have some of us. I soon tired of everlastingly emery papering my Army pair, which had a marked tendency to rust, and bought the nickelled pair in the tiny camp supply shop. During a walk before tea I thought Stafford a clean and fresh-looking town built entirely of red bricks. Nodding to a forbidding-looking building surrounded by an unscalable wall Bunker said, 'I hope you'll never go in there. That's Stafford jail.' The Bunkers were homely and made me very welcome. Mr Bunker, a watch-maker, is going to repair my wrist-watch and return it to me in a few days. There were two sisters senior to Cyril. The face of the elder was a caricature of Cyril's, while her sister, considerably younger, was a vivacious girl with vivid red hair. The brother, younger than Cyril, in the acquisitive period of youth, displayed to us unusually large collections of cigarette cards, postage stamps, postcards and bird eggs. The girls invited us to go for a walk with them, but Cyril declined and grinned eloquently, but we accompanied them as far as the shopping area after which Cyril told me a lot about the craft of pottery.

23 September (Sunday)

Of the draft of 250 men going abroad today 35 are Signallers. We shall miss some very fine friends including a few from Hut 22. After church parade this morning we strolled up to the gun park to see them parade and hear the Commandant speak to them. Those going to the East have been issued with khaki drill clothing and helmets. Back in the hut I borrowed one of the helmets and intrigued by its graceful curves and the contrast of cream exterior and the olive-green interior, I enjoyed immensely making a water-colour sketch of it in several different positions. Corporal Walton was chief among its admirers. He showed it to everyone and finally begged it from me.

Today I have been warned for the musketry course to commence a week tomorrow and am delighted because it will be a complete change of work and will bring me that much nearer the end of my training and to service overseas.

27 September (Thursday)

We've had plenty of night work lately. Monday night I was on duty at the Brigade Office telephone exchange. Tuesday evening at the Signal School we started a telephone-exchange scheme which lasted continuously for 28 hours. Between our periods of duty we slept grubbily on the floor in the school. Then tonight we had night lamp signalling after which we look forward to a restful weekend. The Brigade Office job is a sinecure affording a capital opportunity for answering letters. Letter writing for some of the fellows is a colossal task.

After having laboriously set down the initial greetings we watch them gazing interminably into space. Sometimes they plead for help and are invariably advised to write: 'Dear Mother, I am sending you 5s, but not this week.' Letter writing was once for me a distasteful task to be procrastinated continually. Now, as I become a little more proficient at it and value the incoming letters more than ever, writing becomes easier and pleasanter. My diary jottings provide an ample reserve, always ready to be tapped when memory proves inadequate.

30 September (Sunday)

Today I have attended church twice, this morning through compulsion and this evening voluntarily. At this morning's parade service a Minister from Ellesmere preached finely from the text: 'This is he that cometh from Edom' (Isaiah). He was a small, pale, scholarly man with a benign expression. After the service Gunner Lewis, another Welshman, and I went for a walk. Lewis is our beautiful 'C' Battery tenor and I felt proud to be in his company and listen to his silver-toned speaking voice. It has been a glorious day, kept cool by soft breezes. This evening a Hut 22 friend and I went to Horseman's Green chapel. I think there are three reasons why I go, reasons that surmount the occasional desire to gaze at members of the opposite sex. They are: force of habit, desire to please my relatives and a diversion from the monotony of camp life on a Sunday.

I find the average sermon thin after the excellent ones I have been used to hearing in Wales. To get to this little Wesleyan chapel we have to traverse a piece of the most sylvan scenery. Hedges now have patches of the most brilliant russets and reds and the topmost branches bear most inviting blackberries. Hawthorn bushes are ablaze with clusters of scarlet berries and clumps of campion stand out vividly amid the vigorous grass at the hedge bottoms. The oaks are laden with acorns, the pleasant smell of hay fills our nostrils and near a farm, snow-white geese challenge with wide open beaks our approach. Prevailed upon, we stayed behind for the first time to drink cups of coffee kindly provided for the soldiers by the chapel people each Sunday evening.

Chapter 8

MUSKETRY

1 October (Monday)

Today commenced musketry course. Assembled outside the armoury hut
our squad was issued with rifles by a mild Corporal. One Signaller dropped
his rifle and with a pained expression the Corporal said, 'In the regular
Army you'd have been given fourteen days "CB"[1] for that offence.' We
spent the morning learning the rifle parts, some of which can be easily
detached. The rifle is the Lee Enfield Mark III, a magazine rifle with a
calibre of .303in. To our amazement there are 63 parts and before we finish
the course we shall have to remember them all. This afternoon a stupid-
looking Bombardier who spoke with a bad lisp taught us aiming. 'How the
hell did he manage to get a stripe?' my neighbour asked incredulously.
Never willing to hear the Army disparaged, I essayed, 'He's probably a crack
shot', but this was parried by someone else remarking, 'He certainly is a bit
cracked.' We formed a circle around a tripod on which a rifle lay and in
turns aligned it on a given target, the Bombardier checking each man's
effort. We performed various drills and while lying prostrate on the grass
aiming at imaginary Germans, our instructor recited some advice well
known to all Bettisfield Signallers: 'Remember, your rifle is your betht pal,
not the flags on your arm, so align your "thights" and carry on.'

Back in the hut I found a short letter from Abram: 'Sorry cannot tell you
anything concerning my movements since the 16th, save that I left the Base
on the 21st to join my new battalion.' He adds that he is proud of his
regiment which is the 13th King's Liverpools and praises the officers and
even the sergeant major:

1. Confined to Barracks.

So far everything is A1. Could not wish for it to be better (I don't think). If the weather keeps fine it won't be so bad. I am still in the best of health and cheer and take all things as philosophically as possible. You must blame the censor for my brevity. The 13th KLRs – I dismiss from my mind the superstitious thought, for there's no such thing as luck and why should any number be deemed unlucky?

Besides, Abram is too valuable to come to any harm.

2 October (Tuesday)

Continuing the musketry course today we fired on the miniature range, situated in the park. We fired at 100yd range, over the pond where the mascot swan lives. I scored a 2in group which meant placing the five shots allowed us into a 2in space, thereby scoring the maximum number of points required.

I received a letter from Eddie Rogers, our student friend, who is still a Private in the RAMC and now aboard the hospital ship *Araguaya*.[2] The war is providing him with a world tour. In August he was in South Africa, being permitted to land two or three times in Cape Town. On two occasions his ship called at Sierra Leone and from there brought to Avonmouth 800 patients, a large number of them suffering from malaria.

At 7 pm the trumpeters sounded the fire alarm which roused the camp into a state of agitation. According to rule we 'fell in' on the square, silently cursing the skulkers we saw sneaking away behind the huts. The news soon spread that a hayrick was afire and we doubled to a farm well away from the park and arrived there panting and sweating freely. The rick was ablaze and quite beyond salvation. From two duck ponds fortunately situated nearby we formed two ranks and passed canvas buckets of water up one column and they returned empty via the other rank, to which some very knowingly transferred themselves. The object, which was to prevent the

2. The *Araguaya* was built by Workman Clark & Co. in Belfast in 1906 for the Royal Mail Steam Packet Co. She was a 10,537 gross ton ship. In 1917 she was fitted as a hospital ship. After one voyage to Halifax (Nova Scotia) and one to Cape Town, she was handed over to the Canadian government as a Canadian Military Hospital Ship. Between then and 1920 she made 19 voyages between the UK and Canada, transporting 15,000 patients. In 1920 she was handed back to Royal Mail Steam Packet Co. In 1926 she was refitted as a cruise ship with accommodation for 365 first-class passengers. She was sold in 1930 to Jugoslavenska Lloyd (Yugoslav Lloyd) and renamed *Kraljica Marija* (Queen Maria). In 1940 she was again sold, this time being renamed *Savoie*. She was sunk near Casablanca on 8 November 1942 while taking part in Operation Torch, the Allied landings in North Africa.

flames reaching the farmhouse, was achieved after enduring choking fumes and the nauseating smells of smoke and steam. Then the Ellesmere and Whitchurch Fire Brigades arrived to extinguish speedily what was left of the burning rick. We got back into camp about 9.30 pm, very tired, exceedingly dirty and reeking with the obnoxious odour of burned hay.

7 October (Sunday)

Had it not been for the musketry course I should have been home now on leave. 'C' Battery has a new leave system. Application is no longer necessary and when our turns arrive our names will be posted outside the Battery Office. It is very wet today and the YMCA is one of the few alternatives to staying in the hut. At present the YMCA stage is decorated with wheat and wild flowers for the harvest festival. Flowers hang from the stage ceiling, a huge white cloth has been lettered with the text 'We praise Thee O God', while an impoverished altar stands upon the stage. Here last Friday evening we were given a memorable entertaining by some officers and NCOs from Oswestry. Two of the officers were able elocutionists. One recited Kipling's 'Devil May Care' and afterwards the two recited a dialogue from Shakespeare's *Julius Caesar*. One of the NCOs played some stirring music on a cello.

8 October (Monday)

Finished musketry course and for me the week has been the most enjoyable spent in the Army. The ranges are among the marshes near Fenn's Bank,[3] about 4 or 5 miles away, to which we marched carrying our rifles, weighty boxes of ammunition and mid-day rations.

Resolving to sight accurately at the crucial moment when I pressed the trigger and having perfect eyesight and steady nerves, I succeeded in heading the list with my score of 84, which wasn't bad considering the small amount of actual firing we have done. When firing at 200yd one of

3. These marshes are known as Fenn's Moss and combined with the adjoining Bettisfield, Cadney, Wem and Whixall Mosses form a lowland raised bog of 2,340 acres (948 hectares). For over 500 years the area was extensively cut for peat. Between 1856 and 1990 this was done on a commercial scale. The Mosses were then acquired as a National Nature Reserve, managed by Natural England and the Countryside Council for Wales. These bodies are restoring the bogs and the whole area is designated a Site of Special Scientific Interest. Evidence of military activity in the area is still visible in the remains of the musketry butts from the First World War and bombing range set up in the Second World War. For details of how to visit the Mosses, access www.naturalengland.org.uk or telephone the Site Manager on 01948 880362.

the musketry NCOs stood behind me and watched me fire the five shots. Encouragingly he remarked 'Good lad' when the scorers signalled me two bulls and three inners.

After shooting we marked in turns, signalling to the firer his score with different discs on long poles. The canvas targets were stretched on six frames, each frame having two targets designed see-saw fashion, so that while one target was being used its perforated partner was being renovated by us with strips of coloured, adhesive paper. Until we realised that he was aiming at his neighbour's target, we thought one marksman had fired completely off the course. The bullets 'pinged' over us, but we were adequately protected by the huge bank beneath the targets. My score, which though leaving room for improvement, I considered a very good first attempt, was as follows:

Range in Yards	Remarks	Score	Possible
100	4in Group	25	25
200	2 Bulls, 3 Inners	17	20
300	4 Inners, 1 Magpie[4]	14	20
400	3 Inners, 2 Magpies	13	20
200 Rapid Fire (5 shots in 30 seconds)	1 Bull, 3 Inners, 1 Magpie	15	20
Totals		84	105

This evening my cup of happiness was filled to overflowing by being informed with five others that on Saturday next I was to proceed home on six days furlough, this being the usual final leave granted before proceeding on active service. Today I felt that I had upheld the shooting prestige of the Hanson family, for my father and two of his brothers had in bygone days, as members of the local Volunteer Battalion of the Welsh Regiment, won a number of prizes on the rifle ranges. Of these relations by far the best shot was one of my father's elder brothers, Alfred, a Corporal, who won several prizes at Bisley and also the *Western Mail* Fifty Guinea Challenge Bowl.

4. A shot hitting between the inner and outer rings of the target, scoring 3 points.

My father's cousin, Colour Sergeant David John Hanson, had won the Glamorganshire prize for Sergeants, while my father, a Bugler, won a more modest prize of a leg of pork before he was 18 years of age.

9 October (Tuesday)

Another large hayrick caught fire on a farm near Bettisfield railway station. A number of us were detailed as amateur firefighters and on this occasion were on the scene until 2.40 am, by which time the continual passing of buckets of water thoroughly exhausted us. As a precaution against outbreaks of fire in the camp, fire drill is daily practised. The fire squads are provided with tall fire screens for placing between the huts if necessary.

10 October (Wednesday)

To our varied activities that of trench building has now been added. The weather has been so wet recently that portions of our sandbagged trenches collapsed completely and for several days our time has been occupied repairing them.

Received a letter from Bob Palmer, written at the Royal Artillery Base, France. He informs me that 36 of the Bettisfield 'mob' travelled for 14 hours in a cattle truck and arrived at the Base at 1 am on Sunday. They expected to proceed up the Line in a few days. Today a number of us were summoned to the hospital for our last medical inspection here.

I was passed A1 and am now eager to go to France.

12 October (Friday)

Rode out with Battery for a distance of about 15 miles on manoeuvres. When we went into action we (Signallers) laid about a mile of wire, which being insufficient, necessitated us communicating for the remainder of the distance with flags. Turning my mount over to a horseholder and being stationed at the Battery position, the messages I received from the Observation Post were taken by a Runner to the Battery Commander.

13 October (Saturday)

At 8 am went excitedly to the Battery Office for my leave pass, only to be met with a crushing disappointment.

Because I was not yet 19 my leave had been cancelled. The clerks there genuinely regretted their oversight in forgetting to inform me and explained that though many lads have previously gone abroad underage, parents may object to this if they choose and even have the power to have their sons returned to Britain. Lately there has been so much of this recalling that more stringent measures are being adopted at the offices. Terribly disappointed, I enviously watched Bunker and the others proceed home for a glorious week's holiday, while Walton detailed me for the uninspiring job of hut orderly.

15 October (Monday)

Last night and tonight at the YMCA recitals were given by Fred Duxbury, an elocutionist. A large, dramatic-looking man with an infinite variety of facial expressions, voice inflexions, and whose slightest gesture became eloquent, Duxbury last night gave us a sacred recital. To hear his recital of the parable of the Prodigal Son was to imagine three people talking and to be given treasures in the allegory undreamed of previously. Tonight we were delighted with a descriptive and humorous recital. One of the narrations depicted a man and a girl in a balloon.

The man, taking advantage of a unique opportunity, proposed marriage to the girl and forced her to accept by throwing overboard one bag of sand ballast after another until the frightened, desperate girl yielded.

17 October (Wednesday)

During their stay at Hanmer my parents were informed by Miss Copnall that Bettisfield Park Camp contained a very fine standard of men and a decided improvement on the rough elements in previous contingents. My impression of Bettisfield men has also gone up since yesterday after intimate contact with a large draft of RFA men which arrived here from Glasgow. Mostly Scots, they arrived yesterday morning, since when it has been pandemonium here. In Hut 22, I served out breakfast to 42 of them and I might have been dishing out grub at a zoo for the uproar that took place. Today I was not surprised to learn that four of them are already in the Guard Room.

22 October (Monday)

Bob Jones, a genial hut mate, hails from Cardiff and is very proud to talk of his little child. Smilingly he told me that one of her characteristics is a determined stubbornness. 'For doing wrong I sometimes have to smack her sharply', he explained. 'But d'you think she'd cry? Not she. She just sets her little jaw and looks at me defiantly.' Bob always addresses 'Don' J. Jones as 'Aberystwatch', which reminds me that in a very strange way I am becoming linked with Aberystwyth.

'Don' J., during his recent leave at Aberystwyth, had evidently been discussing me with an acquaintance of his, a Mr W.G. Edwards, who it seems makes a hobby of writing to various people serving with the forces. From him I have received a most-friendly letter inviting me to engage in a correspondence with him, a very attractive idea to which I shall most enthusiastically acquiesce.

Today three British aeroplanes, flying at a great height, passed over the camp. An unusual and impressive sight for us here.

24 October (Wednesday)

One Hut 22 man was a professional footballer, playing I think for Huddersfield. He played today for the RFA Signallers' team which, to our immense satisfaction, beat the RGA Signallers by four goals to three. It was our half-holiday, but drizzling rain reduced my enthusiasm for watching sport in favour of spending the afternoon in the hut replying to my letters, including the one from my new Aberystwyth friend. During this procedure the hut became gloomier and gloomier as each window was painted over as a precaution against enemy aircraft.

One of our signalling officers who goes very soon to India went on furlough today. Though quick tempered at times, he has been very popular among us and having served in the South African War, he has always created in our minds an impression of awe.

I am feeling very fit now, probably fitter than ever before. Enjoying perfect health, on the point of going abroad, successful in my training and enjoying the respect of many friends makes me feel tremendously happy to be alive.

25 October (Wednesday)

Twice weekly we have night signalling, successful events owing to the keen interest taken in the work. When commencing tonight the trumpeters sounded the 'Alarm', and we were dismissed immediately to our respective Batteries. It was obvious by the column of smoke trailing upward so near that this time the fire was in the camp, and we soon learned that a large hut used for gunnery instruction was in flames. Assembling in 'C' Battery we were doubled to the hut and helped to wage war on the fire for 2 hours, but in vain, as the hut was completely destroyed and its valuable contents – two 18-pounder guns and a quantity of harness – ruined. To see Major Ford, with a wet handkerchief over his face, in the thick of the fight, was an inspiration. He'll certainly require a new uniform after that. The YMCA was dangerously near, but by means of fire screens it was successfully protected. The frequency of outbreaks of fire in the Bettisfield area has aroused so much suspicion that the number of sentries has been increased.

27 October (Saturday)

This afternoon several of us were photographed in full war paint, on horseback, by Gunner Jack Sharples, who was a professional photographer. Sharples, a Liverpuddlian, looks like a melodramatic actor with a dark, seamed face, but he does very well with his camera in the camp.

When Cyril Bunker's relatives visited the camp Sharples took a family group photograph, but lost the negative. Cyril's comment to me was, 'It's not surprising really. He's an awful boozer and is drunk most of his spare time.' His one redeeming feature is his voice. He's got a fair tenor voice, but he only knows three songs, including 'Little Willie and His Wild Woodbine'. His singing goes well in the Wet Canteen.

This evening enjoyed a walk through the country which, illuminated by a brilliant moon, looked like an indigo fairyland.

2 November (Friday)

From Abram I have received a letter dated 26 October, which lacks his usual optimistic air, but probably there are many excuses for that not mentioned in his epistle.

Just now I feel like a lousy bit of human mud. It's not the first time, and I shouldn't be surprised if one day the vermin carried me away. I have been pulled up by the censor for letters, although I had written nothing to object to and I regret if my letters are somewhat uninteresting. Your enquiry of Maybell [his friend Mabel] comes simultaneously to hers of you. Just now I hear from her pretty often. She is quite well and glad to know that you are still in England. I see you are anxious for that embarkation leave.

I wouldn't be so anxious if I were you. However, when you do go home, don't forget to call at No. 32 Crown Street and spin them a cheerful yarn about me. I only wish I could tell you more about conditions out here, but I suppose one has to grin and bear it, keeping your heart up and your head down. The weather is wretched, even as it was at Builth Wells whither we went a year today. You remember how it poured that Friday night – but everything for us was A1 then.

3 November (Saturday)

Having travelled all night, arrived at Port Talbot at 10 am for my third weekend leave. I had been home barely a half hour when a telegram arrived for me. It bore the imperious command, 'Return Immediately', and the words 'O/C "C" Battery'. During the journey home, at various stations, recipients of similar commands had warned us of what to expect, for it was evident that a general recall of men on leave was taking place. Extremely disappointed, but not surprised, I favoured the idea that the reason for this procedure was a military test rather than a military necessity, caused through some calamity that was being withheld from our knowledge – an opinion that not a few on the train shared.

With a haversack packed with tempting victuals by my good folk, I left Port Talbot at 2.15 pm and during an hour's wait for a connection at Cardiff, I met a schoolfellow, Griff Thomas, who after being badly wounded was discharged some months ago. Walking along St Mary's Street and Queen's Street in drizzling rain I listened to his enviable experiences in the trenches. I failed to remember the Port Talbot man he spoke of who, mortally wounded, and aware of it, had begged Griff to take his money and other belongings, rather than that any looter should be the gainer. There was some consolation in the fact that scores of recalled men left Cardiff with me on the 4.15 pm train. At Whitchurch (Salop), where we had to wait from 10.30pm until 2.55am, a Cambrian railwayman ushered some of us into the porter's room where a cheery fire welcomed. Our party consisted of the porter, a Royal Welsh Fusilier, a Royal Engineer, both recently returned from France, a man of the Labour Corps, another artilleryman and myself. After listening to a few bloodthirsty yarns from the front, I fell asleep on a long tool box with my plump haversack for a pillow.

4 November (Sunday)

Arriving at the hut I found my 'kip' made, so they expected my return. On waking I learned that the Brigade was ready if necessary to move away. We were just units in a mobilisation scheme and each man had been allotted his place or duty if any such move took place.

Corporal Walton, another Signaller, and I were on Brigade Headquarters Staff. The news that Sergeant Major Bonser is doing his best to arrange for the recalled men to proceed home on leave next Tuesday and also an organ recital this afternoon at Hanmer church atoned for all the tediousness of our cancelled leave.

7 November (Wednesday)

This morning the considerable number of men who joined the Signal School brought the total strength up to the usual of about 400. From Woolwich several extra instructors have arrived and one of them, a Corporal, wears the ribbon of the Distinguished Conduct Medal and three gold wound stripes. The hell they have been through seems to have taken all the starch out of these returned heroes. They all seem to be easy going. Instead of breaking their hearts the war has softened them. A perpetual grin hovers on the face of the aforementioned Corporal.

On parade this morning he said to a certain Signaller, 'I say old man, you're standing at ease with one leg and at attention with the other.'

We pumped these survivors for news about our job in France and the descriptions we listened to painted signalling in action as no rosy picture.

One of them said,

The suicide club is not a bad name for us. The lines have got to be kept O.K. If a shell blows 'em up, well, you've got to get 'em mended 'toot sweet'. If lines can't exist in the shell-fire, they make runners of you. If you fail to deliver the message, if in other words you get killed or wounded, they just keep sending out another runner until the message eventually gets through.

I have received a letter from my old companion, Dan Evans, who, having been transferred from the South Wales Borderers into the 51st Battalion of the Cheshire Regiment,[5] is now serving in the Curragh Camp, Ireland. He writes:

Owing to recent disturbances we have been issued with 120 rounds of ammunition. Our Battalion is dying for a scrap with the rebels. Sinn Feiners have caused disturbances in Dublin and Athlone, but there are enough troops in Ireland to make a mess of these rebels and if the same opinion prevails in other battalions as does in ours, it will be a poor look out for De Valera and his crowd.

12 November (Monday)

Abram's letter, dated the 5th, is so strange that it has me guessing. He complains:

I have not read a book since I've been out here. Before you get this letter I shall have gone through a very risky undertaking. What it is I am afraid to tell you as this might get opened. Anyhow, I am going in for it in the full spirit of the thing – and come what may, I am not afraid whichever way I come off, for I have my compensations.

I tell you Ivor, it's strange that the piece of poetry I once wrote used to haunt me in case it came true, because this I tell you of comes off at night. It doesn't worry

5. Up to 27 October 1917, this was known as the 213th Graduated Battalion and had no regimental affiliation. Before that it had been 59th Battalion of the Training Reserve and up to September 1916 the 13th (Reserve) Battalion of the South Wales Borderers. It was a training unit based at the Curragh in Ireland, part of 194th Brigade in 65th Division. It remained at the Curragh when the Division was broken up in March 1918.

me now. You remember the piece I allude to, that about me laying down on my
grassy bed and the stars o'erhead:

Silently, Mother, my tears fall.
Life is going and you gave me all. Etc. Etc.

Then he concludes on a more optimistic note – 'Good old Ivor. Good old Ivor. We will yet meet.'

17 November (Saturday)

The weather has been very cold and wet and mud in the camp is ankle deep. This afternoon those who remained indoors were all asleep with the exception of Signaller Bates and myself, who busied ourselves sketching in each other's autograph albums. Too great a price can be paid even for a well-rested body and I have never forgotten the shock I received when reminded by Baden-Powell in *Scouting for Boys*, I believe, that the average man of 75 has spent about 25 years of that time asleep. Bates has made for me a worthy if rather scratchy copy of a masterly black and white advertisement for mackintosh costs. The original sketch, a consummate drawing by an artist well trained in the art of leaving out, displays a very distinguished looking military officer wearing an elegant trench coat. With the justifiable superiority that the original worker feels over the copyist, I considered my little water colour a greater achievement than Bates', for mine was a sketch of my equipment – a bandolier, haversack, water bottle and mess tin carefully grouped upon my folded blankets.

19 November (Monday)

Received from Abram a letter written on YMCA notepaper and felt relieved that he had stumbled on such an oasis out there. Printed on the sheet top is 'On Active Service', beneath which are the words 'With the British Expeditionary Force' and on the side is the red triangular design of the YMCA. Abram adds to the date, 13 November, 'Dilys' birthday', probably as a gentle reminder that it is high time I wrote to Mabel's charming sister. In her last letter, Dilys, knowing of my approaching embarkation, earnestly desired that I should return safely and also 'the pure boy I had always been'. Well, why not? Abram refers to his recent hazards:

> *On the 5th I gave you a slight hint of a certain venture. Well I am thankfully glad to say I came out of it quite soundly.*[6]
> *This affair was mentioned in The Times of the 8th, from which you will gather it was an entire success. Tho' the experience was a new one for me, somehow I refused to be feared and probably ventured more than I should have. I had two very narrow 'shaves' – one indeed was a hairbreadth affair . . . These last few days I've been on the most cushy job I've had since being in the Army and am at present away from the Battalion with the platoon Lewis Gun team. There are 6 of us. I had better not say too much about it in case I might be relieved sooner than I would like. Sunday afternoon, for the first time out here I went to the pictures at a Corps cinema. The pictures and the music were not so bad, neither was the price of admission – 25 centimes. It's a pity letters are censored, but we must reserve such news for chats 'round that famous fireside at No. 7'.*

The batch of Hut 22 men who recently left here are now at a French Base. Signaller Aldous has written to tell me that they are having a fine time there prior to going up the line. These good friends were soon replaced by a number of youths who I understand have just attained military age. They are a lively lot and always up to some trick or other. One night they built with tables, forms, trestles and bed boards a chute sloping from the ceiling to the bottom of the other end of the hut down which they slid in turns.

---

6. Here Abraham is referring to a trench raid made by 'C' Company, 13th King's Liverpools on the night of 6/7 November in which three German prisoners were taken. The raiders lost one man killed and six wounded. (Details from the battalion war diary – National Archives reference WO/95/1429.)

Chapter 9

EMBARKATION LEAVE

23 November (Friday)

Arrived home for six days embarkation leave. This is now my fourth leave, as it is only about a fortnight since I had my third weekend leave. A few hours after my arrival I answered the door to find there our friend J.E. Rogers smiling broadly. His ship, SS *Araguaya* had brought patients from some theatre of war to Avonmouth, so he decided to come and spend a few days with us. When he is not commandeered by my sister, Nellie, to whom he is now engaged, thanks to Abram's mediation some time ago, I shall be glad of his company as nearly all my pals are in the forces. I thought he looked well in khaki and that the red cross on his sleeve looked impressive.

24 November (Saturday)

J.E. and I walked into town and on the way he remarked, 'My word Ivor, you are a smart soldier.' I could think of no reply but, 'And you're a good soldier, Eddie.' In Day's bookshop he bought me a complete set of the works of Shakespeare in ten volumes, each of a size that I can slip into my pocket if necessary. I am delighted with this unexpected gift. We bought a loaf cake, some chocolates and cigarettes, made of them a compact parcel and posted it to Abram. Acting on the advice of nearly every 'overseas' man I have spoken to about my going abroad, I bought an enamel mug. My mother is suffering acutely from a stomach disorder, probably brought on or worsened by worry about me going to France. To a chemist in Station Road I explained the symptoms and I hope the bottle of medicine he sold me will do the trick.

25 November (Sunday)

The members of my church have presented me with a pocket Bible. On the flyleaf, in beautiful copperplate handwriting, Pa has inscribed, in addition to the name and the donors, the following biblical text – 'Search the scriptures; for in them ye think ye have eternal life: and they are they which testify to me.', St John, Chapter 5, Verse 39.

28 November (Wednesday)

I returned with the 5.50 pm train and was relieved to find that the parting was not too painful. In fact I thought they all kept up very well. I had to go to Crewe to catch a connection, and there, for the first time saw some men of the US Navy, who on closer observation I discovered belonged to the Naval Air Service. I enjoyed a long conversation with one of them and as he had no English money, I exchanged some of mine for his which I intend to keep as mementos. I arrived at Bettisfield at 3.15 am and after a few hours sleep awoke refreshed and ready for the day's work.

This morning my kit was inspected and some comfortable, thick underclothing was added to it. Also I was given a gas helmet and a box respirator, testing the latter in a room full of tear gas.

Abram is in the thick of it again. He wrote the following letter the day Eddie and I despatched the parcel to him.

At the end of five days I was recalled from the Lewis Gun, being relieved by a man just returned from hospital. After that I had about as strenuous a time as ever I had, being out as much as 12 hours some nights, or from dusk to dawn, on rotten jobs, which however could not break my spirit. On one of these jobs my mate was killed and under most pathetic circumstances. On a certain night I got stuck in the muddy trench and once had to be dragged out. We are on the eve of another adventure, much riskier than the last and well, never mind, wait and see. Keep your heart up and your head down. Over the top with the best of luck.

2 December (Sunday)

All day I have been in the curious position of wishing that one of a batch of men would fall sick, as I was 'waiting man' or reserve on a draft going to the Anti-Aircraft Corps at Dunkirk, but no one became ill and I therefore missed a very attractive job abroad.

O'Reilly is being drafted to a depot at Norwich. Having bad eyesight and being in his late thirties, which makes him an elderly man to us teenagers, his medical category has been lowered and he will probably be kept in Britain. In order to have something by which to specially remember him, I asked him to write in my autograph album and he spent a half-holiday composing the following poem:

THE SONG OF 'IDDY UMPTY
Let others sing the glories of
Our peerless infantry,
And sturdy sons who man the guns,
Or our dashing cavalry.
But of the Signallers we sing: -
Although unarmed we be,
Yet ne'ertheless all must confess,
The Army's nerves are we.
Though we're not dressed in War's attire;
And to lonely O P(ips)[1] we retire;
But we flash the spark along the wire,
That sets the battle front on fire!
Heigh ho! We've nothing much to show,
A tattered flag the news to 'wag',
And p'raps a helio.
Slung o'er our shoulders you may see
Our reel of wire and old 'D(on) 3'[2]
Which we 'Iddy umpty, umpty iddy, iddy iddy umpty'.[3]
Night and day we play away,
The song of 'Iddy Umpty',
. . . - - - . . .[4]

1. Observation Posts.
2. The D3 Portable Field Telephone.
3. Terms used by a signalling instructor when teaching the use of flag signalling to send Morse messages.
4. Morse code for SOS.

We are the boys the ladies love,
We win each darling's heart;
No maid unkissed can e'er resist
The 'wagger' gay and smart.
And when the call 'To Arms' is heard,
We march to meet the foe, –
The darlings weep and to us creep,
They would not have us go.
There's many a sigh and tear dim'd eye,
And many a girl would wish to die,
But we laugh and chaff as we ride by
And give them all the glad, glad eye.
Heigh ho! 'Tis hard when we must go
And leave behind the girls so kind,
Who always loved us so.
But we'll return again some day
And gaily chase their tears away,
With our – 'Iddy umpty, umpty iddy, iddy iddy umpty' –
Loud and long we'll sing the song,
The song of 'Iddy Umpty'!
.. - - ..[5]

Upon dread War's encrimsoned field,
We're foremost in the fray;
Through maimed and dead our way we tread,
To keep the lines O.K.
And comrades bid their last 'Good bye', –
Old chums we loved so well,
Who nobly wrought and bravely fought,
Midst shattering blasts of Hell.
Where grim old Death goes stalking on,
And gives 'V(ick) E' to many a one;[6]

5. Morse code for IMI (Repeat).
6. Signalling code for 'The End'.

But bravely every mother's son
Undaunted, waits His last 'R.D(on)'![7]
Heigh ho! Here's to those lads we know
Who fought so well and fighting fell
With faces to the foe.
In mem'ry of each gallant boy,
We sing the song that gave them joy, –
Our – 'Iddy umpty, umpty iddy, iddy iddy umpty' –
Loud and strong, we sing the song,
The song of 'Iddy Umpty'!
. . . - .[8]

Beneath this poem the author wrote:

May you return from your 'Great Adventure' to those that hold you dear, safe,
sound, and full of honours.
At such a time may these few crude lines recall to your memory
Your sincere well wisher,
J.P. O'Reilly.

My other immediate hut neighbour, Gunner Hyde, was drafted away recently. Consistently, he was last to straggle on to his draft parade, causing an irate NCO to bellow, 'Hyde! You'll be late for the resurrection.'

After his departure I saw a military policeman escort a prisoner to the dentist. Thinking the prisoner looked a rare kind of cove, I enquired of someone what had been his crime and was told that he had been confined to a civil prison for desertion. I arrived in the hut one evening to find that this prisoner had succeeded Hyde as my neighbour. A short, squat man with a bald head, slits for eyes and a mouth that produced a leering expression, he certainly looked a hard case. After tea, sitting on our beds, we got into conversation during which he disclosed to me his amazing story. He is Driver Davies, comes from Pontypridd and enlisted early in the

7. Signalling code for 'Read Correctly'.
8. Morse code for V(ick) E (The End).

war. Because an O/C refused to grant him leave he deserted the Army and worked underground (coalmine) for two years and an overworked military records office failed to notice his absence. A quarrel with an in-law resulted in him being reported to the police and he was convicted and sent for 90 days to Bedford jail where he made mail bags and on the whole enjoyed himself thoroughly. Through the prohibition of tobacco he grew to feel so fit that he resolved to abstain from smoking for the rest of his life, but on his release, after the completion of his sentence, a good-intentioned warder offered him a cigarette which he hadn't the heart to refuse and thus was the bad habit resumed.

Finished reading *Life's Ideals* by Rev'd W. Dickie, which my uncle and aunt gave me as a birthday present at Fforestfach during my last leave.

Studiedly chosen by my kind relatives, ever anxious that I tread the straight path, it is a book of essays dealing with the development of moral and spiritual life. 'Life', the author tells us, 'is the greatest of all arts, and in doing the meanest task rightly and well a man demonstrates his capacity for doing the greatest.' In the chapter on Friendship the writer says, 'To the strongest natures persons count less than principles and to be true to great principles leads often into strange and desert paths.'

The chapter entitled 'The Ethics of Work' contained a sentence that shall have a permanent home in my memory – 'It is said of Amiel that he went to his desk as to an altar.' Then comes the noble suggestion that if we cannot rise out of our environment we can rise above it. A great book and one to be re-read.

5 December (Wednesday)

The Signal School has presented its O/C, Lieutenant Ince, who will soon be leaving for France, with a silver inkstand. He responded with feeling and afterwards shook hands with a number of us.

Church members at Port Talbot are doing their best to ease the lot of lads in khaki and blue. They collect donations and form sewing classes for the benefit of the men who are away serving their country. From my own chapel I have received a very welcome Postal Order for 5s, while the friends of Dyffryn Welsh Calvinistic Methodist Chapel, to which my grandfather attends, have sent me a parcel containing a knitted scarf.

8 December (Saturday)

Our friend from Bedford jail can neither read nor write, but I have taken him in hand. Am teaching him to write his name and to read small words like at, bat, cat, and numbers up to 12.

I advised him never if possible to admit his inability to read or write for there are numerous ways by which he could be duped on account of that, although he has other wits very well sharpened. He is an expert at opening sealed letters or removing an unfranked postage stamp. Since being in the Army I have heard some choice language, but never anything to compare with his. As Walton observed to me, 'He either coins new oaths or gives abominable twists to the already generous selection of swear words available.'

At the Dry Canteen this afternoon I performed for him what he considered an important piece of work, writing a letter that he dictated. It concerned his domestic affairs and ended affectionately with the words, 'With lots of love to little Annie', Annie being his young child. One of the sentences was so intimate that I had to question, 'Do you really want me to write that?' 'Yes', he replied definitely. Such devotion have I earned from him for such simple services that I believe he would strangle anyone who would try to do me an injury, and in a way it is a misfortune that I cannot take him to France with me. What a bodyguard he would be.

9 December (Sunday)

Among our hut mates who recently left for France was Signaller Crosby, a bald-headed, clean-shaven, powerfully built market gardener who bought a steel body protector prior to leaving. Crosby always displayed a remarkable ability for looking after number one and this unorthodox purchase was a manifestation of it. He was unmercifully teased about it, but possessing superb self-confidence he treated his laughing critics with disdain. 'D'you expect that to stop a bullet?' enquired an experienced warrior. 'It may not stop a bullet, but it may stop it going too far,' replied Crosby in his usual deliberate way. Then he continued effectively, 'Well, if a steel hat is good enough to protect my head, a steel waistcoat is good enough to protect the rest of me.' 'Why not go in for a pair of steel leggings?' asked someone else, but Crosby, realising that even logic is sometimes useless against humour, retired with disgust from the argument and proceeded hastily with his packing.

11 December (Tuesday)

With another senior Signaller placed in charge of one of the junior squads numbering about 20. After marching them to an empty hut we gave them buzzer reading and afterwards flag drill outdoors. The latter was a real test of our ability since we had been given no warning and had certainly received no practice, but realising that we had to proceed with the job, we willed ourselves into command and of course we relieved each other at intervals. I shall always feel grateful to the old-timer in the front row who on those few occasions when I hesitated for the right word, smilingly became a whispering prompter.

15 December (Saturday)

It is rumoured that our draft leaves for France next Tuesday. On the draft are many Gunners and Drivers, but only three Signallers – Herring, better known as 'Fish', which he prefers to be called, Ainscow, a dark, handsome fellow, in his thirties, I imagine, and myself. 'Fish' is a Liverpool man and was a bank clerk. At one time he was in the Liverpool Scottish Territorials. He is fresh complexioned and always looks as if his tender skin suffers from its daily shave. He is sturdily built as also Ainscow is, but Ainscow has a sallow complexion and has a small, neat moustache. Ainscow is quiet and reserved and wherever he would be placed you would imagine him behaving like a gentleman.

Our kit has been inspected and we have been issued with new underclothing, boots, field dressing, gas helmet and respirator and two identification discs, one circular and one angular and both about the size of a penny. The circular one is to suspend around your neck and the angular to be worn on the wrist. On them is stamped rank, name, regiment and religion, the last (cheerful thought) for burial purposes.

16 December (Sunday)

Today is my mother's birthday, her fiftieth. At home they are expecting me to go abroad any day, for today I received from Nellie a box of cigarettes. Also a letter came from our friend, Eddie Rogers, who is aboard the hospital ship SS *Braemer Castle* at Liverpool, waiting to take American and Canadian wounded and sick across the Atlantic. As a theological student at Aberystwyth, he answered his country's call, with several fellow students and joined the Royal Army Medical Corps. After a period of training they were placed aboard a hospital ship and are seeing much of the world.

This evening a draft leaves Bettisfield for Egypt.

17 December (Monday)

Assembled with the other 'C' Battery draft men at the canteen where Major Ford, our O/C, addressed us. There was genuine feeling in his parting message this morning, when he wished us the best of luck and a speedy and safe return with honour and glory. I think Driver Davies is sorry to lose me for he will now have to find someone else to read and write his letters. He has given me his own cigarette case as a keepsake.

Our draft left Bettisfield Park Camp at 10 pm without any fuss or excitement, for such exoduses are frequent.

18 December (Tuesday)

In the early morning, during frequent awakenings from fitful slumber, I once looked out, when passing through a large station to find it was Luton. Our train arrived at Waterloo station, London about 6 am and we learned that we were to leave for Southampton at 1 pm. The youthful subaltern in charge of us ordered us not to leave the station. What a hope he had. No sooner had he stridden away than Fish, Ainscow and I went to the Union Jack Club nearby, where we shaved, washed, polished up and had a substantial ham and egg breakfast. Afterwards feeling fresh and satisfied we walked to the Strand where the theatres, whose names are household words, claimed much of our attention, as also did some ruined buildings, the result of a recent air raid. At Trafalgar Square I sent home a postcard, then we strolled around Westminster, returning by bus to St Paul's, which we inspected even to the crypt. Before entraining there was a roll call and it was found that one man had deserted. The young officer who will have to answer for it was visibly upset, but he did grin when he overheard Fish say, 'We can win the war without him.'

At Southampton, passing through a large shed near the quay, we each received a sickly, yellow, rock-cake. I ate mine but immediately regretted it.

About 4 pm we left Southampton on a small ship named *Mona's Queen* and as we steamed away it dawned upon me what infinite comfort and security was being left behind. The crew moved among us distributing lifebelts. On board many regiments were represented and there were also some USA soldiers with one of whom we conversed. We passed a large liner, probably the *Aquitania* or *Mauretania*, lying at anchor, painted grey, with a large red cross on her side. Nearby a dummy battleship looked quite dwarfed in comparison. Farther out seaplanes swooned about. As dusk approached we 'came to' and on our starboard were assembled a flotilla of destroyers, looking efficient and purposeful. A captive balloon was moored to one of them. We gazed proudly at these silent allies silhouetted against the blue haze. Presently one of the destroyers steamed ahead of us and signalled two 'Don Don' messages, messages sent twice, and to which no reply must be sent, for in this instance we faced the Channel and possibly hostile attack. With ease we read those messages flashed by an electric signalling lamp fixed on the vessel's mast, the signalling being slow, deliberate and splendid. The first message gave instructions concerning our ship's navigation lights and the other read:

LOOK OUT FOR SCATTERED CONVOY IN CHANNEL.

Darkness had now enveloped us and we stepped below into the saloon where we dined on biscuits and tinned fruit. We steamed into very rough weather as we laid down on the deck in the hope of sleep. We shipped abundant water, the companion way looking like a miniature waterfall if the ship's bow dipped forward when one of the crew came in. With most of the others I was sick, but not very badly, although the crew were not able to tell us as their ancestors told Robinson Crusoe that it was 'but a capful of wind', for some of them were sick too. We were glad to reach port about midnight and we climbed on deck to have a glimpse of France, but all that was visible were dull-looking sheds and warehouses along the quayside. My impulse was to step ashore so that if for some reason our ship was ordered elsewhere, I could then proudly boast that I had been to France. We returned below to our kits, made ourselves as comfortable as possible on the hard deck and slept for a few hours.

1918

With the coming of 1918 the war was building towards its climax and the major test would be for Germany. Could she capitalise on the defeat of Russia and win the war on the Western Front before US manpower decisively tipped the balance in favour of the Allies? A further problem for Germany was the fact that the other members of the Central Powers were increasingly unable to support the demands of total war. Austria-Hungary had become dependent on direct German military support, Turkey was losing ground all over the Middle East and Bulgaria was satisfied with her conquests and wanted nothing more than to get herself out of the war. Germany's war leaders also realised that problems on the home front, severe food shortages, riots and strikes, would undermine any further prolonged military effort. The Allies too were increasingly war weary but they at least had the knowledge that the USA was now on side and in the near future more than 1 million of her troops would be in France.

Between 21 March and 15 July, Ludendorff had the German Army launch a series of offensives. Transferring numerous divisions from Russia, Ludendorff achieved a superior concentration of manpower for his offensive. However, he was forced to leave over one million troops in the East to further German territorial ambitions in the chaos of Bolshevik Russia. Ludendorff's first blow fell on the weakened British Fifth Army, which was thrown into confusion by the speed of the German assault. In a pattern that played itself out in each of the major German attacks of 1918, a hurricane artillery bombardment of high-explosive and gas shells was followed by an initial successful breakthrough and advance, which was gradually checked by a combination of stiffening resistance by Allied forces, tiredness among the German infantry and the inability of their artillery and logistic support to keep pace. Even so, this advance was the greatest since the initial German invasion of France and Belgium in 1914. The seriousness of the situation can be seen in Haig's 'Backs to the Wall' order to his troops following the German offensive push in Flanders launched on 9 April. In this order the British commander called for his men to stand their ground and fight to the death. His biggest fear was of a German breakthrough to the Channel ports, the loss of which would spell defeat for the BEF as they would be cut off from Britain. However, with each attack, German casualties among her key stormtroop units and assault divisions weakened the ability to successfully undertake the next attack. By the time the Germans were halted by French troops on the Marne in July, Ludendorff's war-winning strategy was in ruins and his army no longer had any reserves of manpower to make good their heavy losses.

When the Allies went over to the offensive in August, the lead role was played by Haig's forces. The British attack at Amiens on 8 August by General Sir Henry Rawlinson's Fourth Army, in conjunction with the French First Army, was supported by more than 400 tanks and the massed use of British and French aircraft flying ground-attack sorties. Spearheaded by the Australian Corps and Canadian Corps, by nightfall the advance could be measured at between 6 and 8 miles and more than 30,000 German prisoners were taken. The tide of war had now turned. Ludendorff called 8 August 'The Black Day of the German Army' and declared to his nation's political leaders that Germany could no longer win the war and an armistice was needed. From this point, despite suffering a manpower shortage brought on by the heavy losses of late 1917, British, Dominion and Empire troops, supported by the French and Americans, maintained their advance in 100 days of offensive action, including the storming of the strong Hindenburg Line position. On 29 September, following the collapse of Bulgaria, Ludendorff again advised the Kaiser to seek an armistice. This time the wheels were put in motion and on 8 November German and Allied delegates met in Compiègne Forest to discuss terms. The severe armistice terms offered by the overall

Allied commander, Marshal Foch, were designed to ensure that Germany could not resume hostilities.

When the guns fell silent on the Western Front at 11 am on 11 November, victory for the Allies was complete. The process began in the Balkans with the Bulgarians signing an armistice on 30 September. Here Serbian forces, supported by the French, managed to scale the 4,500ft Moglena Mountains and break the Bulgarian Line by late afternoon on 17 September. Next day the British, with Greek support, attacked at Doiran and for two days battered away at the defences. Once again the Bulgarians held firm at Doiran, but had been unable to send troops to reinforce against the continued Franco-Serbian advance. On 20 September, with their lines of communication threatened, the Bulgarians were forced to withdraw all along their line. Pursued by Allied forces and bombed in mountain passes by the RAF, this retreat became a rout and nine days later an armistice was signed, coming into effect on 30 September.

A month later it was the turn of Turkey to follow suit. Lloyd George ordered General Allenby to advance on Damascus and Aleppo, the capture of which would not only clear Turkish forces from Palestine but also trap the remaining Turkish forces still operating in Mesopotamia. Although losing the equivalent of five divisions to the Western Front, making up for casualties suffered in the German spring offensives, Allenby was still able to undertake an advance, having been reinforced by troops from Mesopotamia and India. By September 1918, with the Turks expecting a major attack through the Jordan Valley, Allenby moved back toward the Mediterranean for his decisive offensive. On 19 September the advance began with such overwhelming success that three days later the Turkish 7th and 8th Armies ceased to exist. During these operations the Turks were harassed in their rear by raids mounted by Arab irregulars led by the Emir Feisal and T.E. Lawrence. Damascus fell to Allenby's men on 31 September and the advance continued until checked north of Aleppo. The offensive continued on 26 October and placed Turkish forces in such a poor strategic position that an armistice was asked for two days later. The crisis for Turkey was compounded by the news from Mesopotamia when, on 24 October, General Marshall's troops began operations against the last major Turkish force left in the field. Although slowed by Turkish rearguards in very difficult terrain, by 27 October British forces had the Turks hemmed in south of the town on Sharqat with their line of retreat cut. For two days, while the Turks tried to break through armoured cars, cavalry and infantry to their north, British and Indian infantry attacked from the south to tie as many Turkish units to their line as possible, thus weakening their breakout attempt. On 30 September, with both sides exhausted and the British Line to the north still holding, the Turkish commander surrendered his force. The war in the Middle East was as good as over and confirmation of this came on 31 October, with news that a general armistice with the Turks was now in force.

The final member of the Central Powers to collapse prior to the German armistice was Austria-Hungary. Undertaking an offensive to coincide with German attacks on the Western Front, the increasingly weak Austro-Hungarians made the fatal decision to split their forces and advance from the mountains and along the River Piave. As the offensive only began on 15 June, it failed to draw Allied forces away from the Western Front and met stubborn resistance from the rebuilt Italian Army. Suffering almost 150,000 casualties, the Austro-Hungarians were forced on to the defensive and now lacked the reserves to strengthen their line. Morale collapsed and the various nationalities within the Empire began organising its destruction and the establishment of independent nation states. On 23 October, Allied forces in Italy went on the offensive with British troops seizing vital islands in the River Piave. Four days later, Emperor Karl attempted to negotiate a separate surrender for Austria-Hungary. However this came too late as the Czechs, Hungarians, Croats and Serbs had moved too far down the road to independence and many of their units within the army mutinied. On 4 November, an armistice between Austria-Hungary and the Allies came into force, although the Habsburg Empire in all but name had ceased to exist.

With the war now over, most of Britain's 'civilian soldiers' wanted to go home, having done their bit to secure victory. Unfortunately, the initial demobilisation scheme, drawn up in 1917 by the Secretary of State for War, Lord Derby, proposed that the first men to be released from service were those who worked in key industries. However, it was invariably these men who had been called up in the latter stages of the war. This left many of those with the longest service records at the back of the queue, which was the main cause of resentment. Soldiers from the Dominions also suffered delays, many waiting months in camps in Britain for transportation home. Once Churchill was appointed Secretary of State for War in January 1919, he amended the demobilisation programme, making sure that age, length of service and wounds were taken into account when selecting the order in which men were sent home. But until then the authorities worried about unrest in the ranks as small-scale mutinies broke out in Calais and Folkestone and a demonstration of 3,000 soldiers occurred in central London. There were also problems with Australian and Canadian troops stuck in Army camps in England who wanted nothing more than to get a troopship journey home. The most serious incident occurred on 4–5 March 1919 at Kinmel Camp in North Wales where Canadian discontentment ended with 5 men killed, 23 wounded and 78 arrested. Of the latter, 25 were convicted of mutiny and given sentences of between 90 days' detention and 10 years' penal servitude.

Some of those awaiting demobilisation were part of Allied occupation forces sent to enforce terms of the armistice in Germany, Austria, Turkey and Bulgaria. Others found themselves in 1918 committed to far-flung parts of the former Tsarist Empire in an attempt to curb German territorial ambitions and to secure large stockpiles of arms and munitions that had been sent to aid the Russian war effort. Once Germany surrendered, the threat of their pre-eminence in the region was at an end. However, the Allied governments, rather than pull their forces out of Russia, became embroiled in a muddled and half-hearted attempt to support anti-Bolshevik 'White' forces. At the North Russian ports of Archangel and Murmansk could be found some 30,000 men, almost half of which were British, under General Edmund Ironside. In South Russia former members of the British Salonika Force could be found at Sevastopol in the Crimea, Batoum in Georgia and even Baku on the Caspian Sea; the latter two locations being important for their oil. Troops from Mesopotamia were also involved in these operations, forming the largest contingent of the occupation force at Baku. Finally, there was a multi-national Allied force, under General Alfred Knox, operating in Siberia along the Trans-Siberian Railway from the port of Vladivostok. These politically inspired expeditions would drag on into 1920 before the wartime Allies pulled out and left Russia to Lenin and the Bolsheviks.

Chapter 10

FRANCE AND THE FIFTH ARMY

19 December (Wednesday)

When we awoke it was daylight and from the deck Le Havre was dimly visible across the water. Slowly the haze lifted, buildings loomed into sight, tramcars plied to and fro, traffic increased and people hastened to their work. Two French naval patrol boats ploughed rapidly up the Seine. Near us on the quay a French naval man sauntered to and fro with fixed bayonet. A small red woollen ball of wool crowned his cap. About 10 am we commenced discharging rations, consisting of weighty boxes of bully beef, biscuits and jam, after which we disembarked, were rallied on the quay by a Scots Sergeant Major and then marched away. The storm had so penetrated our systems that we could still feel the rocking and rolling of the ship. In the streets, with their numerous cafes and estaminets, blue-uniformed poilus were conspicuous amid the drab clad civilians, and yet more conspicuous a Zouave[1] in red pantaloons and fez, lounging at a street corner. We had an exhausting march to Harfleur, halting and resting after each mile. Carrying a full pack and a rifle is no joke and although it is December, perspiration oozed from us and when the rests came we were glad to lay down at the roadside in the snow. At such times we were besieged by apple and chocolate vendors who demanded exorbitant prices for their commodities, but a shrewd indifference on our part quickly resulted in a reduction in prices. The slab of chocolate I bought (Chocolat Menier) had a stale, earthy taste. We passed a colony of refugees housed in sheds and shacks of all

---

1. Zouaves were light infantry recruited from French settlers in Algeria. From 1915, with the French Army changing to horizon-blue uniforms for their home army and khaki for colonial troops, the Zouaves adopted the latter as service dress. The soldier spotted by Ivor was wearing the traditional uniform of short blue jacket decorated with braid, baggy red trousers and red chéchia (fez) then worn as a dress uniform.

descriptions. Replying to inquiries as to how far Harfleur was 'Tommy', riding a bicycle, replied impressively, 'About half a kilometre.'

This cheered us a little, but not so much as the brass band which met us and played us up a steep hill into the camp, for the magic of music rendered our packs weightless and transformed our shuffling into a rhythmic march. Harfleur, the name brings memories of schooldays and Henry V, is the Base Depot of the Royal Horse and the Royal Field Artillery; we hear it is noted for the severity of its discipline and for the number of musicians and entertainers that comprise its permanent staff. The fathers among us swear that their boys shall learn to sing or play a musical instrument in preparation for future wars. Here everyone moves at the double, so that after the band detached itself from us, we were doubled to a square where a colossal Sergeant Major awaited us. His moustache was perfectly waxed and he reminded me of a pouter pigeon. Skilfully he marshalled us into ranks, stood us at ease, strode away and after a few minutes returned with the Commanding Officer and the Orderly Officer. The CO was a fatherly old gent with rows of medal ribbons on his breast. 'Pouter', with a stentorian voice, bawled 'Shown' (Attention) and at the request of the CO we again stood 'at ease' and underwent an inspection, each man having to turn up the flap of his tunic and display the field-ambulance dressing deposited there in a special provided pocket, and state his occupation in civilian life, musicians and entertainers take one pace to the rear. This over, we were allotted to different camps and tents. There were 17 stuffed into our bell tent, besides kit and equipment and we heard that some tents had more. God help them. My address now is:

203348, Signaller J.I. Hanson,
L. Troop, No. II Camp,
Royal Horse and Royal Field Artillery,
Base Depot,
HARFLEUR

20 December (Thursday)

When sharing a bell tent with 16 others one has to be an incorrigible optimist to expect a night's sound sleep, nevertheless we squeezed ourselves into the small circle and closed our eyes, for as the poet says, 'Hope springs eternal in the human breast.'

It was a night of frequent awakenings, to find oneself pinned beneath another's legs, having to push from one's face a sweaty foot, easing an elbow from one's ribs or finding oneself half outside the tent curtain.

Our hours of duty are from 7 am to 4 pm and today we have had a thorough course of gas drill, a revision of the course we had in England. As no plates or basins are provided for meals we make use of our mess tins and mugs.

This evening we attended a dance at the YMCA but being unable to dance I was merely an onlooker. Had a conversation with a Coldstream Guard whose experience in the Line had taught him that the average British Tommy was more than a match for the average German, a statement that I found very reassuring. Sent Ma a souvenir handkerchief.

21 December (Friday)

This morning on the snow-clad cliffs, where a stiff breeze blew and the misty Channel lay below, we did flag signalling and in the afternoon we were tested in the various methods of signalling. We received our first overseas pay, each being paid a clean, crisp, 10 franc note, magnificently designed, the procedure taking place in the approved Army fashion, outdoors. My pay is now 1s 6d per day, the extra sixpence being proficiency money. I shall soon be entitled to another small increase, as a penny a day is added for each year's service. This evening, in a large hut, a chaplain gave a lantern lecture on Dickens' *A Christmas Carol*, after which he distributed from the stage a number of gifts such as tins of fruit. The precious articles were hurled from the stage, but unfortunately none came near us. I have bought a book of postcard views of Le Havre. It looks a fine city, but we are not allowed to leave the camp.

22 December (Saturday)

After a medical inspection we received our 'Up-Line' equipment – steel hat, high boots, blanket, groundsheet and iron rations, the last consisting of a fist-full of small biscuits and a tin of bully beef, these being issued in a small, white calico bag, with strict instructions that they were not to be eaten except in emergency. The groundsheet is made so that it can also be used as a cape. Today, for travelling, we had to roll the blanket into the groundsheet lengthwise and then bend it into shape resembling a horse collar, this being worn like a huge bandolier. For the last time we paraded at the Base Camp in the afternoon, had a roll call, then in the fading light a Corporal read out rules and regulations affecting men on active service, each paragraph ending with the warning that offenders would be severely dealt with. Then our field dressings were inspected again, after which we were informed of the name of the unit to which we were being posted. Fish, Ainscow and I were consigned to the 5th Cavalry Corps and we felt proud and satisfied. We marched to Le Havre railway station and were dumped on a platform used only by troops. A small canteen selling tea, buns and chocolate was like an oasis in a railroad desert. It was a relief to extricate ourselves from our weighty equipment and after a wait of several hours our train shunted slowly in, a chain of goods vans, each lettered 'Huit chevaux ou trente hommes'.[2] We exceeded this limit, for 36 of us were packed into each vehicle, in which we spent the night travelling at a very slow pace. Sleeping or even resting was difficult, there being insufficient room for stretching one's limbs, so we chatted for hours in the light of candles stuck on the ledges, the flames having to fight a desperate battle with the draughts.

23 December (Sunday)

Awaken from a doze by the jolting of the train as it stopped at a station which was our destination. We found it was Rouen. As we walked alongside our train some passenger carriages provided for officers caused grumbling in the ranks. After the usual wait, we were marshalled into our squads and marched through some streets alongside the Seine, to a Church Army Rest Camp, which we appreciated after the uncomfortable night. The building looked like an ex-factory and it was capable of accommodating a large

---

2. 'Eight horses or thirty men'. Ivor may be mistaken here for the standard capacity of French railway wagons was marked as 'Huit chevaux ou quarante hommes' – 'Eight horses or forty men'.

number. One large shed was fitted with rows of wire-netting beds fixed in tiers. We annexed one each depositing thereon our equipment. The adjoining room contained a large canteen selling various military necessities besides refreshments. At a table a chaplain busily censored letters. Outside, in the wash house we had a refreshing shave, wash and brush-up, afterwards enjoying the good things served up by beaming English ladies at the canteen. My conversation with a friendly Australian soldier ended when the chaplain expressed a desire to have a short service. He trusted that on this Christmas Sunday all would remain to take part, and very soon hundreds were heartily singing the good old Christmas hymns. After that we paused to listen to a French boy sing 'Apres la guerre fini', accompanying himself with a concertina. Having learned that we were to remain for the whole day at Rouen, Fish, Ainscow and I secured passes and after dinner went into the city, walking alongside the river with its ships, barges and stately bridges. Sunday here is like a Saturday at home. The main streets were thronged with soldiers, most French, but there was a good sprinkling of French colonials, Belgians, Americans, Chinese and scores of British soldiers and WAACs, the last two making the scene less unfamiliar.

It seemed to me that all the civilians wore black. After passing through a few streets, interesting ourselves in the people, shops and buildings, we came to the Cathedral, a building of towering magnificence. We entered and joined a group of sightseers who were being shown around by a ghostly looking verger. He was uniformed, and dangling from his gilded belt was a dirk. With subdued voice and gesture he elucidated each object, such as a tomb, a statue or painting and other sickly sights that confront one in such edifices and cause them to resemble sepulchres. Sunbeams tinted into many hues by the stained glass illumined the bowed heads of praying people. The innocent sound of children singing wafted in from some cloister, and we saw some of these children afterwards and in contrasting them with our own bonny bairns in the homeland they seemed to be delicate and refined. When we came out we lost Fish for a considerable time, but finding him eventually and chaffing him as to where he really had been, we decided to remain in the city for tea enquiring of several Tommies for a suitable restaurant. All the ones recommended us were packed, with long queues waiting outside some of them, so guessing that those on the outskirts might be less busy, we recrossed the Seine and passing along several streets we found a decent-looking cafe. Sitting alone at the next table to ours was a British Royal Marine, who it appeared was stationed at Rouen and could speak French fairly well. He gave our order and advised us not to display our franc notes. Realising that our opportunity for another spread of this kind would be negligible for an indefinite time, we dined well for our financial resources. An encore of fish and chips was followed by chicken, other foods and a bottle of vin rouge, the victuals being sent up to our 'garcon' in a small lift. The proprietor decorously bowed us out with profuse 'Merci monsieurs' and handed our notes to his cashier, a dark, plump lady who reminded me of Dickens 'Madame Defarge',[3] and who sat at a desk at the entrance. Feeling contented and fit to continue the Up-Line journey, we returned to camp and left soon afterwards at 9 pm, entraining in the same kind of vans. The French railmen use horns as ours use whistles and the tooting of them raised much laughter in the vans. There are very few bags of iron rations left. A brawny, sullen Welshman, squatting near us in the van, described in detail the brief affair he had had with a prostitute in Rouen. On behalf of the woman he had been solicited in a street by a small boy.

24 December (Monday)

Still ambling along we entered some of the old battlefields, scarred with winding trenches, barbed wire entanglements and dug-outs. Snow lay everywhere, the scenery being monotonous, dreary and uninviting. Occasionally we saw a tank or gun, *hors de combat*, lying at unusual angles in shell holes. We passed through scores of villages, some completely destroyed. During one long halt of our train we kindled a fire alongside the railroad, drew water from the engine tank and in spite of its stale oily taste, boiled it in a huge biscuit tin and made tea.

Peronne, our destination, was a mass of ruins and looked a scene of utter desolation, especially under its mantle of snow. Arriving there in the afternoon we cautiously marched along the slippery road. Several of us fell

3. Wife of the proprietor of a wine shop in Charles Dickens' novel *A Tale of Two Cities*.

but came down on our kit bags and as they were filled mostly with clothing we were unhurt. The roads had been cleared of debris and shattered masonry which was piled high on the roadsides. The artillerymen of the detachment numbered about a hundred and were billeted by the Town Major in a wooden shed in the yard of a ruined house. The shed was patched with canvas which kept some of the draught out, and was fitted with the usual tiers of wire bed.

I felt slightly apprehensive. Real values were now asserting themselves and the real, practical men – the 'Admirable Crichtons' – rose to the top like cream.[4] A fire was soon blazing and we dined on tea, biscuits and jam. Afterwards, rejoining Fish and Ainscow, we went for a walk, crossing a narrow but turbulent river which someone said was the Somme. Very few civilians remain, but a large number of soldiers are billeted here, including Indians with their turbans and smocks, bravely enduring the extremely cold weather. Some of them were mounted on lithe, well-groomed horses. Motor lorries passed us in what seemed an endless convoy, loaded with men, munitions, food and stores. We heard the 'cheerful' news that Peronne is bombed frequently.

Gravitating to the YMCA hut, we did some letter writing as the people at home will be anxious just now. We spin a very cheerful tale, but oh! What a Christmas Eve.

25 December (Tuesday)

Christmas Day. Early ironic greetings were exchanged, and one realist exclaimed disgustingly, 'Merry Christmas by damn.' As we arose two lively fellows occupying the beds beneath us sang 'Burlington Bertie'. After breakfast continued our journey on foot, but had an early halt owing to an enemy plane flying over. It flew at a tremendous height and was soon gone. We marched 3 or 4 miles along icy roads to a transport depot, passing several military cemeteries crowded with small white crosses. The weighty

4. *The Admirable Crichton* is a comic stage play written in 1902 by J.M. Barrie. In the play, Crichton, butler to Lord Loam, assumes the role of leader after the family is shipwrecked on a deserted tropical island and he proves to be the only one with any practical survival knowledge and skills. After two years on the island Crichton becomes 'the Gov' and has all the trappings of privileges and power that his master had in England. He is on the verge of marrying Lord Loam's daughter, Lady Mary, when a rescue ship arrives and he has to resume his role as butler. Back at Loam Hall, where the status quo is uneasily restored, Crichton announces he is leaving service. He does this to protect the reputation of Lady Mary of whom there are rumours of her having being unfaithful to her fiancé Lord Brocklehurst. The play ends with the regretful final parting of Crichton and Lady Mary.

equipment cut into our shoulders and during the halts we were glad to prostrate ourselves in the snow for a rest. Waiting is one of the banes of a soldier's life, but this of today, at a roadside in the Transport Camp, for about 3 hours was a severe trial of our patience. Then two lorries belonging to our new unit arrived for us. They bore the red and black colours of the artillery, and the red, running fox sign of the Fifth Army.

After a jolting, swaying journey, during which we were forced to stand owing to our number, we were deposited at Hancourt about 5 pm. Here snow was a foot deep. Not many walls of Hancourt had escaped destruction by shell fire and the scene reminded me of pictures of Scott's expedition to the Antarctic. Here our unit was resting, a misnomer. At this particular time they were watering the horses, both men and horses having a shabby appearance. We learned that they had only recently arrived on this front after a period in the Ypres sector which fully accounted for their condition. It was hard to believe that the very ordinary looking officer who was among the first to meet us was the Colonel. 'Are there any cooks or stewards among you?' he enquired. Like a shot up went Fish's arm, which amused Ainscow and me, but to our derision he reacted by pointing knowingly to his head and saying, 'Up here you want it.' Immediately he was appointed assistant cook at our Brigade Headquarters. Eventually our separation was complete for Ainscow was sent to 'A' Battery and I to 'B' Battery. A Bombardier escorted our squad to 'B' Battery, where we found the men dwelling in bell tents, but nearby bow huts were being erected. The horses and the guns were as yet shelterless. A youthful officer, hammer in hand, put his head out of the window of a nearby almost completed hut and gave instructions to a Sergeant who cheered us up by the generous remark, 'You're just in time for the Christmas dinner.' Our squad, alluded to as 'the reinforcements', had the first sitting at the Christmas spread which had been paid for by the officers and Sergeants of the Battery. We greatly appreciated this very considerate kindness to ourselves as newcomers. A whole pig had been roasted and there were potatoes, onions, Brussels sprouts, Christmas pudding, apples, oranges, dates, nuts, cigarettes, a cigar and a double rum issue. During this orgy musical selections were given on a portable Decca gramophone, manipulated by a Sergeant wearing an

Australian 'bush' hat, broad brimmed and turned up at one side. It appeared that at some time our Brigade had been attached to the Australians. One of the songs chosen by the Sergeant was 'Where my Caravan has Rested', composed by Hermann Lohr. During the rum issue teetotallers were eagerly requested by beaming drinkers to draw their ration since they were not at all averse to a little extra. A crude entertainment followed in an adjoining hut which was nearly completed. A driver tried to do a solo dance, the cook, a stolid fellow with a good bass voice, sang, 'Asleep in the Deep'. The aforementioned officer is the Captain, at present in charge of the Battery, during the absence of the Major. He shared in the fun. Slept the night in a bell tent which luckily possessed a little stove.

26 December (Wednesday)

Reinforcements escorted to the Brigade Medical Officer, a dark man with a small moustache. He examined between our fingers for signs of scabies, we were told, and took particulars from our pay books. The guns at the Front boom continuously, gun flashes preceding them and Verey lights dangle against a vermilion background. We learn that Hancourt is about 5 miles behind the Front-Line trenches. Last night Driver Callon imbibed too much rum, slept the night among the horses and mules, probably mistaking their legs for bedposts. He survived unhurt but lost his dentures. When someone heard that a mule had interred the teeth with a dainty hoof, his reaction was 'Lucky Callon wa'nt interred too.'

Captain A.F. Hollingworth,[5] who is O/C our Battery at the moment, is quite young and seems very keen. He has risen from a Gunner and we hear that in 1917 he led a Naval Brigade raid after its own officers had been knocked out. For that exploit he was awarded the Military Cross and the French Croix de Guerre, while Signaller Womersley, who accompanied him, received the Military Medal. My address now is:

---

5. Albert Hollingworth from Bolton in Lancashire was born on 8 October 1893. When war was declared he was working as a machinist in Edmonton, Canada, and signed up as a Private in the 4th Canadian Infantry Battalion on 5 January 1915. In January 1917 he applied for a commission in the Royal Artillery and was sent to 311 Brigade. On 14 August the award of his Military Cross was announced in the *London Gazette*. On 12 November he was made acting Captain and officer in charge of 'B' Battery, 311 Brigade. On 6 January 1918, he gained promotion to Lieutenant. Hollingworth held the rank of acting Major from 10 February until 17 March, when he again became an acting Captain. He returned to England for demobilisation on 12 May 1919.

203348, Signaller J.I. Hanson,
'B' Battery,
311th Army Brigade, R.F.A.,
British Expeditionary Force, FRANCE

Army Brigade, or Flying Column – an invention by GHQ in 1917. Army Brigades were transferred from their original Divisions and placed under the direct command of an Army. This was claimed to be deleterious for the awards of decorations and other desirable attentions from the Big Brass, but had the advantage of such Brigades being fussed over less by Divisional Commanders.

27 December (Thursday)

Had a tough job getting into my high boots this morning. As the weather is so cold we are forced to sleep in our clothes, taking off only our boots and tunic. I hadn't learned the trick of keeping my boots near my body, so that this morning I found them frozen stiff. We each have two blankets and a groundsheet, and sleeping in pairs we share four blankets and two greatcoats, with tunics and kit bags for pillows. This morning a pile of snow, drifting through a narrow crack during the night, lay quite near me, but this Nissen hut is a great improvement on a bell tent. In one of the empty bell tents Callon sat staring at nothing with glassy eyes, for he has been in a semi trance since Christmas night when he got very drunk on rum. When he recovered he vowed never to touch rum again.

I am on the look out for my friend Abram Marienberg, making numerous inquiries about his regiment – the King's Liverpools, and scrutinise every cap badge I see, but the regiment is not in this sector.

30th December (Sunday)

This morning attended Divine Service at the YMCA hut, not far from our camp. The subject of the sermon was gratefulness, the chaplain reminding us that as it was the last Sunday of the year we should feel grateful for being kept safely through a year of strange experiences.

Hancourt is so near the Front that we have to wear our gas respirators at the 'ready' position, that is, slung over the shoulder and hanging at the side. In the Line they have to be worn on the chest in the alert position.

1918

1 January (Tuesday)

Reinforcement Signallers tested in buzzer reading by Captain Hollingworth and Corporal Swallow. Swallow is in charge of 'B' Battery Signallers. Most of us had 'R.Don' (Read correctly) and Hollingworth, glancing through the message forms, picked out one and enquired, 'Which is Hanson?'

I signified and he remarked, 'Yours is very neatly done, Hanson.' Not a bad start, I thought.

2 January (Wednesday)

We are medically inspected by the Brigade Doctor once a week. When he arrives we heard the command, 'Fall in everybody', at which we undress in the open, for there are no civilians within miles of us, and then the doctor and a Royal Army Medical Corps NCO inspect our hands, peering between our fingers for any signs of scabies and at our abdominal regions for any signs of lice.

The weather is fine but exceedingly cold. For several days we have been cleaning, polishing and improving everything in the camp for General Sir Hubert Gough's[6] inspection, which took place today. During his inspection the Signallers did flag drill under Corporal Swallow. The greatest problem confronting 'B' Battery was how to deal with Jacko, the 'D' Subsection mule, in time for the inspection. Jacko has never been broken in. His place is back in the wilds, or in a zoo, providing the barricades were powerful enough. He has never been saddled or harnessed and the only time I have ever seen him groomed was during the last few days. He looked a sight with his hide caked with mud and to remove that the 'B' Battery Farrier enlisted the help of Farriers from the other Batteries who bound him with ropes. When that dangerous procedure had been accomplished he looked a queer sight, lying on the ground like a trussed fowl for Christmas, and with

6. General Sir Hubert de la Poer Gough (1870–1963) was, at 44, the youngest British Army commander of the First World War. He shouldered much of the blame for the retreat of his 5th Army in March 1918. Gough was a sharp-tongued man, given to sarcasm and not one to suffer fools. This character somewhat belied his chummy nickname of 'Goughie'.

an expression of hate in his wild eyes. He is a parasite and a disgrace to the British Army. Everyone except Farriers give him a wide berth normally, and he goes to the water troughs, a mile away, alone, well behind the column, his tethering chain which is never used trailing between his dainty forefeet. The Signallers imagine he does semaphore signalling with his long ears.

The 311th is a Yorkshire Brigade raised in the West Riding. The Battery is sprinkled with Scots, Irish and Welsh. At present we are attached to the Cavalry Corps of the Fifth Army. In the neighbourhood are Indian Cavalry, the 10th Hussars and the 9th Dragoon Guards. At present these cavalry regiments serve in the trenches as infantry, their horses being stabled farther behind the lines than we are.

Did my first guard on active service. I was surprised to see how splendidly some of the Yorkshiremen polished up for the occasion. I shall have my work cut out to beat them for the job of 'waiting man'. Captain Hollingworth inspected us in the dusk and rightly chose one of the Yorkshiremen as waiting man, for he was easily the smartest. It was a dull, uneventful guard, futile and unnecessary as most guarding is, and spent pacing to and fro alongside the guns during an interminable night.

6 January (Sunday)

There is no compulsory church parade, but anyone may apply for time off as I did this morning in order to attend the service at the YMCA. Prior to that and before breakfast we were out exercising the horses, having three each and riding the centre one without saddles. Had a long jog-trot through the snow.

7 January (Monday)

Reveille blows at 6 am every day and we tear ourselves reluctantly from our beds, hard as they are. Our time is spent doing fatigues such as grooming, all kinds of stable work, loading and unloading GS wagons, cleaning bicycles and water carrying. The Drivers have each two horses to look after and their harness, but Gunners and Signallers out of the Line are like fish out of water and at everyone's beck and call. We have entered a period of continuous rain and mud lies everywhere.

In an encounter with a hard ration biscuit I broke one of my front teeth, feel vexed over it, imagine I look hideous when I grin and should have used a hammer on that flinty biscuit.

This evening a concert took place at the YMCA, celebrating the anniversary of arrival of the Brigade in France. We were early in our seats and full of cheery expectancy. The best turn was that of a staff captain, a gallant, dashing fellow who captivated everyone by the way he sang:

Oh! Oh! Oh! It's a lovely war.
Who wouldn't be a soldier, eh?
Oh! it's a shame to take the pay.
As soon as reveille has gone
You feel just as heavy as lead,
But you never get up 'til the Sergeant
Brings your breakfast up to bed,
Oh! oh! oh! It's a lovely war,
What do we want with eggs and ham
When we've got plum and apple jam?
Form fours! Right turn!
How can we spend the money we earn?
Oh! oh! oh! It's a lovely war.

The Brigade comedian followed with 'Good-byee', which he sang so mischievously that he had everyone roaring with laughter.

Good byee, don't sighee,
Wipe the tear baby dear from your eye-ee.
Though it's hard to part I know,
I'll be tickled to death to go.
Good-byee, don't sighee,
There's a silver lining in the skyee.
Bon soir, old thing, cheerio, chin chin,
Napoo, toodle-oo, pork and beans.

The next artiste, who arrived with eyes shining a little too much I fancied, was greeted with thunderous applause. 'The Brigade Caruso', I was informed. At any rate he was a tenor who sang very well 'The Trumpeter', which the audience had loudly demanded. Among the other items were two solos, 'The Battle Eve' and 'Tommy Lad', rendered by a splendid baritone. How these celebrities escaped retention at the Base Camp passes my comprehension. What a diversion an event like this is out here, and what a tonic.

8 January (Tuesday)

Near our camp are a number of tree stumps standing about 1ft high. They are the remains of a fruit orchard sawn down by Fritz prior to his evacuation of this locality.

9 January (Wednesday)

One of the fellows who sang 'Burlington Bertie' at Peronne on Christmas morning is now a 'B' Battery Signaller. His name is Jack Bradburn, just a little my senior in age and we have become friends. For days I have been pestering Bombardier Kingsland, the Battery Orderly, to know whether any letter had arrived for me. At last mail for me arrived today and having received from my mother a half-crown postal order, and learning that a Field Post Office was situated between us and the line, Jack Bradburn and I set out after tea on a path illuminated by gun flashes and Verey lights, which gave us a curious longing to see beyond the dark ridges of the uplands before us.

An infantryman accosted us inquiring the way to the railway station, and detecting a Welsh accent I asked him where he came from. 'Ireland' he lied. 'Where do you come from?' 'Port Talbot in Wales', I answered. He then astounded me by asking if I knew where Margam was and then admitted that his home was there. 'My name is Ace, I'm a Private in the Middlesex Regiment and am going home on leave now, and if you'd like me to call and give your people a message, now's your chance.' I gave him my address, told him to tell my people exactly where I was and to spin them a pleasant yarn about this quiet front and the pleasant comforts we enjoy. We directed him to the station and smilingly he left us to wonder at one of life's most remarkable coincidences. I do not remember having seen or heard of him before, but am very pleased of this opportunity of reassuring my folk of my safety and of my whereabouts.

Farther up the road two Indian soldiers stopped us and began jabbering. 'They take it for granted that every British soldier understands their lingo', protested Bradburn. Realising our ignorance of their language, one of them uttered a cooing sound which closely resembled the whistle of a railway locomotive, so they too, but by signs this time, were directed to the same goal as Private Ace. Among a group of huts, with duckboard paths laid between, I found the smallest Post Office I had ever seen and there exchange my order.

The Signallers are now all housed in one hut and some of the personalities already stand out prominently. One of the most interesting is Signaller Brain, a well-knit, curly headed fellow with a mischievous expression. Recently he made a lone raid at night on a trench-wader dump and finding the sentry asleep, helped himself generously, returning with as many as he could carry. When he laid them out there were five pairs and an odd one, but all size tens. For 5 francs he sold me a pair, but to wear them in comfort I have to encase my small size seven feet in two pairs of thick socks and bind each rubber instep with a coat strap. They are invaluable as the mud here is now knee deep. Brain comes from Burton upon Trent and is very proud of it.

He maintains that the gallant Staffords were the first to enter Jerusalem,[7] a statement that is usually received with prolonged ironic cheers, followed by someone asking, 'But who let the Bosche through at Cambrai?', and by all the hut occupants answering in chorus, 'The gallant Staffords', at which Brain furiously consigns us all to hell.

Another Signaller named Oram has lived for some time at Ystalyfera, but his present home is at Bristol. He has a large head, and fair hair.

We hear some grim tales of the Ypres sector which this Brigade was so glad to leave recently. We reinforcements replaced the casualties they sustained there, for they suffered something of a mauling. They tell us of

7. The only Staffordshire unit in Palestine at the time of the capture of Jerusalem in December 1917 was the 1/1st Staffordshire Yeomanry serving with the Yeomanry Mounted Division. They were not among the forward British units advancing on the city. Small groups of men from the 60th (London) Division, including the 2/19th and 2/20th Londons, were the first to reach Jerusalem. However, the first formed body of troops to enter the city were the Westminster Dragoons acting as advanced guard for the 53rd Division.

plank roads built through quagmires of mud, roads on which a false step by one of the horse teams would probably have meant drowning in a sea of mud. We heard of the Australian dead lying nude in no-man's-land, their clothing being desperately needed by the survivors. One was seen to have had a finger amputated by a bayonet so as to more easily remove his gold ring. We heard of the pillboxes, concrete dug-outs, around which shells fell so thickly, that in order to relieve their bodies, men had to unloose their clothing inside and dash out during a quiet moment. One Signaller related the tale of a certain 'B' Battery Driver who wished to acquaint his relatives of his whereabouts in France, in a letter inserted in code the name of the place and actually added the key to the code at the end of the same letter. He was saved a court martial, it was assumed, by the censor's sense of humour.

Another night after lights out the uproar exceeded all limits and Bastow's mighty bass voice, which dominated all the others put together, could be heard singing in a melancholy way and to the tune of 'Love I am lonely':

Far far from Ypres I want to be,
Where German snipers can't snipe at me.
Cold is my dug-out, wet are my feet,
Waiting for whizz-bangs to send me to sleep

When the Orderly Sergeant burst in and demanded angrily what we meant by kicking up such a row after light's out, the reply he got was a chorus of snores, but Brain overdid his and by the aid of his torch the Sergeant found him.

'All right Brain,' he said, 'don't try and come the old soldier', to which Brain, with a realistic bit of acting, stirred slowly, yawned and sleepily replied, 'Oh! Go away, it's not time to get up yet. Reveille hasn't sounded.' Dubiously the Sergeant then singled out Bastow and said to him, 'Now Bastow, your voice could be heard above all the rest. Let me see, your turn for leave is soon due. Well, for this we'll have it stopped.' 'All right Sergeant,' replied Bastow coolly, 'I've done one year out here without leave, I suppose I can do another bloody year.'

Chapter 11

UP THE LINE

11 January (Friday)

My first experience up the line, from which it is evident that the Brigade will go into action soon. A party of us went mounted through Bernes to Vendelles. At Bernes there were a large number of troops billeted in huts. The original buildings had been blown to smithereens and crossroad signs were the only indications of former localities.

Saw 4.5 howitzers firing, and their Signallers at work in action gave me a proud thrill. Our mounts were taken back by Drivers (horseholders) and in a rear position we dug gun-pits. We were situated in a small valley hidden from enemy view, but we worked beneath a camouflage of netting which had strips of green cloth tied to its meshes and so were concealed from view of enemy aircraft. At dusk two GS wagons arrived and took us back to camp. A field gun battery was in action on the brow of a hill and firing like blazes. We watched the flashes spitting from their muzzles.

12 January (Saturday)

Another day of gun-pit digging at Vendelles. On returning to the hut a letter awaited me. It was from my father, a welcome, lengthy epistle written on the buff, lined foolscap paper of the Great Western Railway. Joyfully I sat down to drink in its contents, but the news the letter bore wounded me more deeply than I had ever been wounded before.

My friend Abram Marienberg had been killed in action.[1] Then came faint hopes that it wasn't really true. Perhaps a mistake had been made. Badly wounded and thought to be dead, or perhaps missing and thought to be killed, for I cannot imagine this promising young life ended. Then I realised that it had happened to other noble and brilliant men. It had happened to the very best of men. This news had on me a sickening effect which I could never fully describe. I was now fed up with the war, fed up to the teeth with War and with France. One of my first reactions was to write a letter of sympathy to Mabel, his Builth Wells friend, but I shall need a little more time before I can attempt the far harder task of writing to Abram's people.

13 January (Sunday)

My first stable picket overseas. It surprised me how miraculously some horses managed to break loose from seemingly unloosable chains. Some slipped out of their head collar time after time, although the worst offenders have been fitted with specially made head collars.

The only redeeming feature about guard and picket duties is that supper is provided. The stables are much improved now and between duties we slept at the end of the horse lines.

15 January (Tuesday)

Detailed with a few others to do some timber shifting. Boarding our Brigade motor lorries we were taken to a huge timber dump from which we brought loads to our Brigade Headquarters. I like these different fatigues especially when done away from the Battery where there is so much stable work. Anything rather than groom horses, for I thoroughly detest the drudgery. A Major has arrived to take command of 'B' Battery. He is a small, confident-looking man with a large head and he looks about 35 years of age.

---

1. Between 3 pm and 10.30 pm on 11 December 1917, the 13 King's Liverpools relieved the 1st Royal Scots Fusiliers in the Noreuil sector of the line, some 6 miles north east of Bapaume. 'A', 'B' and 'C' Companies went into the front line. At 6 am the following morning the Germans put down an intensive barrage on the battalion that lasted for 40 minutes. This was followed by a strong infantry attack, which was eventually driven off by rifle and Lewis Gun fire. A second barrage and infantry attack hit the Liverpools between 7.15 am and 8.40 am. Two hours later the Germans shelled the sector again for half an hour, although this time there was no follow-up attack. Further shelling occurred at 2.30 pm and at 4.15 pm. Between these intensive bombardments the Germans kept up an intermittent shelling of the Noreuil sector. Abraham Marienburg was among 21 men of the battalion killed that day. Other casualties were 1 officer killed and 3 officers wounded along with 48 other ranks. Abraham is buried in Favreuil British Military Cemetery just north of Bapaume. He was aged 19 when he died.

Missing from our midst a sallow, dark-haired Corporal, I enquired of someone what had become of him and was surprised to learn that he had been sent to hospital with a venereal disease contracted during his recent leave.

16 January (Wednesday)

Yesterday the weather was wet, but today it is wet and windy and several of our tents were blown down (they are still retained for certain purposes). The camp is a lake of mud.

I am becoming more used to the general routine here now, and try to relax in the hut in the evenings, talking to my mates, reading, or writing letters around the stove.

18 January (Friday)

Last night our guns went up the line. I joined them today and felt highly pleased at being detailed to go as I notice that a number of Signallers senior to me have been left at the Wagon Lines.

I have not yet felt any fear and regard the experience as a very fine adventure. I also have the feeling that I shall come through the war safely.

Four of 'B' Battery's guns are situated beyond Vendelles and Bihecourt at a place called Vadencourt, the other two guns, known as the Forward Section, being on our left front. Our station code call is N.R. 37, and the Forward Section – 'B.C.'. At N.R. 37 there are seven Signallers including Corporal Swallow, who is in charge of the Signallers; and at 'B.C.' there are three Signallers including Bombardier Cannon, who is in charge. Corporal Swallow has a vigorous mop of curly, red hair, a bovine expression, but he seems very efficient.

Bombardier Cannon, so aptly named for his regiment, also has red hair, but of a bronze hue. He has a divergent squint so that when he looks at you one eye looks beyond you. I heard Signaller Robertshaw address Swallow thus: 'Linnet, Sparrow, Chaffinch or whatever your name is, you're wanted at the Officer's Mess.' Our dug-outs are in a small wood, facing the enemy, but the Officer's Mess is in a safer position, around the corner, so to speak, built into a little hill, and facing the Wagon Lines. Near it is one deep dug-out reached by descending 20 or 30 steps. The four guns are on our right, just outside the wood and a narrow-gauge railroad slopes down to them from the road, small trucks like colliery trams being used to convey ammunition and supplies that come to the road on GS wagons. The whole position is hidden from enemy view by the land before us rising gently. When I arrived the guns were registering. The net camouflage had been rolled back like a veil from a woman's face and the guns were painted with patches of green and brown. The pieces projected from the gun-pits and recoiled each time they viciously spat a shell.

19 January (Saturday)

My first experience at an observation post, familiarly known to us as an O Pip, pip being the sound given to the letter P in the signalling world to avoid confusion with the letter B. Signaller Pomeroy and I accompanied a Lieutenant. Pomeroy is a pale-faced, taciturn Londoner. In appearance the Lieutenant closely resembled Jack Holt the film actor.[2] The O Pip was a rough dug-out, situated on a ridge, overlooking the trenches. All we had to do at this station was to keep a constant lookout for any unusual occurrences on the Front and especially for the SOS signal, which is given by firing a rocket the colours of which are changed periodically. At present the colours are two red lights bursting into two green lights. We brought two of these rockets with us and should we need to use them they can be fixed into the rifle muzzle and sent aloft by firing a cartridge. We observed in turns during the night, which turned out to be a quiet one. From the trenches Verey lights shot up continually, vividly lighting up the Front for a few seconds, then descending slowly as if dangling from a parachute, then dropping to the ground to flicker out. One of them set fire to something that burned for a considerable time and the officer noted it in his log book. Many lights of various hues ascended from the German trenches. On our right front a terrific bombardment took place the Lieutenant saying that it was on the St Quentin front. We are in the Line between Cambrai and St

2. Jack Holt (1888–1951) was an American leading actor of silent and early talkie films. He is most associated with westerns, getting stunt jobs and bit parts before his big break in 1917 with Paramount Studios when he starred in a series of westerns based on the novels of Zane Gray. During the Second World War, Holt served in the US Army as a horse buyer for the cavalry. He continued his acting career after the war alternating between character roles in major films and lead roles in minor westerns. On 18 January 1951 he died of a heart attack at Los Angeles Veterans Hospital, Sawtelle.

Quentin. The sky was afire and the din like the continuous rumbling of thunder. Between us and the trenches a hare screamed pitifully much like a human baby and we wondered if it had been caught in a gin. 'Jack Holt' was most kind to us, we had several interesting chats and he shared with us some deliciously cut, thin slices of bread and butter and cold, sweet tea in his water bottle.

20 January (Sunday)

This morning returned from the O Pip to the Battery and after breakfast went to bed. Before settling down to sleep I was reading when one side of the dug-out collapsed and I was half buried with earth. The vibration caused by gunfire must have loosened it. Prospects of sleep were ended for some time and Oram and I did the necessary repairs.

This dug-out has three beds, the frames of each being made of two stout tree branches with sandbags tacked across them. We are unable to stand up in it and the entrance is like a large rat hole through which we go and come head first, a slimy procedure during wet weather. Our life out here is similar to that of a rat. We are in constant danger of death or mutilation; food, or the lack of it, is our chief problem and instinctively we retire to our holes for sleep or in the event of any bombing or shelling. This dug-out isn't much of a shelter either. Sandbags filled with chalky earth lay on the corrugated iron sheet roof. It might be proof against small shell splinters, but a small shell would pierce it as easily as if it were tissue paper.

My dug-out mates are Signallers Brain and Oram. Oram was an assistant in a grocery shop, but what Brain was I have yet to discover. Spent hours scraping dried, caked mud from my greatcoat, which had got badly splashed at the Wagon Lines by a horse squelching behind me, returning from the water troughs. When wet the chalky soil becomes like cement and dries as hard as flint.

Today I made the depressing discovery that I was lousy, so I am quite in the fashion. I discovered them in my pubic hair when urinating.

Each dug-out is issued nightly with a few small candles about 3in long and known as siege candles. Tonight, in their gloomy light, we took off our shirts and for the first time I joined my mates in the hunt for lice.

If the candles give little light they perform another useful purpose, for we draw across the flame the seams of our underclothing, the spluttering sound reminding us of distant machine-guns. Re-donning the garments we suffer a new and disgusting torture, the sawing against our inflamed flesh of the hard singed creases. This will be a nightly horror now until we can get a bath and a clean change, for vermin increase at an incredible rate. We learn that when we are lucky enough to enjoy a bath and clean change we may have only a brief respite from these pests for the dug-outs are infested with them. In fact they are everywhere and many are convinced that they are in the air out here.

At night the entrance of each dug-out is carefully covered with a blanket soaked in some anti-gas chemical. This blanket also serves to shield our candlelight from the watchful gaze of enemy airmen. During the day the blanket is rolled up and tied to the lintel. At night it is so cold that we kindle a fire in a perforated tin can, having to tolerate dense columns of tear-jerking smoke or the alternative of a near freeze.

21 January (Monday)

With another Signaller commenced a 24-hour duty at the Battery Telephone Pit, a dug-out entered by descending about six steps. Unlike our own badly designed dug-out, it is sufficiently high enough for us to stand in, but two beds, a rough table and a seat leave little room to move about in. The roof is made of logs covered with earth-filled sandbags. Two Signallers are always on duty here as telephone operators and during the night divide the time between them, that is if the situation is normal. The Pit contains a D3 (pronounced Don 3) telephone, a Fullerphone and a Four-plus-three exchange.[3] The Fullerphone, an invention by a Captain Fuller, is used extensively out here. Unless another Fullerphone is used within 30yd, earth-current messages cannot be picked up. Here we are in communication with our Brigade Headquarters which can switch us through to any of the other Batteries that compose our Brigade. We also have lines to 'B.C.' (our Forward Section), our O Pips, the Officers' dug-outs and to our gun-pits. All messages are tapped on the buzzer and in Morse

3. This portable field telephone exchange created in miniature the same service rendered by an ordinary permanent exchange. The field exchange could take four incoming lines, all of which could be connected to each other by the exchange operator, who could also send and receive calls on each of the four lines.

code. Every 2 hours we inquiringly tap 'OK'? to each station and if any line is broken or 'Dis', to use the Signaller's jargon, two Signallers set out immediately and repair the wires. The lines run out over the ground and are 'aired' or buried at paths or roads. In addition to various communications, we receive twice daily in code, weather particulars called 'Meteors'. Weather conditions have important effects on the flight of a projectile and various calculations and adjustments are made from them by the officers.

25 January (Friday)

Again on duty at Battery Telephone Pit from 5 pip-emma today until 5 pip-emma tomorrow. Someone scrounged a load of 3in-diameter pit props, used out here in the erection of barbed wire entanglements. So, quickly learning to wield effectively a sharp axe, I helped to chop a substantial load of firewood in readiness for the chilly night. Left behind a quantity of white splinters which brought us a rebuke from Lieutenant Sampson, who reminded us that such litter might be plainly seen by enemy aircraft.

26 January (Saturday)

Signaller Pomeroy and I detailed to accompany Captain Hollingworth and Lieutenant Sampson to an O Pip called 'Rum' (I must have been relieved from telephone pit duty prior to this). Each O Pip has a name in addition to a telephone code call. 'Rum', a camouflaged shack, was situated in Le Verguier, a wilderness of battered buildings and debris on the uplands that conceal our gun positions from enemy view. 'Rum', on the brow of Le Verguier, looks down at the trenches commanding a fine view of miles of plains occupied by the Germans. Telephone lines, running along the ground or along trench sides, with wooden identification labels tied here and there when there are other sets of lines, connect us to the Battery. We connected our Don 3 portable telephone and tapped to the Battery range and degrees left or right, which Hollingworth, peering through binoculars, called out. Sampson, spectacled and leaning on the ledge of the observing aperture, watched also with binoculars the operations, but it seemed with slight difficulty. The phone, only needing one to operate, enabled Pom and I to share in turns in the sightseeing. A few seconds after each message was buzzed the barking of our guns could be heard behind us, followed by the rushing sound of the flight of the shells overhead. Captain Hollingworth called Lieutenant Sampson 'Sammy'. 'D'you see that Sammy?' he asked, referring to the black smoke of a high-explosive shell in the area of enemy dug-outs or the white, cotton-wool puffs of shrapnel bursting above their trenches.

Sampson, moustached, mild and anxious looking, referred to the Germans as 'The Boche'. No movement could be seen anywhere, but they were manning those trenches all right, and if anyone this side exposed himself above the parapet for the briefest moment he stood the risk of having a bullet through him. Through the narrow slit before us we studied the drab, uninteresting landscape rolling interminably away before us. The occasional sharp crack of a rifle shot, the short, spasmodic rattling of a machine-gun reminding us that between those mounds of earth flung up from zig-zagging trenches on both sides, infantry of armies at war were keeping each other on the alert.

Returning to the dug-out at the Battery I finished reading a most-enjoyable novel, *The Ne'er do Well* by Rex Beach. Books of all kinds circularise among the troops, but usually there are not many to choose from, although occasionally a good one turns up.

Out here time passes very slowly, a day seeming like a week, and a month like a year, partly, I think, because we have to spend so much of our time in the same places, whereas our time in civilian life was split up into so many departments – home, work, church, sport, theatres, etc. Therefore something readable is a boon; it passes an otherwise monotonous hour and helps us to forget. At night, lying so near Mother Earth, we sometimes hear strange noises, as though someone were digging or tunnelling under us. The thought of being blown up by a mine isn't wholesome, so we do not dwell on it and trust the noises are connected with something less harmful. Another strange fear I have is of complete darkness, a very deep-seated fear I imagine. I first became aware of it when passing through Cockett tunnel in an unlighted railway carriage and shall never forget the feeling of relief I had when, almost in a panic, I saw faint streaks of light stealing across the tunnel walls. I suffered the same fear in this dug-out after the candles were blown out at night and found relief in watching Oram's lighted 'fag' passing to and from his lips, but mercifully I discovered that the face of my wrist-watch was illuminated, this reassuring me that I still possessed my sight.

27 January (Sunday)

In the Line on a Sunday is no different from any other day and one sometimes has to think hard or refer to one's diary to ascertain the day and date. Today went to 'Gin' O Pip with Lieutenant Sabaston who is known among us as 'Sabby'. It is said that he hails from the Orkney Islands and that in civilian life he was a police constable.[4]

He certainly has a pronounced Scots accent. On the outward journey we passed a shrine of the Virgin Mary, went through a marsh, skirted an old sugar refinery and encountered an Indian machine-gun post, the gun pointing in a businesslike way through a hole near the base of a high wall. At last we came to 'Gin', a dilapidated shanty erected in a cutting that 'Sabby' informed me was situated in no-man's-land. The hut was perched near the top of a side of the cutting nearer the enemy, its frail roof sloping from the crest. 'Sabby' is a tall, lean, fresh-complexioned and clean-shaven man, very genial, although speech does not come easily and readily to him. After I had connected up my Don 3 telephone and buzzed N.R. II, the code call of Brigade Headquarters, Sabaston's attention was immediately arrested. 'Ah!' he exclaimed, 'I remember the Signaller who came here with me last time buzzing those sounds. Goes with a swing doesn't it?' he added, singing in a monotone the Morse sounds. The Front was blurred by a quickly gathering mist which in a short time became so dense that observation was rendered impossible. Most of the time Sabby spent renovating the roof of the hut. As he did not ask me to assist him I offered to, but he said he preferred if I would keep near the phone in case anyone rang up.

If 'Jerry' came over now we would not be able to see him, I speculated, but perhaps 'Jerry' was thinking the same way. Anyway, I thought, 'Sabby' with his revolver, and I with my rifle could possibly defend ourselves very well. Returning in the afternoon, 'Sabby' decided to try a short cut, we lost

4. Possibly 2nd Lieutenant John Sabiston of Over House, Sandwick, South Ronaldsay, Orkney. Unfortunately, no service record appears to be available for this officer at the National Archives.

our bearings completely, and trudged miles in the wrong direction, through misty marshland. My steel hat made my head ache, and my box respirator, phone, rifle, and 50 rounds of 'ammo' in my bandolier made my shoulders ache. Keeping up with the long strides of 'Sabby' who was unencumbered except for his revolver and ammunition, I silently cursed him. He seemed to sense it too. He did a most unusual thing for an officer. He apologised to me, and in a most kindly way. It was dark when streaming with perspiration I trudged wearily into Vadencourt. After tea, resting in the dug-out, I was surprised to be visited by Sabaston who had actually come to see how I was, and again to offer more genuine apologies for his mistake. This unorthodox gesture on the part of an officer made me feel awkward, but I shall as a consequence of it always cherish a deep regard for 'Sabby'. 'Sabby' is blessed with such a double portion of natural kindliness that not even the military distinction – officers and men – has been able to dilute it.

29 January (Tuesday)

When we go on O Pip duties we draw rations of limited variety from the cook. We are given bread or biscuits and tinned bully beef or jam. Sometimes we get a tinned soup called Maconachie, and sometimes tinned pork and beans. Maconochie and pork and beans are not so bad after being warmed.

This evening, with 2nd Lieutenant Smith and Signaller Bradburn set out for 'Rum' O Pip. Between us and Le Verguier a British aeroplane stood *hors de combat*. An unexploded finned aerial bomb, around which we gingerly detoured, lay near it. We had settled down for some time at 'Rum' when I discovered that one of the telephone batteries had run out. Smith, naturally not very pleased, wanted to know why we hadn't tested the phone at the Battery. I explained that we had asked Corporal Swallow, who handed us the phone, if the batteries were OK and he assured us that they had only recently been put in. Smith chose me to return to the Forward Section for a new battery and I set off hurriedly as dusk was approaching. When I left the Forward Section it was quite dark and as landmarks were few I missed the path and wandered almost into the German lines, being saved only by a Verey light, the first of the nightly fireworks, which swished up quite near me. This enabled me to judge my approximate position, so I altered my direction and made for a small, dim light which proved to be an infantry dug-out, the occupants of which were able to assist me a little. On re-entering Le Verguier I was abruptly challenged by a sentry:

'Halt! Who comes there?'
'Friend.'
'Advance friend and give the password.'

Expecting to be back at 'Rum' well before nightfall I had not bothered to ascertain the password for the night, so here I was now, in a serious fix undergoing some careful interrogation from the sceptical machine-gunners before they felt it safe to release me. Approaching the well-concealed and camouflaged 'Rum' from a different angle made difficult its discovery, but eventually I reached it.

Connecting up, I found 'B.C.' (Forward Section) lines OK but Infantry Brigade Headquarters had the unmistakable hollow sound of lines 'dis'.

Smith sent me out again, alone, to make the repair, unfairly I thought, but anyway, orders are orders, so I set out, trailing through my hand the lines that led to the left of our position. After a few hundred yards walk I came to the cause of the trouble. Recently struck by a shell, a huge wall had collapsed in a long tremendous heap over the wires. It was too big a job for me and my resources, so back at Rum we reported it to the Battery who later sent out two Signallers with a sufficient supply of wire. I have a feeling that Smith dislikes me, and probably that is the reason the feeling is mutual. I cannot remember giving him any cause for disliking me. He usually addresses me with a mild and studied sarcasm and occasionally he is quite uncivil. Smith is very short in stature and I suspect that gives him an inferiority complex. On the way up to 'Rum', Bradburn and I had to look down at him during our conversation. He is a 'ranker', winning the Distinguished Conduct Medal when a Sergeant. He also has the French Croix de Guerre.

He told us that he was educated at the famous Chaterhouse School, that he had been a settler in the Soloman Islands and that his brother was a Lieutenant Commander in the Royal Navy. His Colt-Eley service revolver lay on the ledge of the small aperture through which we observed, a weighty, cumbersome, but deadly looking weapon, with stumpy bullets. Smith has recently been down the Line on a trench-mortar course. When I asked him to tell us for what he had been awarded his decorations he said that he had the British medal for successfully extricating some guns from a difficult situation. 'As for the Croix de Guerre,' he said, 'it was sent to my former Battery by the French. The O/C didn't know who the hell to give it to, so we tossed up for it and I won.' Bradburn and I laughed outright, but Smith's face was so inscrutable that we did not know whether he was telling us the truth or pulling our legs. Speaking of Captain Hollingworth, he said, 'Oh yes, I like Holly. He's a good Gunner too,' and then he added thoughtfully, 'a good gunner, but not an excellent gunner.' Though Smith's conceit is markedly apparent, I imagine him to be a good sport, and he is certainly a handy, resourceful and experienced man. During an uneventful night we kept watch of the Front in turns, gazing for hours at innumerable Verey lights lingering dazzlingly in mid air, then plunging us into a darkness deeper than ever and to which our eyes took a little time to adapt themselves. Sometimes we fancy their brilliant light reveals figures crouching in no-man's-land, but probably it is only fancy. I don't think Smith will have much to report this time.

5 February (Tuesday)

Set out with Lieutenant Gascoyne and Signaller Bradburn for 24-hour duty at Dragoon Post which is in the Front-Line trenches, and we felt that we were in for an interesting time. On the way we met a Signaller from another of our Batteries whom Bradburn knew. They stopped to speak and when Bradburn rejoined us he said, 'That's Russell. Hell of a boy. Told General Brancker[5] to go to hell, after the General had criticised him for some offence during manoeuvres on Salisbury Plain. Got off because he was underage at the time. The other night,' continued Bradburn, 'while on duty at his Signal Pit, he fell asleep and a candle set on fire the "4 plus 3" telephone exchange. Had they not hushed up the offence, he would have been shot.'

---

5. Major General and later Air Vice Marshal Sir William Sefton Brancker. He was one of 54 men killed in the loss of the airship R 101 on 5 October 1930 at Allone in France. The airship had left Cardington in Bedfordshire the previous day on its maiden flight to Karachi.

Nearing the communication trench we met two cavalry observers whom we discovered were coming from Dragoon Post. They stopped to show us a telescope with which they had been observing back areas. It had been hit by a sniper's bullet, the front lens being smashed and the brass casing torn.

'Brad' asked me if I had made my will. Gascoyne is a short, pink-faced man with a sandy moustache. He doesn't look a soldier, but a civilian dressed up in an officer's uniform. He is a dry and secretive man and slightly miserable. He withers with an occasional snub any attempt we make at conversation, but I fancy this is not snobbery, but due to a natural tendency to keep aloof. Trudging along, we entered the shallow communication trench which gradually deepened until it was well over our heads as we neared Dragoon Post. In single file we clattered along the duckboards (wooden gratings laid on the floor of trenches) in the traversing trench, Gascoyne leading. If we met anyone we had to tilt ourselves against the trench wall in order to let him pass. We passed the cavalry O Pip, which was now discreetly empty. At Dragoon Post we descended a deep sap, sinking into darkness deeper than the blackest night, steadying ourselves on the steps by means of a hand rope. We descended 32 steps before we reached the bottom, a shaft that proceeded forward like a tunnel or coal mine. As our eyes adjusted themselves to the scene, we first beheld dim shards of light, then candles, then men off duty resting or sleeping here and there on wire-netting beds. At the end of the shaft we ascended a few steps and came to a narrow loophole through which burst dazzling daylight.

Through the narrow slit – about 24in long and about 1in deep – Gascoyne surveyed the front, while Bradburn and I unburdened ourselves of our kit and equipment. Afterwards Brad and I had a long look through the loophole. Grass wavering in the breeze, growing on the earth sloping down from the aperture acted as a natural camouflage. The land dipped steeply to the German trenches and it was obvious that in this position we were very advantageously situated for observation purposes. Actually we were now in no-man's-land and if they decided to attack us at this moment, we should be trapped like rats in a hole. In several places portions of the enemy trenches had been badly smashed by shell fire and when we kept a constant watch on these openings, we could see grey figures flitting rapidly back and forth. Gascoyne observed for some time here, wrote some notes, then led us back into the trench where the light temporarily blinded us. Our own labelled wires hung near the sap entrance and we connected up our phone.

Gascoyne stuck his periscope on the parapet and peered through it for a long time and then he took it down and rapped his khaki handkerchief around it. That's what the cavalry observers should have done, I thought, for we were facing an easterly direction and the lenses of these instruments and possibly their shiny casing could well reflect the bright sunshine. We registered our guns, by giving ranges, increasing or decreasing ranges, and reaching our targets by giving degrees right or left. Then Gascoyne left us, probably for the Officer's Mess, which of course would be a dug-out somewhere in the trench. During his absence we made good use of the periscope, which disclosed a wider and entirely different landscape from that seen through the loophole. Through that small lens could be seen a mirror-like panorama of the front, the earth-rimmed Front-Line trenches and support trenches of the enemy, a few shattered buildings and many ghoulish tree stumps with spiked extremities. Later we learned that the buildings were the remains of Ascension Farm. The name is apt for most of the farm has ascended. This and a group of trees known as Eleven Trees were regarded as important landmarks. During the morning, which was fresh and sunny, our wires went 'Dis' once. They were new wires with red insulation which made them easy to follow down the trench side and then back over the parados[6] from which the land sloped downwards, so that it was only for a briefest moment that I exposed myself in order to avoid a lengthy detour. Between the trench and B.C. I found the two wires severed by a shell, a new shell hole nearby. I repaired the break, tapped in with a pin on the end of a wire, found everything OK and returned to the O Pip. The trenches here are manned by Indians and normally one sees few on duty in the trenches. Just a detachment here and there with a machine, Lewis or Stokes gun. The regiment is the 10th Hodson's Horse. They have black, bobbed hair which is oiled and carefully dressed. They have several

---

6. A parados is an elevation of earth or sandbags built along the rear of a trench to provide additional protection from bullets, shrapnel and shell splinters. A parapet constructed in a similar manner does the same job along the front of a trench.

native subalterns, but the senior officers I have seen are British, splendid-looking men, serious, experienced and capable. This afternoon some of the natives in the trench became quite friendly with us. Their dark faces accentuated the whiteness of their teeth. One of them was anxious to teach me his lingo, so phonetically and I wrote a number of words for such things as water, food, horse, artillery, infantry and numbers up to 15. The only words I now recall are pawnee for water, resallah, a squadron of native Indian cavalry, and of course chapatti. When I called back the words he was so delighted that he smiled broadly, and he must have praised me to his mates for when teatime came, they brought me some very sweet chapattis, pancake-like food. They told us that the pancakes were called chapattis. We found them dry and not half so tasty as our pancakes and they were much more difficult to chew. In fact an observer of the 9th Dragoon Guards, seeing me eating one, predicted for me a month's indigestion. A native, carrying before him a small bowl of water, passed by and disappeared into an alley leading from the trench. In soldier's language the guardsman explained to me how much more hygienic than we the natives were, at least in this particular act for which we, their would-be superiors, generally made use of a piece of newspaper. I learned that artillery warfare baffles them because they are not used to it. For instance, during a raid on the enemy trenches they made recently, they mistook our barrage for enemy fire, and retreated into our own trenches on the right flank. They have endured our wintry climate heroically.

Boxes of Mill's bombs and Verey lights lay in convenient places, and near the sap was a clumsy looking brass pistol called an elephant gun used for firing Verey lights. At dusk we saw a unique sight – a patrol go over the top. The men (Indians) lined up in the trench while an English officer stood on the firing step and scanned the hazy Front for a few moments and then led his party forward in single file. They were going into no-man's-land to relieve a listening post.

6 February (Wednesday)
Finished reading *A Tale of Two Cities*, which I found much more readable than any of the other works of Dickens I have read.

10 February (Sunday)

In readiness for tonight's duty at the Telephone Pit, I have chopped a number of logs. Through practice, and by observing experts, I can now wield a large axe with confidence and skill.

11 February (Monday)

After handing me a despatch for our Wagon Lines, Corporal Swallow suggested that I should make use of the Battery bicycle. Jumped at the opportunity, visualised a pleasant ride in the sunshine but soon discovered that the stout, heavy, military machine was stiff for the want of use and oil and needed to be pedalled even down hills. Captain Hollingworth, who has returned from leave to the Wagon Lines, studied the message form on which there is a space for the insertion of the time the message was sent and complained of the time I had taken to bring it. I put the fault on the bicycle, adding that I regretted not having walked. He looked unconvinced, but said no more. When preparing to return I was conscious of someone standing behind me. I looked over my shoulder and saw a short, dapper man staring at the bike. Without shifting his glance he enquired slowly and with a trace of Yorkshire accent,

'Wot's your name?'
'Hanson', I replied.
'I suppose you Signallers up the Line have so much to do that you haven't time to clean bikes', he complained.
For once I was at a loss for words.
'You tell Corporal Swallow to see that it's done', he commanded, walking away as quietly as he had come.

I guessed he was the Sergeant Major Hanson of whom I had heard the Signallers speak and whom I was anxious to meet because he bore my name. When I joined the Brigade at Hancourt at Christmas time, he was on leave. They tell me that in civilian life Hanson was a railwayman whose work was the marshalling of traffic and that such training enables him to marshal troops with the same skill and efficiency. As a rigid disciplinarian he is regarded by the men with more respect than affection.

12 February (Tuesday)

This open-air life creates tremendous appetites so that food becomes an obsession, because we never receive sufficient. Occasionally there is a small surplus of rice, which enables the cook to ration us out sufficient with which to make a supper. After boiling it we are unable to sweeten it as sugar cannot be spared us. We have experimented with pozzy (Army slang for jam) and marmalade and tonight we Signallers sweetened our supply with a tin of pineapple chunks. One night after our efforts to obtain anything from neighbouring canteens had failed and no one had received from home a parcel, we sat silent, miserable and suffering a gnawing hunger within. Signaller Brain is the finest scrounger I have ever met, but tonight even he had failed. 'I've a good mind to make a raid on the bloody cookhouse', he said. Having our entire immoral support he waited until he thought the cook was asleep (his bunk is in the cookhouse), then slunk out alone and returned with a small tin of small, hard biscuits, a daring feat, which meant getting in and out, under the cookhouse door where a curved hole had been worn, without waking the cook. We dined on this dry food without any feeling of guilt, for we were starving, and when I realised the story of David, the psalmist, in a similar plight, filching holy bread from the temple, we all felt even better.

20 February (Wednesday)

Removed to another dug-out which is far superior to our first rat hole. Our present one is 14ft by 10ft and we can stand upright in it. Best of all it has a steel, elephant-arched roof which is level with the surface of the earth. We have much more elbow room. The occupants are Signallers Bradburn, Oram, Willis and myself.

Willis is the Battery Runner or despatch carrier, but has only recently come up from the Wagon Lines. He is a solidly built, bluff fellow with whom I get on splendidly, although I have had to tell him off for borrowing my trench waders without asking my permission. He walks about with a huge staff, a popular habit out here and of much use in muddy regions.

During his training in England he was so captivated by two famous lady singers whom he heard in concert that he wrote them appreciative letters which has resulted in him enjoying with them a charming correspondence ever since. In 'civvy' life he kept a bicycle repair shop.

22 February (Friday)

Visitors other than Signallers to the Telephone Pit have become so numerous that Corporal Swallow asked me to letter the word PRIVATE for him. Limited to paint of one colour and an unworthy brush, I did it on a flat piece of wood which is now nailed above the Pit entrance.

Recently two decent books drifted here: *The Street of the Flute Player*, by H. De Vere Stacpoole, which I finished today and which reminded me of this author's controversial novel, *The Blue Lagoon*, loaned me by my friend Ted Preston in more peaceful days. Its daring but fascinating situation made it a best seller. I have enjoyed reading *The Street of the Flute Player*, a classical story, exquisitely written. The other book, *Secret Service*, by Cyrus Townsend Braby, I finished on Monday and enjoyed it immensely.

25 February (Monday)

The weather now is quite seasonable. Up to a week ago things had become rather dry and dusty, but a week tonight heavy rain commenced and freshened everything. Anyway, we have had enough rain for the narrow paths running between the trees and dug-outs are now little canals of mud. It is also very windy at present. From the 'crocked' aeroplane that rots between us and 'Rum' O Pip, I recently brought back a lath-like piece of timber out of which, with my jackknife, I have made a paper knife after the pattern taught us in school. I hope to keep it as a souvenir.

In this dug-out we usually end up the day with a sing-song. Lying on our wire-netting bunks, we sing selections ranging from hymns to ragtimes.

The present favourites are 'Come ye thankful people come', 'It is Well with my Soul' and 'Cock Robin'.

1st March (Friday)

I am on duty at the Telephone Pit. It is a very fine night, but bitterly cold. During the quiet, uneventful hours I replied to my correspondence. On the 18th February I received a letter from Italy, from Signaller Jones, a

Bettisfield hut mate who is on the Piave front. On the 20 February I received a letter that I had written to Abram Marienberg. It looked the worse for wear and bore various remarks such as, 'No trace' and 'Unknown'. Its arrival finally dispelled the hope I had entertained that the report of his death might have been a mistake. Pa has sent me some 'British weeklies' and Hilaire Belloc's magazine, *Land and Water*. I find much to interest me in the British weeklies, especially the competitions in which I was successful in winning a book prize and several commendations in the painting section.

It is with resentment that I learn that our letters are censored by our own officers and I shall henceforth have to censor myself when referring to Hollingworth, Sampson, Smith, Sabaston and Gascoyne, for I fear that I have described them rather candidly in my letters home. For instance, in one letter to my parents I described Smith as conceited and suffering from an inferiority complex, owing to the shortness of his stature. Is that the reason why he does not appear to like me? If so, I can hardly blame him. Anyway, it would be an easy matter for our letters to be transferred to another Battery for censoring and vice versa. Occasionally we are issued with 'Blue Envelopes', large enough for the enclosure of several other letters. These are sent to the Base for censoring. Blue Envelopes are very popular.

2 March (Saturday)

We have had a snowfall.

Recently the Infantry sent up 'SOS' rockets, and for such contingencies our guns have definite points to fire on, points constantly checked by us each time we man the O Pips. On this occasion, Gunner Clarke, who is a real soldier, was on duty at the gun-pit, and who, without a moment's delay, after we passed on to the gun position the message, pulled the firing lever of his gun which roused the other Gunners to man the guns.

The following day, Sabaston, inspecting the gun, asked what had become of the muzzle cover, a leather cap, strapped around the muzzle between bouts of firing. Clarke promptly replied, 'It's in the Jerries' lines, Sir.'

3 March (Sunday)

When we are sent behind the lines on errands, we are always on the look out for canteens, where biscuits, tinned foods, chocolate and stationery may be bought. Tinned café-au-lait is sometimes obtainable and being so delicious and easy to prepare, it is a great favourite. One night recently I found a canteen at Vendelles, where I bought 14 francs worth of *2d* and *3d* packets of biscuits, which I carried back in a new sandbag. On my return journey a thick fog gathered and I landed in a lane of barbed wire entanglements and found it difficult extricating myself from the barbs. First my breeches got caught, then the sandbag, and after I had succeeded in freeing myself from them I found the tail of my greatcoat was caught, and so on. I knew the Battery was somewhere near, for this wire entanglement runs like a road on the left of us, so that soon after liberating myself I quickly reached my destination, where the Signallers bought the contents of the sandbag and grumbled because I had not brought more, but 14 francs was all I possessed at the time.

Between Vadencourt and Vendelles there is a dummy battery. Out of each gun-pit points a timber prop that looks exactly like the piece of a gun.

From a distance it looks very realistic and it must certainly do from the air.

6 March (Wednesday)

For 24 hours on duty at Dragoon Post O Pip, to which we set out well clad, for the weather is wintry.

Trench waders and leather jerkins make us look bigger than we really are and today the waders were invaluable, for water in the communication trench was knee deep. We squelched along the submerged duckboards.

Setting down our supplies at Dragoon Post, we found that, among the many necessities for a duty like this, candles had been forgotten. Bradburn rang up the Battery, asking them to send a Signaller to meet me with a supply, while I set off to meet him via a landmark called Lone Tree.

Met Signaller Hey with the candles at a place called Quaker's Quarry. Hey is a quiet, harmless fellow, a good practical Signaller, but hampered in telephone by slight deafness.

We are here to link the infantry with the Field Artillery, to supply a barrage if necessary or to strafe the enemy if he attacks, but it was a quiet night. Too quiet to be good we suspect. Our officer retired to the infantry officers' dug-out and we to a dug-out in the trench, near the deep sap, but we slept little owing to the intense cold. Deep breathing no doubt saved me from pneumonia, but there were times when my feet felt almost frostbitten.

7 March (Thursday)

We were glad to get on our feet early, and from Dragoon Post we observed activities above the normal all day and we greeted them with plenty of shelling. After transmitting the commands we carefully watched the stampedes our salvoes caused, but in spite of this, movement opposite increased and became most daring, especially as the light began to wane. Rifles cracked from our parapet and I joined a Private on my right in firing a large number of rounds, he and I entering into the business with enthusiasm. As was expected, they retaliated and their bullets 'pinged' savagely over our heads. An infantry officer arrived and received from the Private an exact account of the daring activities we had witnessed. Probably he knew what they had been up to over there, but we never found out. For today's shooting I had some excellent practice quite recently, for in order to clean the bores of some rifles, a squad of us at the Battery position were detailed to do some firing. The targets were empty biscuit tins and the range about a hundred yards. I had the satisfaction of bowling over one of the tins.

8 March (Friday)

White frost this morning, so it is small wonder why we were nearly frozen at Dragoon Post yesterday.

Bradburn and I on duty at Battery Telephone Pit and as we were not warned until late of the duty, we had to chop our supply of firewood by the limited light of the stars.

13 March (Wednesday)

I overheard the following conversation take place between two of our Signallers, Pomeroy and Robertshaw, the latter being usually addressed by his mates as 'Robby'. The subject was the eternal one out here – food. In broad 'Yorksheer' dialect Robby asked Pomeroy, 'Hast out t'ate?' 'Yes,' replied Pomeroy admirably. 'Eat the currents in this telephone.' The original number of Signallers proved insufficient for the duties here in the line, so our number has been increased by the arrival recently of a few more from the Wagon Lines. Robertshaw was one of them.

He has a weak-looking head and mouth, but he possesses a quiet and unfailing self-confidence. Criticism is lost on him, affecting him as little as water on a duck's back. He has a lazy, easy going manner and judges himself with great leniency.

Finished reading *The Court of the Angels* by Justus Miles Forman.

14 March (Thursday)

Bradburn and I gun-pit digging near our gun position. At this spot the land begins to rise and beneath the turf we encountered chalk, which is hard to dig and shovel. We toiled beneath the usual camouflage of netting and strips of cloth and were left entirely on our own, a situation in which I work best and am happiest. Bradburn is a handsome, wavy haired boy, just slightly older than I. He has an intelligent face, rather full lips and is a good, emphatic speaker. He has a splendid figure which I guess would be good enough for him to become an artist's model. Today he was in a bad mood, the result, I think of being teased. He confessed to me despairingly, 'I'm sure there's a few slates missing from my roof.' I pooh-poohed the idea, following that by listing his strong points. Previously he had modestly told me of his success in school, so I reminded him of that. Also I reminded him of his lovely flowing penmanship, which was all I could think of at the time. 'There's no one in the Battery to touch you at it', I stressed, but he was not much impressed and continued dismally,

Our family was born wrong somehow. I should have been a girl and my sister a boy. I come from a coalmining area (Ashton-in-Makerfield, Lancashire) and as you know subsidence occurs frequently in such areas. When our house was damaged by one of them, who d'you think did the repairs. My sister. She handled the bricks and mortar like a man. She ought to be wearing trousers and I skirts.

We both escaped from the unpleasant conversation by attacking the flinty chalk.

18 March (Monday)

This morning two or three small shells landed a few yards in front of our position. At the time I was near the cookhouse, the cook shook his head forebodingly and said, 'I don't like the look of that.' 'Registering,' I exclaimed. 'Sure,' he added. As I walked away, thinking of own constant registering, I thought, 'Two can play at that game.' Back in the dug-out we reminded ourselves of the expected offensive by the enemy which has been talked about ever since we came up the line. Things seem to be warming up for it.

The Colonel visits us about once a week, accompanied by the Adjutant and a batman. The Colonel, a blonde, fresh-complexioned and rather horsey looking individual, has very thin legs, which his high boots do not improve very much. He is known among us as 'Legs Eleven'. He leads the way, smilingly, bareheaded, with his silky hair blown about by the breeze. His handsome, but effeminate Adjutant follows, and is a regular soldier and wears the red and black ribbon of the DSO. It is said that he sometimes studies our sector from an observation 'plane'. It is also said that he is a strict disciplinarian. For his birthday sent Pa a postcard embroidered with the Allied flags.

19 March (Tuesday)

Setting out with 2nd Lieutenant Smith and Signaller Bradburn for Dragoon Post this evening, we had just left the Battery when we spotted a small balloon drifting over us. German propaganda in the form of leaflets fluttered from it. We had heard of but not seen such a thing until now. Bradburn and I would have liked to have picked up some of the sheets, being terribly curious to know their contents, but Smith forbade us to touch them, fearing that they might be deliberately infected with disease germs.

20 March (Wednesday)

Since our arrival last evening we have had an exciting time at Dragoon Post. I have never experienced anything like it. The German trenches

Ivor, aged 14, and his sister, Nellie, in 1912. (Hanson Family Archive)

Ivor's best friend, Abraham Gerald Marienberg, in 1916. (Hanson Family Archive)

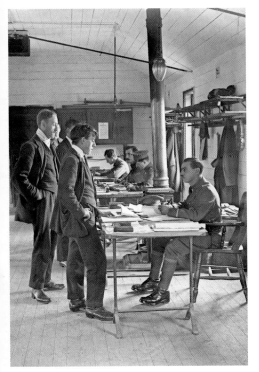

Volunteers, newly arrived at an Army recruitment office, have their details recorded as part of the enlistment process, 1915. Ivor's first attempt to join up, on 20 November 1916, failed when he forgot to take his birth certificate to Swansea Recruitment Office. He returned two days later and was attested as a volunteer under the Derby Scheme. (Imperial War Museum Q 30074)

Part of the British military camp at Harfleur, March 1916. Ivor was at the Royal Artillery Base Depot, Harfleur, between 19 December, when he landed at Le Harve, and 22 December, when he was posted to 311 Army Brigade, RFA. (Imperial War Museum HU 99051)

Officers and Signallers man a signals
station during an exercise in England
during 1915. Ivor applied to train as
a Signaller on 14 March 1917. His
training, at Bettisfield Park Camp,
included semaphore and Morse code flag
work, lamp and heliograph signalling
and the use of field telephones.
(Imperial War Museum HU 99793)

Recruits engaged in PT/Swedish Drill at a
Royal Artillery training camp in England,
1917. Such exercise was very much part
of daily life for new recruits such as Ivor.
(Imperial War Museum HU 100350)

Sunday morning Church Parade at Bettisfield Park Camp.
(Reg Meredith Collection)

Soldiers outside a canteen, Bettisfield Park Camp, c.1917.
(Reg Meredith Collection)

The Queen's Head at Sarn, built in 1912. Ivor visited it on 6 April 1917 with Gunners Evans and Pritchard for a memorable afternoon tea. (Alan Wakefield)

Remains of one of the First World War musketry butts on Fenn's Moss, used for rifle training by Bettisfield Park and Prees Heath Camps. (Alan Wakefield)

A sergeant instructor leads a group of inexperienced horsemen during a lesson at an Army Service Corps riding school in England, c. 1917. Ivor's riding course at Bettisfield ran for two weeks from 10 August 1917. He passed without once falling off. (Imperial War Museum HU 87700)

British soldiers on a rifle range during a musketry course in England in 1915. Ivor's musketry course, on the ranges at Fenn's Moss, ran between 1 and 8 October 1917. He enjoyed the course and discovered that he was a good shot. (Imperial War Museum HU 89801)

Hanmer Mere, seen from the village church. Ivor recorded: 'From whatever angle you view it Hanmer Mere is always a picture of loveliness'. The Mere was a favourite bathing spot for troops from Bettisfield Park Camp.
(Alan Wakefield)

One of the few surviving huts from Bettisfield Park Camp. This is currently used as a community hall in the village of Penley. (Alan Wakefield)

Copnall's store in Hanmer is still a butcher's shop. The present owner is John Roberts. His uncle, Joseph Roberts, married Maud Copnall, daughter of Thomas Copnall who owned the shop during the First World War. The shop passed from Joseph to his brother Jack, who was John Roberts' father. The Copnalls took in short-term lodgers and proved popular with families of men training at the nearby artillery camp. Ivor's parents visited during July 1917. (Alan Wakefield)

Men of the Royal Field Artillery practise respirator drill during an anti-gas course at a training camp in England, 1917. All soldiers had to undergo an anti-gas course, which included instruction in both the PH/PHG helmet and box respirator. (Imperial War Museum Q 30109)

British soldiers relaxing in the YMCA hut at Rouen, 1917. Both at home and in the theatres of war, the YMCA offered soldiers a few welcome comforts and recreation. These included games, libraries and canteens. YMCA huts were also places in which to write letters and to enjoy concerts. (Imperial War Museum Q 5457)

Artillery officers and Signallers direct battery fire in 1917. This was typical of the front-line work undertaken by Signallers such as Ivor. (Imperial War Museum Q 5095)

Artillery Signallers practise sending messages in Morse code while wearing anti-gas respirators, 1918. (Imperial War Museum Q 36095)

The ruins of Ascension Farm after capture by the 45th Battalion, Australian Imperial Force, on 18 September 1918. These buildings were first viewed by Ivor from Dragoon Post observation post on 5 February 1918.
(Imperial War Museum E (AUS) 3252)

A battery of 18-pounder field guns of the Royal Field Artillery moves up towards Mailly-Maillet to meet the German advance. On this day, 26 March 1918, 311 Army Brigade, RFA, withdrew to positions near Beaufort and were quickly in action after their arrival. (Imperial War Museum Q 8631)

British aerial reconnaissance photograph of Blangy village near Arras. 'B' Battery, 311 Army Brigade, RFA, went into action here on 29 April 1918. During this time Ivor's duties saw him working in the Battery Signals dug-out and in an observation post. (Imperial War Museum 1900-03)

Gas-mask drill for horses of the Royal Field Artillery at Mont St Eloi, 15 May 1918. Ivor spent a few days near here, in Stuart Camp, before his battery was sent to Blangy. (Imperial War Museum Q 8794)

Shell-damaged buildings in the centre of Arras, 13 June 1918. When Ivor rejoined his battery after detached duty at a signals dug-out, they were located close to the railway station. This gave him a chance to visit the centre of the battered city. (Imperial War Museum 6732)

British aerial reconnaissance photograph of Oppy Wood, looking south-east towards Fresnes. This IWM photograph was taken at 6pm on 26 June 1917. When Ivor first saw the wood from 'Horror' observation post, on 8 August 1918, he recorded: 'In front of us is the renowned Oppy Wood, now a miserable row of branchless tree stumps, blighted, ghoulish and forlorn and which has been captured and lost so many times'. (Imperial War Museum 1900-03)

The village of Roclincourt, north of Arras, 1918. Ivor was here with 'B' Battery when they came out of the line on 26 September 1918. Here the battery rejoined 311 Army Brigade for training. (Imperial War Museum HU 96202)

A battery of 18-pounder field guns of the Royal Field Artillery prepare for action near Moulain on 17 October 1918, during the final Allied offensive on the Western Front. (Imperial War Museum Q 55067)

Canadian troops march through the streets of Mons accompanied by Belgian civilians, to celebrate the end of the war, 11 November 1918. 311 Army Brigade, RFA, was attached to the Canadian Corps from 2 November 1918. Ivor visited Mons on 13 November and witnessed the funeral of Private George Price, the last Canadian soldier to be killed in the First World War. (Imperial War Museum CO 3660)

Ivor with his father, John Hanson, Traffic Inspector, Great Western Railway. The photograph was taken on 3 February 1919, the day after Ivor returned home for demobilisation from the Army. (Hanson Family Archive)

George Kingsland and Ivor at Kew Gardens during a joint family holiday in 1959. (Hanson Family Archive)

The wedding of Leighton and Ann Hanson. Ivor is standing behind his son.
(Hanson Family Archive)

Port Talbot Railway Station, 10 July 1962. Farewell to Leighton, Ann and their
children Michael and Eileen, who were leaving for three years in Fiji. Back
row (from left), Margaret Hanson, Sylvia Williams and baby Kevin, Leighton
Hanson, Enid David and baby Eileen Hanson and Ann Hanson. Front row
(from left), Michael Hanson, J. Ivor Hanson, Susan Williams and Will Cowell.
(Hanson Family Archive)

teemed with movement and we assumed we had spotted a relief coming into the Line. With our guns, especially the two at the Forward Section, we sniped all day, firing salvo after salvo. Working at the phone in turns, Brad and I shouted time after time the commands, 'Get ready' and 'Fire'. Smith, watching certain spots in the trenches, became impatient if the gunners delayed a second and on such occasions swore vigorously. On one occasion he shouted to us excitedly, 'There goes their bloody sergeant major. Come on! Let 'em rip.' Recently the Indians were relieved by the 8th Division and a group of officers of the Rifle Brigade stood near us in the trench for hours, fascinated by the abnormal activity opposite and the effects of our firing.

Returning via the Forward Section we were accosted by a group of grumbling Gunners who wanted to know 'what all the fuss was about?', Smith having given them a hard day's work. The Signallers too had been well occupied there. One of them, Forman, was naturally anxious to have all the news.

Forman comes from Newcastle upon Tyne and boasts legitimately of the beauties of Jesmond Dene. He is a lean, shrivelled man, as hard as nails and has travelled in Canada and the USA, where he lived the life of a rolling stone, staying at each place just long enough to save enough dollars to proceed to another place. Among the places he worked at were a tinned salmon factory and the Force patent food works.

After tea at the Battery, Sergeant Mellor visited every dug-out, with the serious warning that a gas attack was expected during the night or early morning. We were to take special care that our respirators were placed near at hand.

Each of the combatants seem to be almost completely aware of the designs of the other. Observation from the air, captured prisoners, listening posts, intercepted messages, the Intelligence Department and I may add observation officers and Signallers, all help to make the information complete.

Chapter 12

THE MARCH RETREAT
(2ND BATTLE OF THE SOMME)

War Diary entry, 311 Army Field Artillery Brigade: 21 March 1918:

About 5am hostile barrage opened. All Batteries fired counter preparation for one hour. Report received from tank gun of enemy patrol seen about 9am, confirmation being obtained later from infantry. Before 12 noon B/311 main position evacuated with loss of 2 guns; 2 anti-tank guns and 2 18-pounders in B/311 forward section also fell into enemy's hands. D/311 lost 2 howitzers destroyed by shell fire in the morning with 2 officers and 8 other ranks killed, wounded and prisoners. At 2pm D/311 withdrew remaining 3 howitzers to rear positions. Lt Seagrave assumed command of D/311 as Major Hay wounded. At 4.20pm D/311 withdrew under group orders to Jenaves Farm and was reinforced by 4th howitzer from wagon lines. At 11am Red Line barrage came into force, all available batteries firing continuously. This barrage was shortened as information was received during the day. In the evening 1 gun of C/311 forward section was withdrawn to main position, the others falling into enemy hands and A/311 withdrew all guns to rear position.[1]

21 March (Thursday)

About 4 or 5 am we were awakened into a most trouble world. My first impression was of the sound of rapid cannonading in the distance and shells crashing and smashing all around us. I knew I wasn't dreaming for I could hear my dug-out mates stirring and fumbling for matches.

Hastily we lit the candles, but the concussion of shells bursting so near kept extinguishing the flames. 'Wot the 'ells up?' asked Oram, rubbing his eyes. 'Must be the big stunt we've heard so much about lately', suggested

1. National Archives reference WO 95/205: 311 Army Field Artillery Brigade, January 1917–May 1919.

someone. Hurriedly we slipped on our clothes and began to realise that we were being peppered with shells. We felt that the whole German artillery was shooting directly at our Battery. Over the shells rained, projectiles of all calibres, shrieking, screeching, whining and moaning. Amid the hail of steel we could detect gas shells by their peculiar whine and sloppy bursting sound. This was the hottest bombardment I had ever experienced, and they had our Battery position perfectly ranged. Any moment we expected death, for the shells seemed to be making straight for us and as they screamed forward we crouched together against the side of the dug-out nearer the enemy. We speculated on the withstanding power of our elephant arched roof. 'Wouldn't stand a bloody Verey light', said someone hopelessly. A man brushed aside the gas curtain, tumbled into the dug-out and sprawled upon a bed, panting, with his head in his hands. He was one of our Bombardiers. He was too breathless to answer our eager questions, but when he cooled down we found that he had not been wounded, but merely winded in his dash for shelter. Gallantly Lieutenant Sabaston paid us two visits, the first time shouting into the dug-out, 'Are you all right boys?', and the second time bawling out excitedly 'Gas!' The gas gong had already sounded and we were already steaming inside our respirators. 'Run to the deep sap around the corner', he commanded. This meaning running the gauntlet with a vengeance, but if we succeeded we'd be safe, at least for a time. How Sabaston escaped death was a miracle. Taking a full breath each we made a desperate dash for the sap, plunging over trees felled by the shell bursts, and into steaming shell holes. That 30 or 40yd race was hellish.

The ground was churned up and every tree felled or broken. How unnaturally light the sinister scene looked with all those trees down. Within a few yards of the sap I felt myself choking and not being able to bare the respirator for a moment longer, frantically I tore it off letting myself in for a good dose of gas. It stank like strong pineapple. That worried me a bit, but I hope that my present fine condition will be able to shake off any evil effects of gas. Reaching the sap we dived past the gas curtain and stumblingly we arrived at the bottom where we found most of the other men. Corporal Swallow told us that one of the first shells landed outside the Signal Pit blowing up every wire except the pair to a howitzer battery on our left.

This battery heroically kept firing for a considerable time. With long strides Sabaston rushed wildly about and it looked as though he were organising a rally to our own guns. 'We'll blow the buggers to hell', he shouted savagely. Bombardier Redfearn, with a Mephistophelian expression, was one of the party that ventured back to the guns and for some time we heard at least one of our 18-pounders barking a puny defiance at the on-coming hordes. The Major, who had a reputation among us for being extremely 'windy', remained unusually calm through it all. He sent Willis with a despatch to the Forward Section, a suicidal journey from which few expected him to return, but he did come back, with a wound on the back of his head which was soon bandaged with a field dressing. I heard him ask of the people bandaging him if Hanson and Bradburn were safe, and felt touched by his concern for his dug-out mates. We hope he'll be sent to Blighty and that he'll be recommended for a decoration, for that trip was at least worth a Military Medal. A telephone was needed and volunteers were sought to get one from the Signal Pit. Oram and I made a dash for it and found Pomeroy alone in the Pit, looking very pale and afraid to budge, but we persuaded him to return with us and after some hesitation he raced with us back to the sap.

Lieutenant 'Jack Holt', who had been reconnoitring, arrived excitedly and when he had regained his breath informed us that 'the Jerries are just around the corner'. He added that at Quaker's Quarry they were marching forward in columns of fours. There was a hurried consultation among the officers who ordered us all to retreat to a railway cutting. 'At the double', one of them added. Corporal Swallow asked Lieutenant Sabaston if we could go back to the Signal Pit for the Fullerphone and other signalling equipment, but Sabaston angrily refused and after looking at him in amazement we obeyed the order and joined in the stampede across a field into which German salvoes crashed, with precise intervals between the shell bursts. Near here the infantry were now digging themselves in and as we arrived one of their officers was having a slight wound dressed. The wound was situated in that region admirably suited for youthful chastisement and his breeches were down about his knees. We all laughed at the sight and he smiled back at us good humouredly.

Two of our Signallers, Womersly and Deakin, returned to the Battery position for the Lewis Gun which the Signallers are responsible for. They must have gone without the knowledge of the officers. Womersly came back with the gun, but alone. 'Dek's gone west', he said. 'I wasn't with him when it happened,' he continued, 'but an 8in burst near him and piece caught him in the stomach. He must have crawled into the dug-out where I found him already dead.'

In a hut in the cutting we assembled and placed all that we had been able to salvage from the guns – the breech blocks and dial sights, but later the horse teams arrived from the Wagon Lines and under German machine-gun and rifle fire we managed to extricate two of our guns from the Vadencourt position. Thus we lost four of our guns, two at the Forward Section and two at the Vadencourt Battery position. I have a feeling, which I am afraid to express, that the order given for our retreat to this cutting was precipitate. As for personal belongings, I like many others possess only what I stand in, as few of us thought when fleeing to the sap that we would not be given a chance to return to our dug-outs during a lull, for our haversacks, greatcoat and equipment. Callon, one of our Forward Section Signallers, has had his nose peeled by a fragment of a gas shell and looks like a red-nosed comedian.

The brilliant morning sun dispersed the fog and the bombardment, though less fierce, continued throughout the day. Infantry advanced in small batches which were sometimes obscured by the smoke of the bursting shells. The wounded being borne back through the cutting were a pitiful and distressing sight. One badly wounded fellow had had it beneath the abdomen and looked a hopeless case. A few of us were perched with Lieutenant 'Jack Holt' on the edge of the cutting and had a wonderful view of the proceedings. Impotent with the loss of four of our guns and all kinds of equipment, we had become little more than spectators. On our right front we spotted a Battery of Field Artillery galloping towards our lines. 'Holt' was agitated until he had, by the aid of his binoculars, satisfied himself that it was a British Battery in full retreat and not a German Battery in full advance.

'A' Battery of our Brigade brought up several guns to the rear edge of the cutting and kept up a continuous fire. The explosions resounded through the cutting and tore our nerves to shreds. It is not the result of 'windiness' but of continuous physical strain. The Major of 'A' Battery looks a hard-boiled, competent fellow, is stout and so bloated and dark skinned that he reminds me of a certain Indian rajah. A turban would suit him perfectly.

Towards evening, in a large dug-out in the cutting we had a roll call and it was found that Osmond and Vaughan were missing. We learned that Osmond, who was the Major's batman, had been badly wounded at the Battery position, but that no trace of him or Vaughan had been found since, so it was decided that a party should go back in search of them. A Sergeant asked for volunteers and as no one offered after he had waited a long time he said, 'If there are no volunteers we'd have to toss up for it.' Eventually five of us decided to risk it. We searched the cutting for a stretcher, but they were all in use, so we decided to use a door or a duckboard or anything available. We advanced from the cutting under a terrific machine-gun barrage from our own detachments situated just behind the cutting, the racket being like that of a hundred threshing machines. The bullets rained over us, the smell of cordite was terribly strong and the general atmosphere ominous. We filed beyond the infantry trench that we had crossed this morning and which was now the Front Line and came to a listening post. The three men here informed us that Vadencourt was now in the hands of the enemy and they expressed a doubt whether they would have allowed us to proceed any farther forward even if it was not. We might be attempting to desert for all they knew. Treating us with suspicion and our mission as crazy, they sent us back to see their Captain in the aforementioned trench. This officer questioned us very carefully and after some consideration ordered us back to the cutting where we found our men ready to move back to Hancourt as the bombardment had abated. We walked across the fields to Bernes, which bore signs of having been well strafed. In turns we carried the weighty breech blocks and were relieved when our Ammunition Column overtook us near Bernes and carried us back at a brisk trot to Hancourt, where, joining our comrades of the Wagon Lines, we were given a meal, having eaten nothing all day except a few biscuits. 'Nobby' Clarke, the cooks'-cart driver, beamed on us and called us heroes. With a huge carving knife he cut the delicious white bread loaves into thick slices and jammed them with the same article, asking each one of us, 'Now, what can I do for you?' as though he had a variety to choose from. 'Nobby' must have imbibed a generous rum ration tonight. Bradburn told me that Russell, the Signaller who swore at General Branker, had reported sick with trench fever. 'Of course,' he added, 'he's only swinging the lead. He's as fit as you or me, but he's just fed up and wants a change.' How nice it was to lay down in a hut again with plenty of headroom and elbow room. In the darkness I wondered what had happened to the officer and the pair of Signallers who had succeeded us at Dragoon Post and who were there when the storm broke. Wondered which of the batteries had been represented there, following our 24-hour duty. Some fellows reckoned that this morning's bombardment was worse than those they had suffered at Ypres. Prior to falling asleep I silently vowed that should I ever be lucky enough to return to 'civvy' life, I shall never grumble again.

22 March (Friday)

This morning we (Up-Liners) saw what a transformation had taken place at the Wagon Lines since our departure Up Line two months ago, for the camp is spic and span and the Nissen huts freshly painted. We Up-Liners paraded for a bath, which was the second we had been able to enjoy during three months, except for a few cold sponges with water carried up the Line in a petrol tin. What if my mother knew? The warm water of the improvised bath house soothed our vermin-inflamed skin and we glowed inside our clean underclothes. Ours was the last batch to get a bath, for after we left, the frail timbered structure, erected by Gunner Page, was demolished by a shell. This calamity drove into a panic some Portuguese troops who were in the vicinity. Page said that they looked like advancing Jerries in their field-grey uniforms.

Everybody seems to be hurriedly retreating and we hear that many of our tanks have been captured. We left Hancourt ourselves at noon, the order coming through so suddenly that there was no time to serve dinner, the cooks having to throw away the contents of the dixies, while in record time we loaded up our GS wagons, hitched the horse teams to our remaining two guns and our limbers and moved away. One of the cooks and I had been given bicycles to ride and just before moving off I discovered that the saddle was loose, a nut being missing, but I secured it with a piece of rope.

The roads were congested with retreating troops and at one place we (cyclists) became detached from the Battery. The cook thought he knew the route, but he blundered badly and we rode a mile in the wrong direction.

The farther we travel from the line, the more intact and taller the buildings become. Some of them are whitewashed and gleam brilliantly in the spring sunshine. After much trouble we discovered our Battery. I am taking particular notice of the names of the places we pass through, for I look forward to the time when I can trace on a map the ground I have already covered and the route we are now taking. Among today's places were Bouvincourt, Mons and Estrees. During the evening we were bombarded with shrapnel. We were trekking along when the perfectly timed shells burst above us. The white smoke had a copper coloured fringe, the bullets sang around us and bespattered the cobbled road. We came to an airfield where the staff were loading aeroplane parts on lorries. Shortly afterwards we saw the hangars in flames, after being deliberately set afire in order to cheat Jerry of them.

Towards dusk we left the road, I soon tired of pushing the bike over plough fields and soft turf, so during the first halt I roped it to a GS wagon. Slept the night in a field with only the gun limbers as inadequate shelters should it rain. Shared someone else's blankets and though the night was cold, we are hardened to it and also feel lucky to be alive.

23 March (Saturday)

Royal Engineers lay mines under bridges and on roads after we leave. At one place we passed a stand on which a number of conical amplifiers gaped towards the front. It was an aeroplane sound detector. On the opposite side of the road was a hospital, a large Red Cross flag proclaiming the fact. Opposite in a field a number of blanketed corpses were laid out ready for burial, a grim sight. Passed through St Christ and came to a place called Misery where we had our first decent meal for the day at 9 pm. What know the well-fed and comfortable hosts of civilian life of hunger and the keenness of appetite and smell produced by circumstances out here? The meanest slum fare would provide a banquet for us. We all stood around the steaming dixie, watching the head cook pouring tins of condensed milk into the huge cauldron of tea from which an enchanting aroma arose.

We had bread and bacon and did bacon ever taste so good? Most of us Up-Liners lost all our equipment at Vadencourt, including water bottles, bandoliers, greatcoats, leather jerkin and haversacks containing small kit such as cutlery and shaving tackle. Even our mugs and mess tins were lost so that tonight we had to drink in turns the most delicious tea we had ever tasted, out of condensed milk tins.

24 March (Sunday)

Bright and sunny day. Still retreating, we left Misery after dinner. Gunner Turner, who also arrived at Hancourt Christmas time with our group of reinforcements, played me a mean trick today. He has I think a cadaverous face which does not correspond to his fairly broad body and sturdy legs. I always judged him to be a superior fellow, but was mistaken. Just before we left Misery he came to me offering a horse for me to ride as he said he had two. I gratefully accepted, but soon discovered the reason for his generosity. The horse was sick and had to be goaded along after every few steps, an exhausting job. At Marchelepot we met a contingent of the Chinese Labour Corps. They seemed larger than the Chinamen I had previously seen at home. Some of them wore straw, sailor hats. Their belongings, wrapped in blankets, dangled from the ends of a long pole carried over the shoulder.

Frequently our column had long waits on the congested roads, especially at crossroads for other elongated units to pass. Each time we had to dismount and during one of these halts I fell instantly asleep on the roadside, due to sheer exhaustion. At Fresnes our two-gun Battery fired 'open sights' or point-blank at the enemy and at Soyecourt we received two new guns and here, with the four guns, we fired many rounds, being repaid by being bombed by aeroplanes, but we suffered no casualties. In this locality a stray mule was found and to everyone's relief, Jacko, the recalcitrant mule was dumped.

For some time we have missed the presence of our Major and today we heard the disconcerting news that he had been killed in action. It happened in a wood near here, but we have not yet been given any details. Captain Hollingworth is in England on leave and during this difficult testing time we are commanded by Lieutenant Sampson, who comes from Pontardulais, which is in my county of Glamorganshire. He rides a black horse with a white, diamond-shaped blaze on its forehead. Prior to this war he belonged to the Yeomanry and he rides his horse with that ease and grace produced only by long practice. He is considered one of the finest horsemen in the Brigade.

Here at Soyecourt, and for the first time since the 21 March, our Battery is split up into gun position and Wagon Lines. Another Signaller and I were sent from the Wagon Lines to the gun position with a despatch.

We walked both ways. Near the gun position I met Driver Howells, a Llanelli man whom I became acquainted with at Bettisfield to which he came from the Eastern Front where he had served in the famous 29th Division. Our Battery was in a warm spot, for the German infantry were near and advancing rapidly. Seeing us returning, an infantry officer asked us rather anxiously if we intended pulling out the guns from their present position.

One of our own Drivers, sitting astride his horse in a team waiting the order to hitch up to a gun limber and retreat, seemed to be losing control of himself. He is a Scot. He trembled convulsively and in an emotional voice appealed to me as I passed by, 'I don't know what to do with myself', he babbled, almost in tears. I could only remind him that we'd be pulling out almost immediately and that there was really nothing to worry about.

Wounded being borne back were a pitiable sight. The less-serious cases walked. One white-faced man had been wounded in the arm which was swathed in bandages, but at each step the blood dripped from his fingers.

I remembered it was Dad's birthday and sent him a Field Card to let him know that I was all right. However, the postal services were so dislocated by this battle that they did not hear from me for 6 weeks, and every day they expected to hear the worst.

We are retreating through the fertile valley of the River Somme, charming country, looking its best in the spring sunshine. It is a country of rich, rolling downland.

As Signallers our rightful place is at the head of the column with the Battery staff, but the number of horses is at present below strength, so we ride with the Gunners on the limbers. We are now seeing civilians for the first time in three months, an interesting change from the military. The first civilian I saw was a girl of about 14. After having seen only the masculine sex for so long she looked to me like a fairy. The civilians evacuate their villages before we enter, but one or two, allowed to remain – probably for special reasons – a little longer than the others, we see at close range occasionally. It is a pathetic sight seeing them taking away as many of their belongings as they possibly can, in small carts, handcarts and wheelbarrows, each man, woman and child being responsible for a share.

They will probably never see their charming homes again, for by tomorrow they are likely to be blown to smithereens.

Passed through Fouceaucourt, Vadvillers to Vrely where we were again bombed by Boche planes. At Vrely I picked up a picture postcard of Peronne. It is a photograph of La Grande Place, looking rather imposing in peace time. The very wide square between the shops must be the market place. I also found a small newspaper map of this department of France and now have an idea of the front we served on, where we now are and the direction – westward – in which we are being driven.

26 March (Tuesday)

Our journey during this sunny but cold day took us through Rosières, Warvillers to Beaufort. This afternoon I saw a calf being unwillingly dragged behind one of our limbers, several necks of chickens wrung and an abandoned tavern raided and robbed of its bottled attractions. I was told that one section had a young pig. What a feast there'll be tonight. The civilians have evacuated this locality and what is left is probably what was beyond their capacity to take with them, so why leave it all to Jerry? Beaufort, which we reached this evening, is a picture, quite the prettiest spot I have seen in France. No wonder artists make for France, like pilgrims to Mecca. A few civilians ventured back for some cows, pigs and miscellaneous belongings. We are billeted in a house near the guns, and for once we can each eat and drink as much as we want. Tonight had a memorable meal of potatoes, peas, cabbage and bully beef. In the cellar were several casks of cider. With it we filled a huge earthenware bread pan and bore it upstairs and placed it on the parlour table, each man dipping in his receptacle whenever he desired. This celestial interlude in the hell that is our normal life was speedily terminated for me by being informed that I was to be on guard during the night, with Signaller Brain, a 'beauty' to be with on guard, for once he falls asleep he is as one dead. To wake him you have to roll, shake, pinch and punch him for about 5 minutes. It was a strange, unofficial sort of guard with just Brain and I on it. No inspection, no rifles and no parading to and fro. Our instructions were to stop at intervals passing men, enquire as to the state of things in case of any unexpected developments. This we did through a long, uneventful night while the rest of the Battery fed to their hearts content and no doubt snored like gorged beasts. How we could have slept too, but I realised that were we both to do so it was possible that the whole Battery could be captured in a sudden nocturnal advance of which we, the appointed guards, had not given the alarm. If that happened, God help Brain and me. Sitting there alone during my turns on duty I tried to weigh up the situation. The Germans seemed to be able to do what they like with us and were doing it so successfully during the day that mercifully they had to take a rest at night. I imagined them pushing us back to the coast and then visualised our retreat across to England. At least they'd find it difficult to land there. I imagined a victorious Germany, but what then?

27 March (Wednesday)

This morning our concealed position enabled us to communicate with another section of the Battery by flag signalling – a rare occurrence during my experience in France. An aeroplane dropped us a message on a streamer which was taken to an officer from whom we learned that it was a map reference and on the place it indicated we fired a lot of shells. How we longed to know what we were firing at and if the result was successful. After this, when I was standing between the guns and the village, an infantry officer came up to me and said, 'D'you mind getting a box of matches out of my greatcoat for me? I've a bullet through my elbow.' I had noticed that his face was ashen, but had guessed nothing for ashen faces are very common among men out here these days. In the right pocket of his coat a service revolver pointed dangerously upwards and beneath it was the box of matches. His right arm hung limply and near the elbow of his Burberry was a small bullet hole, singed around its edge. I lit his cigarette, he thanked me and asked me if I could get him a drink. I asked him if cider would do, smiling at the thought of the pan of plenty in our billet.

The house was near and after skimming the dust from the surface I filled a glass with cider and took it to him. He gulped it down quickly, thanked me again and continued his walk down the Line in search of a Dressing Station.

A triplane flew over us, the first I had ever seen. Here we were badly bombed and shelled and we suffered a few casualties. We were bombed by one of our own planes, which surprised us until we realised that it had been captured by the enemy. Fragments of shells flew about unhealthily, and while chatting to Sergeant Mellor, a piece about as big as my fist whizzed between our heads and struck a garden fence post with terrific force. This ugly, jagged piece of steel dropped into a puddle and sizzled, for it seemed to be nearly red hot. It is the narrowest escape I and probably Mellor have ever had.

A horseman galloped towards us in the distance. When he came nearer I could see it was Jack Bradburn, who is acting as Mounted Orderly, and it was apparent that he bore an important despatch from Headquarters. Like wildfire the news spread around that the German Cavalry had broken through. He who fights and runs away lives to fight another day. He who fights and stays is either killed or captured. Four guns are enough to be captured from any Battery, so we received excited orders to 'Limber up!' and never was an order carried out so swiftly, but just as we moved away one vehicle wedged into a tree, holding up the whole column for a few minutes which seemed hours to us.

How queer that such things like that happen sometimes at the worst-possible times. We galloped across a field of shell holes and we who were riding the limbers had the roughest ride of our lives, having to cling onto the handgrips like grim death and with all our might to avoid being flung off. When we reached the road a limber pole broke under the strain and the limber had to be abandoned. In the excitement a fellow named Wright slipped on his limber and one of his legs got entangled in a wheel. We haven't heard the extent of the injury but it must be considerable. Arrived at Le Quesnel where we went into action about 150yd behind our Howitzer Battery.

When these howitzers fired (almost perpendicularly), for the fraction of a second we could see the shells leave the pieces. The land in front of us rolls out and rises to uplands at the base of which are thick woods.

Chapter 13

MEETING WITH THE FRENCH ARMY

28 March (Thursday)

Early this morning Signaller Hey and I laid a telephone wire. A beautiful moon lit up the land. Once the wire became inextricably tangled and badly delayed our progress. This afternoon the British and French Infantry retreated and left our Batteries completely uncovered. It seemed to me that it was a disorderly and undisciplined scuttle and this was proved by a British Infantry officer arriving at the Battery position to ask very anxiously for the loan of a horse with which to round up his men who were fleeing in all directions. We could not oblige, having lost quite a number either killed, wounded or sick. I steel myself to remember that these infantrymen have, like ourselves, had little proper sleep since the 21st.

Probing, advanced German detachments soon acquainted the main attacking units of the situation, and the rising land before us bristled with enemy activity. The atmosphere seemed electrified. Into this ample target we fired 'open sights' and continued doing so until the carefully directed bombardment we were being subjected to grew hotter and hotter. We could imagine their own artillery observers working excitedly from those uplands or on the fringes of those woods. A barrage crept up to us like a gigantic approaching storm and our situation was critical. The horse teams stood nobly near, in fact just a few yards behind the guns. My heart warmed to those patient, calm and wonderful animals. At the welcomed command we hitched up the guns to the limbers and galloped out of range, but only in the nick of time.

We rode into Mézières, which was congested with troops and we stayed there just long enough for the cooks to make a hurried tea. Here I found a

223

fine German helmet, but reluctantly dumped it as it would be too inconvenient to carry about, especially during these desperately mobile times. A Boche plane flew very low over our Battery. The pilot and the observer looked over the side of the fuselage at us and we could distinctly see their goggle-covered eyes and the big, black, mournful crosses on the wings. It looked like a monstrous bird of prey, after our blood, and almost every one of us shot at it with our rifles or Lewis Gun, but the surprising thing was that they didn't bomb or machine-gun us in those congested streets. Had they done so, the casualties would have been enormous. Afterwards we guessed that it was purely an observation flight or that their ammunition was expended.

Anyway, it won't be safe to stay in this place from now on, for there'll be some strafing once those Jerries get their wireless message through to their Batteries.

We were relieved to get away from Mézières. We travelled all night in torrential rain, for the weather, which has been glorious up until now, suddenly changed. On we trekked relentlessly with heads bowed to the driving rain.

Doubled up on the limber footboard I got soaked to the skin, the rain running down my back like a miniature waterfall. I had no greatcoat and the sack that I scrounged and wrapped around my shoulders was soon saturated.

Two of us stuck this misery for some time before getting into the cooks' cart which was trailing at the rear of the column. We climbed in from behind and the shafts went up like a see-saw. Inside we found 2nd Lieutenant Shaw squatting near the driver. He gave us a look enough to crack a mirror, and mumbled something which was lost on us in the sinister duet of heavy rain and the grinding of steel vehicle tyres against the French pave, but he didn't have the heart to send us back into it. We laid down exhausted amid the rations and slept a deep sleep, after I had noted that our journey had taken us through a place called Athies.

29 March (Friday)

As we reached Castel one of our Gunners helped to wheel in a barrow a fleeing, aged peasant. The old man's last act was an expression of gratitude. He gave the Gunner a franc and then died in the wheelbarrow.

At dusk Bradburn and I were sent out mounted with a despatch for Brigade Headquarters. We were told that Headquarters was situated behind a wood on the right of the road and armed with that vague information we set out. One of the most difficult tasks entrusted to a soldier is despatch riding during a retreat or advance. Everyone is on the move and no one is certain where anyone else is for very long. You are sent to a destination and find when you reach it that the unit you seek had left, no one knows where. When you return you will most likely find your own unit missing too.

Add to this the instinctive reluctance of soldiers to answer questions casually fired at them by strangers and then the difficulties may be imagined. It was quite dark when we reached the main road and I very nearly rode over a drunken soldier sprawling in the middle of the road, but my horse shied and swerved past him and the fellow staggered up and shambled along cursing us as we cursed him. We peered into the inky darkness of the night that now enveloped us, but without success. We retraced our steps time after time without seeing any sign of a wood. We trotted on some distance asking several men where the road led. 'To Jerries' lines' was the curt reply of one of them. We right-about-turned and passed the same way again, riding back for several miles without seeing any sign of a wood on the right of the road. It was now early morning and after making numerous further inquiries without success, we decided to postpone the search until daylight.

We came to a large farm where a squadron of French cavalrymen were billeted; to the best of our ability we explained our situation and they allowed us to stay for the night in one of the barns. We stabled our steeds, gave them plenty of hay, crept under a load of straw and slept, being awakened once or twice by our French comrades walking over us.

30 March (Saturday)

Arose early and continued the search, finding Headquarters at last. The wood was quite near our Battery, but it was well off the main road and too distant to be visible from the road in the darkness. The message could not have been urgent, for no complaint was made regarding its delayed arrival. Returning to the road we met our Battery moving away to another position.

Feeling very thirsty we begged a drink from a French infantryman who had his water bottle filled with vin rouge.

It quenched our thirsts and we were grateful, but I imagined that it tasted like blood.

31 March (Sunday)

We are in action on the brow of a hill and have cut little dug-outs out of the mound that runs along it. Recently the Signallers scrounged a tarpaulin and this now slopes backwards from the open side of the dug-outs, forming an admirable shelter. With a few others slipped down to Castel in search of straw to sleep on. In a deserted farm we found an ample supply. Dead horses of the French cavalry, I think, lay swollen and stiff about the yards. Returning with a big load of straw each, we were ascending towards the hill crest when we saw a German sausage (balloon) up, near enough for us to see the black cross on its side. Its observers spotted us and at that distance we must have looked to them like loaded vehicles moving forward. We were a few hundred yards from our position when their field-gun shells began to screech over and as the sound neared us we dropped the straw and dived into it. We were struck by numerous small shell fragments, but none of us were hurt. In spite of the seriousness of our predicament we were forced to laugh at each other making these undignified plunges every time the shells came over. Some time later, hearing some hearty cheering outside the dug-out, we scrambled out from under the tarpaulin to see the balloon descending amid a volume of black smoke. An Allied plane had shot it down.

Brain, the arch scrounger, produced a safety razor today and we wondered where on earth he found it. I suspect some poor blighter went unshaven this morning because of it. I borrowed it and had my first shave for 11 days. We looked and felt like vagabonds and we used the none-too-sharp, but acceptable razor in turns. During the agony of removing my stubble, tears chased down my cheeks. Oh! For the amenities and comforts of home, such as a luxurious shave followed by a splash in plentiful warm water. I would give much to be able to clean my teeth properly now. They feel tired and aching from lack of thorough brushing and rinsing.

Behind us there is a Battery of French seventy-fives, the finest field guns in the world. They load automatically, fire about 6 to 7 miles, are accurate and have a high rate of fire. The extreme range of our 18-pounders is about 3 miles, so that it is necessary for us to be much more forward in order to be able to reach such targets as communication trenches.

The French 'seventy-five' salvoes are splendid, going off like one gun. This particular French Battery has an arrangement that if a German shell drops within a certain radius of it, it retaliates by firing six shells back, which we imagine the German gunners would find discouraging.

1 April (Monday)

One of the Signallers, probably Brain, scrounged a chicken. In this open position we dare not reveal ourselves by lighting a fire, so the cooking of this fowl became a problem, but where there's a will there's a way, so the difficulty was eventually solved by making a miniature stove out of a cocoa tin, with siege candles and fragments of sandbag for fuel and the tin lid for a frying pan. Quickly feathering and cleaning the chicken, we cut it into pieces and fried it in its own fat as we had no other.

On our right the ridge dips into a small wood. Today this wood was badly shelled and immediately there arose out of it the most terrifying screams we had ever heard in the war. A party of French soldiers had been near the wood at the time of the shelling and several of them were wounded. The cries sent shivers down our spines. Some of our men were despatched to render first aid, returning later to report that the man we had heard screaming had had both his feet blown off.

It is rumoured that the German offensive is now being checked.[1]

4 April (Thursday)

This evening our journey ended with our guns in action in a similar position to that of Castel, for the ridge we occupy is almost identically the same.

---

1. This rumour proved to be correct for it is now widely accepted that the German offensive, 'Operation Michael', began seriously to falter after the fighting on 31 March. That afternoon Ludendorff cabled his Army Group commanders to prepare for a final push towards Amiens on 4 April. However when final objectives were issued for 4 April, they did not even envisage the capture of the city. Amiens, a major Allied transport hub, had been key to the German's original offensive plans. These much more limited objectives reveal that Ludendorff no longer believed he could decisively break the Allied line on this part of the front. On 5 April, Ludendorff called off the offensive, his exhausted troops having been fought to a standstill by increasingly strong British and Australian defence.

Behind us is the town of Dommartin, which looks a large place. Our Wagon Lines are below us at the foot of the hill and as the result of shelling, already several of our men, including Sergeant Major Parker, have been wounded. Parker succeeded Hanson, who is now Regimental Sergeant Major. Driver Bretherick was gassed and it fell to the lot of Brain and I to take him to a French Dressing Station at Dommartin. He was very ill and at times in agony. We had to assist him along as we did not have a stretcher. It was dark when we entered the town where we were directed to the Dressing Station, a villa in its own grounds. We had great hopes of being offered some food for our trouble and we knocked at the door with anticipation. We were led through some wards where wounded or sick lay on the floor, covered with thick, warm-looking clothing. Fires burnt merrily in the huge grates. In an inner room, by gestures and odd words we tried to make the Frenchmen understand the nature of Bletherick's plight, but without success, 'Blesser', a Frenchman repeated, to our repeated Nons. But when Brain suddenly blurted 'Asphyxiate', they immediately understood. We bade Bletherick adieu and good luck as he was led away, and stood uncomfortably long waiting for the good square meal that would be surely offered us, but the Frenchmen looked puzzled. As a last resort Brain resourcefully motioned for a drink, which as we were glad to see was forthcoming. An orderly brought in for each of us a glass of pink, warm liquid, which at least was better than nothing and then we left that comfortable retreat for the exposed ridge of the gun position, feeling terribly disappointed. We arrived back to find that our tarpaulin had been commandeered by the officers and that we poor Signallers were again shelterless during a night of torrential rain. Behind the ridge we made a roof of straw which kept off some of the rain, but did not prevent us becoming soaked to the skin. We risked lighting a fire, kept the smoke down to a minimum and during a temporary cessation of the deluge, steamed ourselves dry in front of the flames. My mother would go insane if I told her about things like this. Hell cannot be much worse than this, for everything contrives to break our spirits. Personally I feel tonight that I don't care which side wins the war.

5 April (Good Friday)

Alongside and behind us are several batteries of French 75mm guns and farther behind are many French batteries of heavier guns and howitzers. I have never seen so many guns massed together.

In one place they were lined up, wheel to wheel, resembling a wall of guns. It looks as though the French mean business now and this massed artillery of theirs strikes me as being impenetrable.

7 April (Sunday)

Our Battery is now in action at Fouencamps, occupying a reserve position for a change. All the civilians have evacuated, but there are hundreds of French troops in the vicinity, some of them transferred from the Italian Front. Among the French soldiers with whom we came into contact one spoke English beautifully and seemed proud to inform me that he had lived in London for a time.

The Signallers are billeted in a cottage that has an apple tree clustered with exquisite blossom at the moment, the branches hanging over the front door.

Today the first mail arrived for a fortnight. It must have been a heavy one, for my share amounted to eight letters and five newspapers, the receipt of which cheered me up considerably and made me feel ashamed of the self-pity with which I inflicted myself a few nights ago. Two of the letters alluded to prayer. One of these was from my aunt, Mrs A.M. Jenkins, who with my uncle, Revd W.M. Jenkins, lives in retirement at Aberystwyth after years of missionary work on the Khasia Hills, Assam, India. She asks, 'Can't you hear them praying for you?' The other letter, from the Revd David John BA, of Port Talbot, contained this more thoughtful remark – 'If prayers have their efficacy, you certainly have ours.'

According to the newspapers, 90 German Divisions took part in this offensive, their object being to sever the British Army from that of the French and drive us into the sea. They did not succeed in their plans, but they certainly overwhelmed the Fifth Army and have driven us back miles.

Marching into the Line the French infantrymen look grimly anxious, but they look healthy troops with ruddy complexions. Many are bearded and that makes them look older than they probably are. The lightheartedness that characterises so many Tommies in similar circumstances is entirely absent from their ranks. On Good Friday the French captured a big batch of Germans and marched them down past our guns. They were a shabby crowd, marshalled along by one Frenchman with a long, spiky bayonet fixed on his rifle.

We miss our British open-fire grates and cheery fires as French kitchens are fitted with cast-iron stoves. At times they become very hot. This evening we cooked on ours some tasty chip-potatoes.

With another Signaller spent the night at a lamp-signalling station, a dug-out of very limited space. A heavy mist gathered and prevented any signalling taking place.

8 April (Easter Monday)

Today our Battery did some rapid firing, one gun fired 23 and another gun 16 rounds in one minute.

French aeroplanes, droning and looking like swarms of flies, flew over us today. We counted 44 of them up at the same time, flying in squadrons at different altitudes.

9 April (Tuesday)

Near us some French soldiers killed a cow and we saw one of them drink the blood flowing from her neck. We Signallers begged a portion of meat and were given the head, which we boiled and with vegetables from the gardens we had a great feast tonight. Gunner Page and some others, having a surplus of trench waders and boots (probably retrieved, found or scrounged) exchanged them with the 'Froggies' for some bottles of vin rouge. We invited a French soldier as a guest, a refined and sensitive fellow whom we learned had been a schoolmaster. We all tried on his grey blue helmet and considered it heavier but of a much smarter design than that of our 'tin hats'. Our attempts at a conversation with fragmentary French caused great mirth and our friend, quite wrongly mistaking the fun to be at his expense, lost his temper and all our remonstrances could not prevent his hasty exit.

The light-blue uniform of the French troops is very conspicuous and can be seen contrasting vividly with the landscape from great distances, so that we wonder why the French ever chose it. We hear it described as horizon blue, a vague classification as the horizon can be of any colour. Some of their regiments are clad in uniforms of darker blue and others wear khaki, which has in it more yellow than ours and is therefore less attractive in my estimation.[2] Our own khaki beats all of them for camouflaging purposes.

10 April (Wednesday)

The cottages of this locality are very weakly built, having walls of laths and plaster with which has been mixed straw. Shells play havoc with them and if one drops anywhere near they collapse like a pack of cards.

Food is still our obsession. This morning, in glorious sunshine, two of us set out in search of anything eatable. We decided to try to buy some bread from the French troops, so approached two likely looking men on a lorry who handed us a round, flat loaf of bread but declined to accept our proffered coin. Spent the afternoon in a barn, chaff cutting.

2. French colonial regiments were given khaki uniforms during 1915 and 1916, while the rest of the French Army changed to horizon blue. This was probably due to the fact that colonial units of the Armée d'Afrique had worn sand/khaki-coloured uniform when serving in Africa prior to 1914.

Chapter 14

TREK TO ANOTHER PART
OF THE FRONT

13 April (Saturday)

On the move again, we came via Boves to St Fuscian where we were issued
with clothing and equipment, Lieutenant Sampson, who superintended the
distribution, grumbling at the quantity missing. Among my equipment I
received a drab, lustreless bandolier, which even with constant polishing
will never attain the mirror-like surface of the one I lost at Vadencourt. We
each now have the allotted load of equipment to carry across our shoulders,
but on trek our blankets are folded in our groundsheets and strapped on
the gun limber. This serves an additional purpose, cushioning the hard,
steel limber seats for us.

14 April (Sunday)

We are trekking to another part of the Line and today we passed through
Salieux, Saleouel, Savesue, Picquigny and St Pierre-à-Gouy. Some claim
that we have passed through Amiens, but I fancy we must have skirted it
as I am sure we did not pass through any place of that size. In a canteen at
Picquigny I met and had a chat with Corporal Judson, who used to be one
of Bettisfield's concert celebrities. At a French Post Office I changed a few
postal orders which Ma had sent me from time to time.

Trekking is very pleasant when the weather is good. Each gun limber is
drawn by six horses or mules, lead, centre and wheel pair. A Driver rides
each near horse and wears a steel shield (leg iron) on his right leg to avoid
crushing against the limber poles.

Occasionally, during a long day's march, we relieve them in the saddle
(voluntarily) for a spell. When they dismount the Drivers appear to be bow-

232

legged. When steep hills have to be negotiated we on the limbers dismount, while on steep declines one man from each vehicle dismounts and applies the brake, which is situated in the rear, an inconvenient arrangement that could be improved upon. We travel at a sharp walk march, having our monotonous meals of bully beef and biscuits on the roadside, after lowering the limber poles and watering and feeding the horses.

15 April (Monday)

Proceed through Legard, Couy, Soues, Quesnoy, Airaines, Allery, Merelessart, to Citernes. At Citernes reinforcements arrived, one of whom, a Corporal, sold me an Army razor for a franc. It shaves very well. The estaminets are doing a roaring trade. I have never been able to whip up any enthusiasm for beer drinking and often marvel why it is so universally popular. Perhaps a taste for French wines and beers has to be cultivated like a taste for tobacco has to be, usually against its initial unpleasantness. So far I cannot say that I really enjoy vin blanc and vin rouge and a few other bitter drinks I have sampled.

16 April (Tuesday)

Billeted in barns, we sleep on top of a huge pile of straw. The nights are cold so we sleep in threes, sharing six blankets. This morning Jack Bradburn was too ill to rise for parade and during my absence on duty the Brigade Doctor arrived and I heard that when he asked him how he felt, all Bradburn could say was, 'I have a queer feeling going round and round.' He was rushed to hospital without my having an opportunity to see him or to find out what the doctor diagnosed.

One of our shoeing smiths, a short, sturdy fellow, has a fine, tenor voice and fortunately for us, sleeps near us, at the other side of the barn. Each morning when cleaning and polishing up ourselves, we are treated to 'Take a Pair of Sparkling Eyes' and 'Come Into the Garden Maud'.

When we stay at a place for a few days the cooks have time to prepare meals which though limited to the barest variety, are an improvement on bully beef and biscuits. In the village we enjoy the luxuries of suppers, for the civilians, at a reasonable price, provide us with that dish so popular with Tommy out here – eggs and chips.

When walking through the village this afternoon with a group of mates, one of our Lieutenants came up to me and greeted me very kindly. This is the officer whom I always think resembles Jack Holt, the star of many Western films. It was he who informed us at Vadencourt, on the 21 March, that 'the Boche is just round the corner', and was thus partly responsible for our precipitate retreat (in my opinion) to the railway cutting. Since then he has been away from the Battery with the Ammunition Column, and I fancy that such a transfer was not a promotion for him. I am terribly sorry for this as he was such a genial fellow to us.

18 April (Thursday)

Our journey took us through Halencourt, Sorel, Liercourt, Pont-Remy, Buigny-L'Abbé, to St Riquier. The name of each town and village may be seen on an iron plate fixed on one of the first buildings of a locality. These sign-plates are painted blue and the raised letters and figures white. Under the placename are the names of neighbouring towns and villages and their distance in kilometres. How useful for all. I record these names in my diary and sometimes, in haste, scribble them on a piece of scrap paper. When that is impossible I deliberately remember them by observing their appearance and by pronouncing them. I believe I have developed a memory for such names. I have also noticed that soldiers develop remarkable memories for placenames and dates, simply by alluding to them repeatedly when reminiscing. We remained at St Riquier for the night, most of the men of the Battery getting drunk and creating a great uproar in the barns. Corporal Stewart looked very funny attempting Indian club swinging with two empty beer bottles, but his short legs were too unsteady to support his long trunk, so the attempt was a failure.

19 April (Friday)

Continuing the trek we passed through Oneux, Hiermont, Auxi-Le-Château, finishing the day's journey at Wavans. Our billets are reserved as usual by the advance party that always precedes us.

Here at Wavans we had a pleasant diversion, for 'D' Battery treated us to a concert in a large barn. Their Sergeant Major, a sinister looking old-timer, with deep seams on his cheeks, did some Indian club swinging and dagger swinging in semi-darkness, the remaining lights reflecting grotesquely on the rotating daggers. We imagined that he had learned all that during service in India. Quarter Master Mailey, possessing an excellent bass voice, sang splendidly, 'My Old Shako'. Returned to our barn to find a violent quarrel taking place between Gunner Turner and Driver Gallagher, known to us as Jock, and who has an awful temper. We arrived at the stage of the brawl when Jock threatened to brain Turner if he uttered another word. Afterwards we learned that the dispute was caused by Turner usurping Jock's bed place in the barn.

20 April (Saturday)

Proceeded through Villers l'Hôpital, Bonnières, Rebreuviette, Etree-Wamin, to Magincourt. During today's trek recognised several Bettisfield men riding on the limbers of a battery which passed us on the route, but was unable to attract their attention owing to the swift pace both columns were travelling at, and the noise of the grinding steel tyres on the pavé. The weather is fair and we were billeted for the night in another huge barn.

Chapter 15

ON THE ARRAS FRONT

22 April (Monday)

Passed through Ambrines, Villers-Sir-Simon, Izel-les-Hameau, Hermaville, Laresser and Etrun. Nearing Etrun, rattling and grinding along the cobbled pave, Corporal Stewart came up to our limber and said, 'I wouldna mind bettin' we're bound for Arras, boys. I've bin heer before.' I hoped he was right, for I had an intense wish to see the old, historical city. The French roads are good everywhere, the principal ones being generally lined with trees which form delightful avenues, dividing vast expanses of undulating cultivated land.

The field boundaries are ditches and we miss our English hedges. Fragile windmills frequently give the landscape a sketchy look and an inevitable tower or spire proclaim to the approaching traveller yet another church and a village clustering around it, such hamlets usually nestling in ample trees. Windows of the cottages are usually shuttered and the walls are painted with fresh colours of various hues. Occasionally, during the brisk march a horse kicks over the traces. When this happens the nearest individual dismounts, unfastens and readjusts the traces, an easy operation as the traces are fitted with a clever but simple quick-release gadget. Our day's journey ended at a depot on the Arras–St. Pol Road, a notice board announcing it to be 'Stuart Camp'. We hear that it is about 5 or 6 kilos behind Arras. The camp consists of Bow huts, dining sheds, stables and water troughs. Looking in the opposite direction from Arras, a tower silhouetted against the western sky immediately arrests the attention.

Old-timers tell us that it is the ruin of an ancient monastery and that its name is Mont St Eloi. Soon its venerable form dissolved into a sky of deepening cobalt blue and we entered our huts and laid out our blankets, for there is no more to be done today and we are tired after a big battle and a long trek. Next to me on the left is Driver Blanchard, a diminutive fellow with ebony coloured hair and eyes. I like him for his amiability and because he rings so truly. We are able to converse without reserve. After 'Lights Out' I pondered on the name Blanchard, which sounds French, but familiar, and then I remembered that Blanchard is the name of a character in Victor Hugo's *Les Miserables*.

23 April (Tuesday)

Walked to Anzin-St-Aubin, a battered locality near the camp. Not many whole houses survive and a big shell hole gapes in the church tower. Anzin's main attraction is a large Canadian YMCA.

Our Brigade is now attached to the Canadians. Sitting in the YMCA I studied the faces of many of these colonials and fancy I saw among them many swarthy men who could be of Red Indian stock. Also of course many French-Canadians.

24 April (Wednesday)

This morning had an hour's signalling drill. This week a half-holiday each day is to be granted to every possible person in order for us to rest and recuperate ourselves. This afternoon it rained very heavily.

25 April (Thursday)

Had more signalling drill for an hour, the remainder of the morning being spent in the stables grooming and harness cleaning.

27 April (Saturday)

This week a Brigade Association Football Tournament has taken place, matches between the different sections of the Brigade having been played each afternoon of the week. This afternoon Brigade Headquarters played 'B' Battery in the final, the result being a draw. Naturally the excitement was great. In the Headquarters eleven was an ex-player of Queens Park Rangers. He is the Veterinary Officer, holds the rank of Captain, is a burly man and a dashing player. On the same side was the Adjutant, a youthful and effeminate individual whose inclusion in the team seemed to me to be a planned joke. He appeared to take the game seriously enough, but his performance was ludicrous and produced much laughter, especially among the officers whom I guess had persuaded him to play.

28 April (Sunday)

Corporal Stewart, who is in charge of our 'C' Subsection, is a Scot and not a bad fellow to deal with. He occupies our hut and though his language is sometimes vile and the songs he sings are of the 'I love my Girl' type, he can rise to higher levels when he chooses.

He possesses a beautifully bound volume of the poetry of Burns which he pronounces 'Burrns', and which he proudly displayed to me today. Formerly he was attached to the 38th (Welsh) Division and he informed me that the Welsh troops are the most pertinacious fighters he has known in France. He is tall, has a long trunk, short legs, has a small moustache and a weak chin. On parade he forces out his narrow chest too much and looks comical.

This afternoon a group of fellows were eagerly reading a Yorkshire newspaper and seemed to be deriving much amusement there from. News spread around that the paper contained Sergeant Preston's own thrilling account of how he won the Military Medal at Vadencourt.

After tea an open-air boxing tournament took place behind our huts. The principal bout was between the Colonel's groom and a Sergeant. The groom was a professional boxer, whose face advertises that fact, for his nose has been pounded flat and his ears into small cauliflowers. On his formidable breast St George and the Dragon has been tattooed in blue and red.

He leathered his challenger, whose defence was game but ineffective. In the audience was a Chaplain, probably there to prove himself a 'sport', but towards the end of this bout, when the 'pro' had his opponent beaten and bloody, the Chaplain arose and left and I fancied there was a pained look on his face.

Ended the day by attending a religious service conducted by the Canadians at the Anzin YMCA.

29 April (Monday)

Our Battery went into action at Blangy, near Arras, through which we had to pass. There is an imposing gateway at the main entrance to this famous old city. Here Military Policemen stand on guard, their depot situated just off the main road. Walking through the cobbled streets we saw a few civilians, but although Arras itself is not so devastated as some places we have been, the suburbs, Blangy, St Catherine and St Nicholas, are badly battered. Our Signal Pit is a cellar among tall, ruined, red-brick buildings, chaotic with debris. On the road, a few yards away there is a quantity of splintered wood, which we learn is the remains of a motor lorry struck directly by a shell. Behind our position is a huge dump of barbed wire, duckboards, etc., which gets badly strafed at intervals. The Signallers of the Brigade we relieved pinched one of our telephones and left a dud in its place, a typical Army trick. Corporal Swallow was vexed about it and told us all off for not being more alert during the changeover.

Received a parcel from a former schoolmistress of mine, Miss Gwladys Penry Edwards BA, containing a kind letter, a box of cigarettes and some 'Studio' magazines from her sister, Ethel. Miss Gwladys remarks that some of the school staff feel quaint and a little older when they realise that the boys they taught are now soldiers in France.

30 April (Tuesday)

On duty at a rear observation post at the top of a high building. The stairs have been destroyed by shell fire, so we climb an iron ladder to reach the small observation room. Sappers of that ingenious regiment the Royal Engineers are responsible for this look out, for it is they who have adapted it from the ruins, reinforcing with concrete the outer wall facing Jerry, leaving an unnoticeable slit in the wall for observing and a trap door in the floor, our only entrance and exit.

This O Pip overlooks many places made historical by the war, including Monchy Hill, now held by the enemy and doubtless a commanding place for their observers. In the foreground is a cemetery which has shared the universal destruction. A small crucifix leans against a tombstone. On the left of this are the remains of a milliner's shop, from which a small signboard hangs perilously by one nail. On it is painted the name, Madame Joly and information likely to attract female shoppers. Many are the speculations on the person of Madame Joly.

1 May (Wednesday)

On this day we read 'The tide of the war has turned'. Music of any kind is so rare here that when we hear any we are unspeakably thrilled. This happened today when we heard a gramophone in a canteen at St Nicholas. On the way over we were accosted by an American soldier who asked us the way to the trenches in the following words, 'Say you guys, where the hell is the goddam shooting gallery?'

Our dug-out is situated on the roadside about a hundred yards from the Signal Pit. From the steps descending to this dug-out we gaze at lonely ruins.

I have made a pencil sketch of the building across the road. It must have been a fine mansion or a public building. Now it is roofless and some of its rafters, caught on the wall edge when their supporting walls were hit, point skywards. Its stucco exterior is pock-marked and from the keystoned windows the shutters hang precariously. The second and third-floor rooms are exposed to view, their fronts having been completely demolished. Islands of plaster cling to the inner walls and the whole tragic remains are appropriately surrounded by huge banks of debris.

6 May (Monday)

Today I was very pleased to receive a letter from Jack Bradburn, dated 29th April and written at the Princess Christian Hospital, Weymouth. It reads as follows:

> Dear Ivor,
> I am pleased to inform you of my presence in 'Blighty' with trench-fever, pneumonia, influenza, bronchitis and various other ailments, but I am progressing as well as can be expected. Just fancy the nurse is on the point of bringing eggs and I have to refuse them because I can't eat.

*I have been in bed since I left you and feel a bit shaky still, so please excuse
scrawl. If I were well I wouldn't mind being beside you once more facing those
dangers which seemed to crop up so very often.*
Au Revoir.
Your sincere friend,
Jack Bradburn.

8 May (Wednesday)

A few readable books have drifted in from somewhere, three of which I
have read and enjoyed. They are *Allan's Wife*, by H. Rider Haggard, which I
finished reading while on duty at the Signal Pit last Thursday; *The Man from
Glengarry*, by Ralph Connor; and *Beyond the City*, by A. Conan Doyle. Haggard
is such a wonderful story-teller that he makes the most improbable
incidents seem actual facts. Ralph Connor was determined to provide a
thrill at the outset, for the opening chapters concern a flight from a
pursuing pack of wolves. In this book you can almost smell the pine forests.
In the selection of books was one of a pornographic kind, the author being
obsessed with the idea of women being flagellated by men. I tried to read
it, but was surprised to find that a repetition of smackings of this kind can
prove boring and nauseating, and I had to abandon it after a few chapters.

9 May (Thursday)

With 2nd Lieutenant Sabaston on duty at a forward observation post,
situated in a trench that the Boche once held, so that the dug-outs and
saps face the wrong way. These trenches are lined with tree branches, far
superior to sandbags, which soon rot and during wet weather often
collapse into the trench. It was a fresh, sunny day, similar to the other
days of this month. German field guns gave us a lively time and Sabaston
surmised that his periscope lens had reflected the sun and attracted the
attention of enemy observers. At one time the shells hailed over and
Sabby dived for the dug-out and slid down the steps to the bottom. He
just laughed and brushed the dust from his breeches. We stood at the
dug-out bottom for some time, hoping that none of those shells would
explode through the door.

Received a letter from Dan Evans, a schoolmate, now a 'category' man and a clerk in the Supreme War Council Offices in Versailles. What an enviable job. Lucky devil! He states that Paris gets bombed occasionally and at the moment of writing the Archies (Anti-Aircraft guns) were busy. Dan was in the infantry, but collapsed on the road during a march up the line.

13 May (Monday)

Informed that Bombardier Cannon and I were to proceed to a dug-out called 'CB' which is between the links up Infantry Brigade Headquarters with our Battery. We are to be there for an indefinite period and our duties will consist simply of keeping the telephone lines between these units OK. Half way to our destination shells had recently exposed the burial place of some horses and the smell was abominable. We had to apply our fingers to our nose. We found 'CB' in a deep trench. It contains two wire beds, two rough chairs, an improvised table and fixed on the wall a box which serves as a cupboard. We had just settled down in the dug-out when we were surprised by the arrival of Signaller Oram, sent to relieve Cannon who was to go down the Line for an anti-gas course. The message had arrived from Brigade Headquarters just after our departure. Cannon is the Battery Gas NCO being responsible for all such appliances. Oram and I are happy to be here, for we can rise when we like and go to bed when we like, with no one to worry us except Jerry. At night we are both permitted to sleep, but one of us has to have the head receiver strapped on. We have brought several books and our rations will be sent us daily. We have to do our own cooking, but Oram shall do most of that as he is a born cook. For tea today he sliced a loaf of bread beautifully with an old razor. The weather has changed and it has rained all day. Oram is 'experienced', and tonight his description of reciprocal orgasm during sexual intercourse was to me a revelation, making me aware of the incompleteness of my knowledge of the subject.

15 May (Wednesday)

Since being here we have repaired our telephone lines several times after they had been severed by shells. My chief need today was a bath, which I accomplished by cutting open a petrol tin and filling it with shell-hole water. After that I felt contented and all aglow, and laying on my bed read one of our books which was entitled *A Fellow of Trinity*, by Alan St Aubyn.

16 May (Thursday)

The weather is fine again and the cloudless sky has the blue of a thrush's egg. We are tormented by mosquitoes. I am not sure what their correct name is but out here they are designated mosquitoes. Our only defence against them is to smoke cigarettes incessantly, which keeps them at bay.

Our position is often shelled. We know the diameter of each projectile by the particular noise it makes coming over, each size having a screech, moan or whine of its own. Gas shells have a unique whine, and burst with a flop, but with little noise. Large shells in flight make noises very similar to approaching express trains. Fragments of shell fly about with a monotone sound.

One jagged piece of hot steel about half the size of my fist landed near my feet today and hissed until it was cooled by the mud. Our Battery fires gas shells now and also shells called 'Delay Action'. The latter burst a few seconds after striking something and are designed chiefly for shelling dug-outs, the pause giving them time to pierce the dug-out roof, the burst taking place inside.

This evening excessive machine-gun fire and three blasts of a whistle at intervals (official warning of enemy aircraft) notified us that a Boche plane was above. Allied planes were conspicuous by their absence and the machine droned unchallenged towards our rear. Unchallenged did I write? Shortly afterwards, hearing a great racket of machine-gun fire, we again rushed outside to see the invader being chased by two British planes which poured into it a hail of machine-gun bullets.

The trio were flying low and at a terrific speed, the German seeming to be in difficulties, was gradually descending. Splinters flew from it and then it was out of sight, beyond our Front Line in land which sloped downwards from our trenches. We felt sure it must have crashed, but were disappointed in not witnessing what really happened. Shortly afterwards our two planes returned proudly, we thought, and we were proud of them too.

We know aeroplanes by sight and better by sound. Boche craft are unmistakable, as their engines throb and sound as if they are of mighty power. On clear nights much bombing takes places on both sides. Some men fear bombing more than shelling and I think I am among them. One has an idea where shells are making for, but not so with bombs. Besides, a plane may be miles away one minute and on top of you the next. Exploding enemy bombs sound as if they have a double burst, like 'crump-crump', or as some insist, 'Krupp-Krupp', as an advertisement for their manufacturer.

20 May (Monday)

I fancy that never in Britain have I experienced such beautiful, warm weather as this we are enjoying now. After all we must be situated a degree or two south of Port Talbot.

Received a letter from W.T. Davies who is a Private in the 45th Field Ambulance, RAMC. As a theological student he preached at our church on many occasions, sometimes staying with us for the weekends. He has proved himself a true, wise and jolly friend. He says that he has enquired of scores of artillerymen for the whereabouts of the 311th Brigade, but with no success.

24 May (Friday)

Rejoined Battery, which is in action in another part of Arras, near the railway station. We are living in cellars that are furnished with expensive, gilded furniture and huge mirrors. The Officer's Mess possesses a piano and the Signallers own a flask of crockery, all inherited from previous dwellers in these subterranean rooms. Bombardier Carpenter and several of our Gunners have been slightly wounded by shell splinters.

Walked into Arras. The 'Square' is made up of some typically Continental buildings which are badly damaged and shaken in places. Stacked furniture bulges out from the second-floor wall of one of them. The cobbled market place is deserted. Near the Square there is a splendid YMCA, beneath the street in cave-like apartments or catacombs. There they have a small lending library. Farther on we see in ruins two noted edifices, the Cathedral and the *Hôtel de Ville*. One of our Gunners is an ex-curate and we like him to show us photographs of himself dressed in his vestments. The unfortunate chap was later killed behind the lines, being hit by a lorry.

The statement 'Enough to make a person swear' certainly applies to this war, for this man's language at times is abominable, but I fully understand him, since I, the former Sunday school teacher, who seldom swore in 'civvy' life, have become a champion at it out here. At times if we didn't do so we might have gone mad. The parson seems to be making up for lost time, whereas my own proficiency is due to a vivid imagination.

After a fine period we now have continuous rain.

27 May (Monday)

2nd Lieutenant Smith asked me if I would make for him a small sketch of Monchy from the rear O Pip. He added that he had spotted there an anti-aircraft battery and felt that the best way of notifying headquarters of its exact position would be by making a drawing of it. He promised to pay me 5 francs for my trouble. This was a commission after my own heart and I succeeded in making an attractive sketch of the famous hill. Signaller Robertshaw thinks I have slender hopes of getting the 5 francs and wanted to know if I had added my name to the drawing. (I had done so.) 'You don't want that bugger to get the credit for it', he said. 'The last time I did O Pip duty with Smithy,' Robertshaw groused, 'he had two qualities of fags in his cigarette case, one quality for himself in one side of the case, and another quality opposite, in case he had to make anyone an offer.'

29 May (Wednesday)

Hollingworth is now Major of 'B' Battery and has been awarded a bar to his Military Cross. This morning he sent for me to appear at the Officer's Mess and on the way there I wondered if I had committed any crime, but I could tell by the pleasant way he received me that I wasn't wanted for anything like that. He sat at a table in a sunny, spacious room in which for the first time I had a glimpse of the piano that I had heard so often. 'Ah! Hanson', he said smiling, 'Are you an artist or a draughtsman?'

'Neither sir, but I have always been fond of drawing and painting.' 'Good! D'you think you could make a sketch of the Front', he asked.

'Nothing would please me better than to have a try at it, sir.'

'Good man', he said in his incisive way. Then he instructed me to proceed to a certain trench from which I would get a good panoramic view and he gave me a generous roll of drawing paper and an ample supply of pencils and a rubber. My destination was a support trench, in which he explained there was a small O Pip which I could make use of, but finding it already overcrowded with an artillery observation officer and two Signallers, I decided to sketch it from the parapet over which I laid prostrate, hidden by tall, glinting grass. I made as many notes as possible, but it was an unattractive landscape, and one I should never have chosen to sketch and it was therefore difficult to draw. On the left was a wood and stretching across the background, spiky tree trunks indicated the Arras–Cambrai Road. Also there were the ruins of Feuchy, a disabled tank and on the extreme right a number of water tanks. These few details and the white chalk rimming the German trenches were the only relief to a monotonous stretch of grey-green desert, but it is surprising what we can do when we must. Degrees were marked on the elegant binoculars the Major had loaned me, so that I could check the correct positions of the landmarks and also insert the degrees beneath them. I completed the drawing in the now vacant O Pip.

30 May (Thursday)

We often walk into Arras. Barbed wire barricades lie on the road sides at strategic places ready to be drawn across the road in the event of an attack. The Arras YMCA is situated in a spacious cellar. From its library I recently borrowed a biography of Sir Robert Baden-Powell, by W.J. Batchelder. I know of no one possessing such amazing versatility as Baden-Powell. He seems to have developed, proportionately and to a high degree, his many talents and he is prepared for almost every emergency. The Boy Scout movement is a remarkable achievement and those of us who were members of it are indebted to the founder for those little scraps of knowledge and experience that have made us more adaptable to this mighty campaign and which will also serve us in good stead in peace time.

31 May (Friday)

Recently I witnessed an air duel to which our attention was first attracted by the sound of machine-gun fire high in the sky, so high that the two planes could only be seen as silver specks when at intervals the sun was reflected by them. Further faint bursts of machine-gun fire could be heard at intervals, then suddenly a thrilling thing happened. One of the machines nosedived, shooting to the earth at a terrific speed with white smoke trailing from it. It was the Allied plane, so Fritz must have had the better of that contest. We held our breath and with awry expressions awaited the crash into the ruined buildings, but just as we expected that to happen it swerved into the horizontal, just clearing the highest walls only a few hundred yards away from us, shooting behind the lines like a bullet.

1 June (Saturday)

Commenced duties at our two-gun Forward Section. Our dug-out is in the centre of a cemetery and there is a stone cross near the dug-out entrance. Like everything else in the vicinity, this cemetery has been badly strafed, some of the tombs and vaults being in smithereens and fragments of granite and stone are strewn everywhere. 2nd Lieutenant Sabaston is in charge and he, his batman, another Signaller, and I occupy the same roomy dug-out. Sabaston told us that he had been writing a letter to his brother and had said that he was now living in an 'eerie' (good word Sabaston) place and he wondered if he would guess it was a cemetery.

The conversation wandered to the March Retreat and Sabby astonished us by blaming the Signal staff for retreating without the signal stores, for it was he himself, in no uncertain manner, dared us to go back to the Signal Pit when we suggested it. He had either forgotten the actual happenings or is deliberately shifting the blame from his own shoulders, but I prefer to think that it is forgetfulness due to the exceptional circumstances.

This evening we had a visitor – Sergeant King, the beefy individual in charge of the Gunners up here. He related boastfully and in sordid detail an affair he had had with a girl. We have heard that Sabaston and Shaw would have each received a decoration for their services during the 'Retreat'.

2 June (Sunday)

Bombardier Kingsland visited us this evening. He is the Battery Orderly or Messenger. He hails from Lewes in Sussex and is a tall, well-built, healthy looking fellow with a dark moustache. He is the soul of honour, always prepared to do a good turn, very sensitive, anxious for people to have a good opinion of him and one who would silently nurse for long a wrong done him. Some of his errands carry him far behind the lines and during these journeys he hunts for canteens and returns laden with biscuits, chocolate and tinned foods, for his many hungry friends.

Army rations do not, by a long way, satisfy our enormous appetites and for that reason canteens, YMCAs and people like Bombardier Kingsland are much sought after. Kingsland is an evangelical Christian and appropriately on this fine Sunday evening in the trench above us he initiated a discussion on religion. Sabaston was present listening respectfully with the air of one who still cherished a warm spot for the old truths. Kingsland was happily confident that Providence and a Purpose could be found in all circumstances – by the Christian – and that this was war simply fulfilling prophecies to be found in the Bible. Therefore we should consider ourselves instruments helping to weave a Divine pattern. Personally I am puzzled by a few things. For instance, the Germans also claim God to be on their side and He most certainly cannot be on both sides. What if He is not on either? But I banish such disturbing thoughts and have faith in our spiritual and political leaders. Asquith, Grey and Lloyd George received the backing of organised religion and their assuring slogan, 'A war to end war', gives some meaning to all this suffering, destruction and death. We are passing through the agony of a temporary hell.

Just outside the Signaller's cellar, at the Battery position, Signaller Robertshaw has been slightly wounded in the leg. He is able to walk and will have to attend the Dressing Station periodically. He chuckles proudly about it.

8 June (Saturday)

Returned to the Wagon Lines for a 'rest'. The countryside looks beautiful and since the end of May the weather has been ideal, very fine, mild and with azure skies. In the mornings the birds sing vivaciously. Roses, peonies and other flowers bloom bravely amid the debris-strewn gardens.

9 June (Sunday)

We wrench ourselves from our hard but welcome beds on the floor when Reveille blows at 5.30 am for the first parade at 6 am. This morning we were out exercising the horses, two each, and we rode the saddled, near one. The morning air was as stimulating as champagne, and the sharp trots and canters through it makes us ravenous for breakfast. Weekdays are usually spent grooming, harness cleaning and various other stable jobs, but having a half-holiday today, a friend and I walked through Anzin and Louez to Maroeuil. At Louez a kite balloon was up, its massive mooring ropes curving gracefully from it. Its seams reminded me of an eiderdown quilt. Farther on some regimental sports were in progress so we leaned on a fence and enjoyed it for some time before returning to Maroeuil for a tasty egg and chip tea.

11 June (Tuesday)

With one or two other men detailed to cut grass for the horses in a field near the camp where I have never seen poppies grow in such profusion. At a distance one of the fields resembled a vermilion lake. The day's work finishes about 5 pm, except for watering and feeding the horses in the evening.

Recently the Colonel's groom, an ex-professional boxer whom I have described on the 28 April, struck a Bombardier, and part of his punishment consists of being strapped to a gun wheel for a few hours each day.

This is known in the Army as Field Punishment No. 1, a futile and degrading penalty having the ignominious appearance of a crucifixion.[1] His rations are biscuits and water, but at night pals smuggle to him more acceptable food.

12 June (Wednesday)

The misery of this monotonous existence at the Wagon Lines is lessened slightly by football and cricket matches, of which there are plenty just now, and by an occasional concert, such as the one that took place in the camp this

1. Field Punishment No. 1 was a British Army punishment imposed for offences such as drunkenness. The soldier in question was attached standing full length to a fixed object, either a post or a gun wheel, for up to 2 hours a day (often 1 hour in the morning and another in the afternoon) for a maximum of 21 days. Within the period of sentence no soldier could be subjected to the punishment for more than three consecutive days. When not tied, the prisoner would undertake fatigues. His pay would be stopped for the duration of the punishment and he was usually confined to a tent under guard and given basic bread and water rations. The punishment was abolished in the 1920s.

evening, given by 'stars' from our Brigade. The programme and the costumes were excellent, the chap taking the part of a girl being a great success. We have a new Sergeant Major named Mailey who was formerly Quartermaster Sergeant of 'D' Battery. He has a squint and when he strides about his body writhes freely and prominently in his tightly fitting uniform. He is a regular and bellows his commands with a stentorian voice. The command 'Attention' always reveals individuality. Given by him it becomes 'Chan' very closely resembling a powerful sneeze. His first words to me were a censure for being unshaved. A squad of us had just come down from the line. Shaving up there had been temporarily impossible and we must have looked like tramps. While up the line, having to wear a steel helmet, my cap had got wet, had shrunk about two sizes, and perched on my head must have looked clownish.

This, together with my hairy face, caught his attention, and protruding his face almost against mine he enquired menacingly:

'Haven't you got a razor?'

'Only an Army one', I replied mischievously.

I had noticed before that my unorthodox replies to such questions generally put my interrogators off balance and this was no exception, for Mailey didn't know what to say for a moment or two. Then he suddenly blustered:

'Well that's no credit to you.'

Then came the final warning, another look of horror at my cap and an order to get a new one immediately from the Quartermaster.

16 June (Sunday)

My previous drawings of the Front must have proved useful, for today I was commissioned to do another, being given 24 hours to do a panoramic sketch of the Line from an Observation Post called 'C.D.'. This post was reached by traversing a communication trench called London Avenue. The view to be drawn was another of unspeakable barrenness and to commence sketching it required will-power. It is amazing what we are capable of doing under compulsion. The result was not at all a bad attempt and should serve the purpose for which it is intended. 2nd Lieutenant Shaw asked me to do a few sketches of any kind for him and has promised to supply me with a quantity of drawing cardboards.

Our Wagon Lines are still here at Stuart Camp and we live in Bow or Nissen huts. Conversing with an elderly, wrinkled Driver in our hut, I learned that in civilian life he is a Great Western Railway carrier. He became very friendly when I told him that my father and I were also GWR men. He had spent a holiday at Mumbles and had enjoyed it very much.

The French edition of the *Daily Mail* reaches us sometimes. It consists of a single sheet and costs 2*d*. From it we learn the encouraging news that the Italians have recently made things warm for the Austrians on the Piave.[2]

19 June (Wednesday)

Having been detailed for gun-pit digging, set out with Bombardier Grill and two Gunners along the main road in the direction of Arras. Walking along I got into conversation with Gunner Page, a tall, lean man of 32 years of age. He has aquiline features, is very conscientious and is a Theosophist.[3] He comes from Folkestone and I have been told is a journalist. When the conversation drifted to sketching he said that he knew the famous black and white artist Dowd, who had 'cartooned' him on one occasion. I told him that I thought Dowd an accomplished draughtsman. We also discussed *Barnaby Rudge*, which I am reading at present. Between Stuart Camp and Arras we veered to the right and dug a gun-pit on the left of a plantation. Grill, a bluff, likeable fellow, comes from Portsmouth and is known as Pompy. During lunch time he talked about leave, and told us that when he walked out with his wife, she decided whom and whom he was not to salute. For instance, if they met an old warrior, well ribboned, she would say, 'Now this old chap has done his bit, so you can salute him.' But if they met a raw, young officer, he was forbidden to salute him.

Page introduced the subject of Theosophy and spoke persuasively about the theory of reincarnation and about the elevating beliefs of this

---

2. Lack of decisive action on the part of Emperor Karl and Chief of General Staff Arz von Straussenburg doomed the Austro-Hungarian summer offensive in Italy to defeat. Both men failed to decide between two plans for an offensive, one on the Piave by Field Marshal Boroević von Bojna and the other, a proposed advance from the mountains of northern Italy led by Field Marshal Conrad von Hötzendorf. Lacking transport, supplies and manpower, the disastrous decision was taken to allow both offensives to run simultaneously. This left no reserve forces to exploit success or reinforce the line when Italian defence stiffened. The offensive quickly floundered and was called off. The heavy losses suffered by many of the most reliable Austro-Hungarian formations proved a terminal blow from which the army did not recover.

3. Theosophy is a doctrine of religious philosophy and metaphysics which holds that all religions are attempts by the 'Spiritual Hierarchy' to help humanity to evolve to greater perfection and that, therefore, each religion has a portion of the truth. Founders of the movement, Helena Petrovna Blavatsky, Henry Steel Olcott and William Quan Judge, established the Theosophical Society in 1875.

philosopher system, and in so doing did a little unobtrusive missionary propaganda. In the afternoon we returned across the fields, lavishly rich with poppies, marguerites and cornflowers. A cornflower, chiefly because of its exquisite shade of blue and its stately slenderness, is my favourite wild flower. We each plucked a large bunch and with them filled the shell-case vases on the tables of the Battery dining hall.

22 June (Saturday)
An epidemic of flu[4] has broken out and a number of men are arriving here at the Wagon Lines from the Line, stricken with it. Except for a slight cold a week ago, I have been feeling exceedingly fit and today was sent up the Line into Arras to replace a sick Signaller.

24 June (Monday)
Parcels have arrived for several Signallers, a beano was arranged for tonight, to which we all looked forward with high spirits, but just as delicious slices of cake were being handed around to us in the candlelit cellar, which is our abode, I began to feel ill and to my chagrin could not eat anything. It began like a bad bilious attack, the sickness creeping over me in increasing intensity, like a fever, and I lay in misery on my bed feeling as though I had been doped. From a gloomy, sickly slumber I was awaken fitfully by gusts of laughter from the diners, now gorged to perfect contentment. Later I returned in the cooks' cart to the Wagon Lines, being met by Corporal Redfearn and a Gunner. 'Can you walk to that hut over there?' Redfearn enquired. 'No', I replied truthfully, for I felt too ill to stand, leave alone walk. They carried me in a groundsheet to a small hut where I laid on the floor in the darkness with a few other cheerless flu victims.

27 June (Thursday)
Almost everyone in our Brigade has been stricken with flu and a number of RAMC men have arrived at the camp to attend on us. I am now in a Nissen hut that is full of flu victims. Every morning each man's temperature is

---

4. This ties in with the outbreak of 'three-day fever' reported in the war diary of 311 Army Field Artillery Brigade during June and July 1918. On 22 June 132 case were reported in the brigade.

taken and they are curing us by starving it out of us. Not that we could eat much had we the chance. For each meal we receive one very thin slice of bread and butter, a drink of tea breakfast and tea time and very thin soup for dinner. Today we were entertained by a daring rat that emerged from a hole in the centre of the hut. It moved stealthily along the sunlit floor, swiftly retreating to the hole at the slightest movement on our part. This was repeated time after time until someone flung a boot at it and we saw it no more. This afternoon I walked to the hut door, swaying a little in the attempt. Near the door there is a mirror in which I beheld a portrait that frightened me. What ravages even a few days of an illness of this kind can make. No wonder the floor boards had felt so hard.

28 June (Friday)

Felt much better and with a few others paraded before the Doctor who inspected us and put us on light duty. The lesson I have learned from this attack of flu is that if a healthy body cannot resist the invasion of flu, it can certainly reduce the period of its occupation.

30 June (Sunday)

In a letter from home I learn that our friend W.T. Davies has been home on leave, and had told my people that he was at Arras. I have replied stating that I am in the same locality. What a surprise that will be for them. Having a half-holiday I went to Douisans where I knew some RAMC men were stationed and from them I learned that W.T's Corps, the 45th Field Ambulance, is stationed at Aubigny, which I shall visit when an opportunity presents itself.

2 July (Tuesday)

Every morning, before breakfast, we are out in the sparkling air exercising the horses. The country looks beautiful now. The French fields are divided by paths and ditches and we look in vain for the familiar sight of a hedge. Trotting along these fields we sometimes see toiling peasants in scenes that remind us of the immortal ones on the canvasses of Millet.[5] Having lived in their land, I shall find Dumas, Hugo and other French novelists no longer

5. Jean-François Millet (1814–75), a French Realist artist famous for his depictions of rural life.

new to me now, for I shall be able to picture the backgrounds and settings so much better. I have breathed the atmosphere and have actually visited some of the places mentioned in their books.

The day has been spent almost entirely in stable work, scrubbing harness and polishing steelwork which bores me stiff. Conversation among the Drivers degenerated into a puerile but violent argument as to whether or not there were ponies down a coalpit.

6 July (Saturday)

On guard at an ammunition dump on a side of the Arras–St Pol road, where there was much traffic, frequent saluting and presenting arms with the rifle making it a tiring business. Motor ambulances scudded swiftly to and fro. In the early morning it was bitterly cold and we suffered the other extreme during the day. Opposite us in a field there is a 6in naval long-range gun, which nearly split our craniums every time it fired.

9 July (Tuesday)

Another Gunner and I detailed to take to an Ordnance Depot at Louez, for chaff cutting, a GS wagon of hay bales. Bombardier Boswell is the Forage NCO and every time I see him or hear his name mentioned I think of Dr Johnson. He has a Jewish countenance, stoops, probably through carrying heavy hay bales daily, and has a benign and fatherly attitude to us all. He assisted us in loading the bales, which weighed about a hundredweight each and made me stagger. He gave us a number of sacks for the chaff and we climbed aloft and the ride to Louez would have been less pleasant if we knew what kind of job awaited us. Yesterday's showers had polished brightly the leaves of the trees lining the roads. Our journey ended in the yard of the Ordnance Factory, a beehive of industry. Near us was a gun-repairing department. The chaffing was done by machinery, our task being to hang the sacks at the mouth of a chute down which the chaff descended in a cloud of dust and remove the sacks when filled. The motor worked too fast and we had to beg for it to be stopped at intervals. This was about the filthiest job I ever did, for the falling chaff was accompanied by dense clouds of blinding and choking dust. Soon our eyes, noses and throats were full of it and we must have swallowed a considerable quantity. Why did nobody warn us of this so that we could have made some preparation for it? We each tied a handkerchief over nose and mouth, but found that far from effective against such continuous volumes of dust. What a relief it was to emerge into the fresh air, where we tied up the sacks and loaded them on the wagon where they reached a great and precarious height, but we had a safe and cushioned ride on top, back to camp where I soon rid myself of the grime by having an open-air bath under a water tap, near our hut, since there are no civilians within miles of us.

10 July (Wednesday)

I have now to look after two outriders, a black called Bobby and a chestnut called Jimmy. Bobby has a white blaze on his forehead, is smart, spirited and much bigger than Jimmy, who is slightly weedy and inclined to hang his head. My other duties comprise looking after, with another chap, a few saddles. The saddles and harness have to be kept scrupulously clean and have to be washed until the stitching is snow white. Then they are soaped. Bits, stirrup irons, links and chains we clean with sand, or if we are lucky, emery-cloth and then we burnish them by rolling them backwards and forwards among strips of paper in a sack. Every Sunday morning the result of our labour is inspected by the Major, who if satisfied, grants us a half-holiday. Most of us (Gunners and Signallers) would prefer being up the Line, in action, to this Wagon Line drudgery, ironically called 'Rest'. In the Wagon Lines we are nobodies and are the general factotums of everybody, whereas the Drivers are quite at home here, for it is their place and work. Grooming takes up an hour every morning and an hour every afternoon, except Sunday. During this most tedious of activities, performed with braces down, an officer or NCO saunters up and down the lines and sees that you do not take too long for a breather. For grooming we have two kinds of brushes, a short-haired oval brush, fitted with a canvas hand band, and the other with longer, stiffer bristles. Sometimes we use wisps of straw and always the curry-comb.[6]

---

6. A tool, now made of rubber or plastic, with short 'teeth' on one side that slides onto the hand of a groom. It is usually the first tool used in daily grooming. The horse is rubbed, 'curried', to help loosen dirt, hair and other detritus. The activity also stimulates the skin to produce natural oils. The curry-comb is generally used in a circular motion. The combs are usually too hard to be used on the legs or head of a horse. Curry-combs with metal 'teeth' are not used on horses as damage to skin and hair can occur. Instead, these combs are used to remove horse hair, dirt, etc. from a 'body brush', which is the main brush used when grooming a horse.

14 July (Sunday)

Set out for Aubigny in search of W.T. Davies. I had not walked far before a motor lorry of the South African Forces agreed to pick me up. A Springbok divisional sign was painted on its sides and rear. But it did not go far in the direction of Aubigny and I soon had to change. In fact, before I eventually reached Aubigny I had ridden in four different lorries. Inquiring at Aubigny for the 45th Field Ambulance, I was directed to a Casualty Clearing Station where, in a dining shed, I soon found W.T., standing before a huge bath, washing dishes. For several moments he was speechless, then characteristically he gripped my hand like a vice and his first words were, 'When did you have grub?' From the cook he procured a liberal dinner of 'gippo' – meat, potatoes, carrots and gravy, followed by a not too sweet rice pudding. This over, we went for a long walk, buying a few picture postcards in a cottage. They were reproductions of water-colour paintings. In another cottage we had a tea of eggs and chips, W.T. having to pay as I was francless. Here we wrote our postcards. I told Ma and Pa that we went for a walk in spite of rain, which later decided to stop on such an historic occasion and that while I had to thank W.T. for two rattling good meals, he had to thank me for being the excuse for an afternoon off. I informed Nellie, my sister, that I was enjoying this Sunday immensely, but not as well as the Sundays of old. We came across a number of French boys playing soccer. They held the ball in until we passed. W.T. said, 'I'd love to bring over a team of Welsh boys to show them how to play football.'

16 July (Tuesday)

Detailed for a scavenging job in Arras. Set out from Stuart Camp with a spirited young shire horse and a cart. The horse's mouth was so hard that it was only by tug-o-war methods we could hold him in. My companion was a Private of the Highland Light Infantry, stationed in Arras. He was a typical-haired Scot[7] and wore a tam.

Along the cobbled highway to the city we both held on to the reins until 'Sandy' decided it was too much like hard work and suggested that we let the animal have his fling. We did and after a spirited canter he settled down to a steady jog-trot. He refused to walk under any circumstances.

7. A reference to the private having red hair, hence the nickname 'Sandy'.

It was a scorching day, with the sunny streets deserted save for occasional Tommies. While engaged in our disgusting job of emptying latrine tins into our cart, two of our Signallers spotted me and giggled when they realised what our work was, but their turn will probably come, and anyway, I was fully compensated by being provided by 'Sandy's' cooks with an excellent midday meal which we enjoyed in a large, cool cellar.

17 July (Wednesday)

Today's duties are decidedly different, for I am Brigade Orderly, the imposing title for the messenger who carries notes from Brigade Headquarters to the Batteries. At present all the Batteries are within short range, so that the work is very light and makes me wish it lasted more than a day.

In a newspaper I read of a strike in England and wonder how such an unpatriotic thing can happen at a time like this.

19 July (Friday)

Our Brigade left Stuart Camp. Parading in the camp, ready to move off, our Battery looked a smart and sparkling sight. Well-groomed horses, shining like satin, burnished steel and polished brass, the sight of which almost compensated us for the weeks of cleaning and scrubbing. At commands given with loud voices we mount and the stout, steel-tyred vehicle wheels are grinding away from Arras. Crowds from neighbouring camps lined the roads to see us march away. We sit uprightly, at attention and feel proud of our regiment. We journeyed through Haute Aveanes to Acq, where I learned that I was to be on guard. It was a wonderful night. Crystal clear, the blue-velvet heavens were congested with a myriad stars, large and shimmering from one hue to another. Standing there alone for interminable hours, rifle in hand, there was naught else to do but gaze up and wonder. The night seemed enchanted and strange emotions surged within me. During one watch great aerial activity developed. The air vibrated with a drone, like the sound of a swarm of gigantic bees. Our plane wings had at each tip a light. It was difficult to locate and follow these lights against the starry background. Our searchlights busily swept the skies, the arcs they described seemed like futile attempts to erase the stars which in scintillating majesty disdained the noisy little interlopers that had so impudently invaded their domain.

22 July (Monday)

Saturday we were granted a half-holiday and yesterday we resumed our trek and have now reached a place called Agny.

Passing through Laresset, Warlus, Berneville, we arrived here yesterday and went into action immediately. In the vicinity are many heavy batteries. On the trails of some of these big guns we noticed some highly polished shells, someone explaining that the polished surface diminishes the noise of their flight, therefore giving less warning to the enemy.

Wherever we go food is our obsession. Today I walked to Achicourt, canteen scrounging. The weather is very hot with occasional thunder.

23 July (Tuesday)

After breakfast met Corporal Swallow and a Signaller. Swallow informed me that I was detailed to report to Brigade Headquarters for duty at a telephone exchange linking the Brigade with the Infantry. The Signaller's sly grin made me sense a plot, and it seemed that I was in for the job he had wangled out of, but I did not object, as I like a quiet life occasionally and I'll be free of irksome discipline for some days. I set out on foot for Brigade Headquarters, somewhere in Arras. The cobblestones of the road were smooth and shone faintly in the brilliant sunshine. Reaching Arras, I spent the whole morning searching for Headquarters and must have trudged miles, but no one knew anything about the whereabouts of an artillery Brigade Headquarters. But then, British Tommies are well schooled in pretending complete ignorance when asked questions by strangers. I reported to the Town Major and explained my mission to the busy but comfortable gentleman, but even he could give me no help and I continued my tiresome hunt up and down the byways of the city. Eventually I luckily recognised a Royal Engineer Signaller of our Headquarters Staff and he directed me to the obscure back alley where Headquarters Staff were billeted. Here I found three other men detailed for the same job and after receiving rations and directions, we set out for the telephone-exchange dug-out known as 'A.X.' and situated in a support trench. 'A.X.' is a roomy dug-out with an excellently built adjoining compartment designed for cooking purposes. Here there are two telephone exchanges, one being a dial instrument, which we soon learned did not respond efficiently to calls, so we shall trust chiefly to the other less-spectacular but more genuine instrument. Here our duties will consist of attending to phone messages and to keeping the lines OK between the Infantry trenches and our Brigade Headquarters. We soon arranged our shifts for duty and decided that two of us would walk each evening to the nearest of our Batteries ('Don') which has been detailed to supply our rations. We have arranged to cook in turn and this will be made easier by our possessing an excellent frying pan, a dixie lid left by our predecessors. The trench that runs by us is manned by the Canadian Scottish. We obtain our water supply from a cistern in this trench.

24 July (Wednesday)

Received a letter dated the 20 July from Eddie Rogers' sister, Nancy. I have never met her, but Eddie must have been speaking to her of me. This letter, written with a racy hand, upon immaculate stone-grey stationery, gave me a thrill and much amusement. It was written in Caersws, Montgomeryshire.

> 'I am a gang-leader', she writes, 'in the Land Girls and one day I was informed that on the morrow I was to cut thistles. Being completely ignorant of the procedure, I cycled that evening to a friendly farmer for a lesson and worked with him cutting thistles until it was dark, so that I might appear less 'green' the following day. My leggings are two sizes too large and each time I put them on I am forced to use strong language. There are about 70 German prisoners here. The guards are awful boozers – it's laughable to see them trying to walk straight after turning-out time.'

25 July (Thursday)

Received letter dated 20 July from Eddie Rogers who is spending his leave at my home at Port Talbot. He writes that in June his hospital ship, the *Braemar Castle*, was stopped in the Mediterranean by a German submarine.

The following is his account of the incident:

> *On this particular day we had left Malta at 8 am and about sunset were not far*
> *from the island of Pantellaria, when the siren sounded the alarm and we rushed*
> *on deck with our lifebelts. Personally I thought it was merely boat-drill, but we*
> *soon found out that a submarine had fired a shot across our bow. We were lined*
> *up on deck and could see the submarine in the distance, a tiny speck approaching*
> *us. At a range of about a hundred yards it fired again and at first we imagined*
> *the ship to be sinking, but it was the signal commanding us to lower a boat.*
> *This was done by two officers and two stokers, the latter doing the rowing. They*
> *brought back the German Commander and two armed men who lined the*
> *officers in the saloon and questioned them. They also questioned some of the*
> *patients and they searched the stores. When asked where they had left their arms*
> *the patients said, 'Salonika'. During this procedure the submarine encircled the*
> *ship and its crew peered at us through binoculars. The German flag flew on its*
> *mast. Finally, after satisfying himself the Commander bade goodbye to our*
> *officers, while some of the crew shouted across from the submarine, 'Cheerio.*
> *Hope the war will soon be over.'[8]*

26 July (Friday)

At dusk this evening a raid was made on the German trenches by 400 men
of the Canadian Scottish. It took place at Orange Hill, just on our right and
we watched the proceedings from the support trench near our dug-out. In
the artillery barrage every gun from an 18-pounder to a 15in must have
taken part. The 18-pounders barked savagely and the heavier guns,
thundering behind, hurled projectiles which passed over us like fast trains.
This is the biggest British bombardment I have ever experienced and our
position was ideal for watching, for we are on rising ground and we were
looking down on the scene which closely resembled a gigantic cauldron of

8. Rogers' account is very close to the record of events written up in the ship's log (TNA WO 95/4142). This states that at 7.30 pm on 29 June a German U-boat fired two shots across the ship's bows. All wounded were got onto the promenade deck ready to abandon ship should the *Braemar Castle* be torpedoed. At 8.15 pm the U-boat signalled for a boat to be sent over. This returned to the hospital ship carrying a young Lieutenant and two ratings. The officer, speaking good English, made a thorough inspection of the ship's radio room, sick berths and cargo hold, which lasted an hour. He also questioned members of the ship's crew, medical personnel and wounded with regard to their military service and particulars of the voyage they were undertaking. On completing his inspection the German officer saluted the ship's officers and stated the *Braemar Castle* could proceed. On departing the U-boat commander is recorded as shouting 'Bon voyage, goodbye, hope the war will be over soon'. It is believed the submarine was *UC-52* under the command of Oberleutnant zur See Hellmuth von Doemming.

molten steel on the boil.[9] Situated slightly to the left, we escaped the retaliating artillery fire. The din was deafening, the sky aflame like an inferno and the gathering darkness heightened the savage flames of bursting shells and the molten fragments that shot in every direction like rockets in a fireworks display. The earth quivered as if timid of the uproar on her surface. German rocket 'SOSs' shot up frenziedly.

Their Front Line must have been churned up to the level of the earth surrounding it, but distance and drifting smoke hid from us the orgy of death, mutilation and agony that took place yonder.

29 July (Monday)

I have finished reading *Barnaby Rudge*, by Charles Dickens. It has taken me five weeks to do so, but there have been many other things to do and also I am a slow reader who never skips, even the driest passages, for fear of missing something good.

Today we finished our duties at 'A.X.' and I had orders to proceed for duty to another telephone exchange called 'F.B.', situated nearer the batteries. 'F.B.' was formerly a German Headquarters and German notice-boards still hang here and there. The exchange consists of two apartments dug out from some high ground and the entrance is liberally fortified with sandbags. The station is staffed by four Signallers including myself. One of the quartet is a Cockney cook who can talk anybody's head off. He has already borrowed my scissors for the purpose of decorating the dug-out walls with a variety of pictures ranging from a birthday card from his sweetheart to a newspaper photograph of Charlie Chaplin. Noise impresses him profoundly and it was with rare joy he discovered in the dug-out a gas alarm – a wooden rattle which made a hell of a row when rotated. In our cavernous abode the din was intolerable, so not to be denied his pleasure, he perched himself at intervals on the sandbagged wall outside and rotated the rattle to his heart's content, accompanying the noise with shouts of 'This way for Charing Cross, Piccadilly or Leicester Square.' The effect on anyone near must have been stunning. Now near us was situated an Officer's Mess from which sauntered across a young subaltern who stood

9. All batteries of 311 Army Field Artillery Brigade were involved in supporting this raid between 9 pm and 10.30 pm.

for a few moments observing the fantastic spectacle, the performer of which was too engrossed in his art to notice any casual observer, but when finally he became aware of the forbidding frown beneath him, the din ended abruptly. With studied politeness the officer enquired, 'Are you training to be a bus conductor or commissionaire?' The humble reply was, 'No Sir.' 'Then let's have no more of that babble.' 'Very good Sir.' He stepped down from his perch and assumed the injured air of one who had been forbidden to express himself in his natural way, but although he occasionally picks up the rattle and fingers it lovingly, there is no doubt that henceforth it will only be employed for the purpose for which it was intended. The other two men on duty at this station are of quiet dispositions. One is about 40 and that seems elderly to those of us who are still teenagers. His name is Booth, so we naturally address him as 'General'.[10] He seems rather browbeaten, but speaks well and he and I have already had a talk about books during a walk back to our respective batteries for our letters. The other fellow is about my own age, is dark haired and swarthy and is an ex-railwayman, formerly employed at the Great Western Railway's Swindon 'Shops'. His bunk lies above mine and tonight he leaned over and talked for a long time of locomotives and rolling stock.

31 July (Wednesday)

Near us there is a glorious lake admirably suited for swimming in. It lies in the grounds of a one-time beautiful château. It is surrounded by trees, fresh and glittering in the sunshine, for these lovely trees have not yet been laid waste by gunfire, although the position gets shelled badly occasionally, for an 18-pounder battery lies on its rear bank and both sides learn where each other's guns are situated. I have seen shells burst in this lake and it seemed that little damage was done to the gunners except to give them a generous shower-bath. A lakeside seems to me to be particularly good for a gun position. This afternoon, however, things were quiet and I had a splendid swim, scores of fellows sharing the enjoyment of a cool dip during sweltering heat. Bathing costumes were conspicuous by their absence, but unnecessary in this wholly masculine setting, so a

10. A reference to William Booth (1829-1912) who founded the Salvation Army in 1865.

host of nude, excited and happy young fellows plunged and splashed in the soothing water. In this Arcadian scene one fellow paddled about in a canoe. The distance to the opposite bank from where I dived I judged to be 250yd and I swum towards it leisurely with a slow side-stroke. I got half way across with ease, for the calm surface offered no resistance, but a gondola came in my direction, its proud prow tearing the placid water, the bow waves receding with silver rims. Some fellows had launched it from the boat house of the château. I about turned, afraid to trust myself to that irresponsible crew who in high spirits shrieked and sported, eventually rocking the gondola so much that it capsized in the centre of the lake, and then the laugh was mine.

My duties at 'F.B.' had ended so I returned to the Battery and told my pals of the wonderful lake. Signaller Brain begged me to show him where it was as he had, to use his own words, 'been fairly roasted by the bloody sun and would give anything for a dip'. I agreed to go back with him, but when Brain saw the water he funked it, making the excuse that it looked too cold, so I went in again without him, for unlike Brain, who came from Southampton, I had been born within sound of the sea, bathed frequently and had learned to swim at an early age.

Chapter 16

VIMY RIDGE

1 August (Thursday)

Our Battery removed to a position near Vimy Ridge. I walked there with Bombardier Cannon, going via Blangy and St Nicholas. We had to carry a 4 + 3 telephone exchange and at first took it in turns, but as its weight seemed to increase, we found a short stick and suspending it on that carried it between us. The heat was terrific and my throat was parched. We tried in vain to find drinking water, but eventually among some huts we found a canteen and the only liquid it possessed was unsweetened tinned milk, in desperation I bought a tin and drank it all. It quenched my thirst but almost turned me sick. Bombardier Cannon told me that Signaller Callon is missing and it is thought that it is because the Battery was recently shelled, for whenever that occurs Callon mysteriously disappears, to slink back when it is quiet. This has happened ever since a shell splinter scratched his nose on the 21 March last.

The Battery position is in a winding trench on the ridge, the gun-pits being bays adjoining the trench. The Signallers have a deep and spacious dug-out next to the Officer's Mess.

5 August (Monday)

Recently it has been so hot that some of us have been wearing trousers, as one feels like a mummy swathed in puttees during the weather like this. 2nd Lieutenant Smith saw me wearing them and with exaggerated gravity told me not to let him see them on me again up the Line. 'What would happen to you if mustard gas came over?' he asked querulously.

At 6 pm commenced duty at the telephone pit and during the night I received from the Infantry 'SOS' signal, and in accordance with instructions well drummed into us Signallers, I relayed the message to the gunners by tapping it on the buzzer key, on a special phone connected to a buzzer in the nearest gun-pit. Instantly a muffled explosion above acquainted me of the fact that the Gunner on guard had heard my alarm call. This first shot aroused the other gunners who were soon at their guns and a good many rounds were fired. Next, I phoned to the Officer's Mess where I was summoned to give details of time of receipt of message and to answer any other questions.

Here I found Lieutenant Sampson, the present Orderly Officer, emerging from the dug-out in his pyjamas. Back at the telephone table I sat wondering what had happened in the trenches. Most probably an enemy raid. I felt bucked at having played my part in the defence and hoped our shelling had been effective.

8 August (Thursday)

A railroad has been laid in our rear, its terminus being quite near our Battery, and its purpose is to bear a long, 15in gun which is shunted up by a locomotive at dusk to fire a few shells on carefully selected targets such as German Headquarters at Douai, and then it retires to safety behind the Lines.

Its report is like the crack of doom, but that worries us less than the thought that 15in guns do too much damage to escape the sound-ranging instruments of Jerry and our position suffers much from retaliating shell fire.

On duty with Lieutenant Sabaston at an Observation Post named 'Horror' and reached by means of an endless communication trench perfectly named 'Tired Alley'. 'Horror' affords a commanding view of miles of plains. In the distance, on the extreme left, pit shafts can be seen in some of the towns and a little farther to the right and much nearer can be seen the ruins of Arleux and a quarry. In front of us is the renowned Oppy Wood, now a miserable row of branchless tree stumps, blighted, ghoulish and forlorn and which has been captured and lost so many times. Also we can see Izel, Esquirchin, Quiery-le-Motte, the German trenches known as the Fresnes-

Rouvroy Line and farther back the famous Hindenburg Line. On the extreme right is Gavrelle, where our Major Hollingworth earned his decorations; and in the background are Drocourt and Douai. Douai is 15 miles away, but can be seen distinctly and on a clear day such as this, we can, by the aid of a telescope, see the hands on the town-hall clock and check our time. At such O Pips as 'Horror' we register or adjust the ranges of our guns on key positions, keep a sharp look out for any unusual occurrences, movements or activities of troops, etc. and gun flashes. By frequent duties at these posts and many consultations with maps, we get to know thoroughly the land around us.

Some sharp salvoes were fired into the trench beneath us, so their observers must have seen some movement there. In places the parapet was badly damaged and clouds of white chalk dust arose from the scene.

11 August (Sunday)

Slept the night at Infantry Brigade Headquarters in order to commence early tomorrow morning at 'Cocoa Tree' O Pip.

This Headquarters is in a deep and spacious sap 40 steps down and ventilated by air shafts. Our subaltern disappeared into the officer's quarters and a sleeping place was found on the floor for my mate and me among the infantrymen. This regiment now in the Line is Scottish of the 52nd Division, which has recently returned from the Eastern Front.[1] One of their officers instructed his batman to get us something to eat and we were pleasantly surprised by a supper of steak and chips, then bread and butter and cheese, rice and tea. We thanked the cook and said we hoped to repay him some day. 'Aye,' he said, 'let's 'ave some more of those barrages of yours.' In this cavernous sap we laid on wire-netting beds. In the good light of siege candles a typical young 'Sandy' on my left became very friendly and talked until midnight of his experiences in Palestine. My eyes wandered to 'Sandy's' cap badge, a rare beauty that I coveted, because at present I have a mania for collecting cap badges and would have paid my last sou for this specimen, but I did not care to ask for it.

1. The 52nd (Lowland) Division came to the Western Front in April 1918. Prior to this the Division had fought at Gallipoli in 1915 and in the Palestine Campaign during 1916 and 1917.

12 August (Monday)

At dawn set out for 'Cocoa Tree'. Every morning 'Stand-to' takes place in the trenches at this dangerous time and the ghostly figures of the infantry stood motionless and expectant as we clattered along the duckboards. The morning air was like iced champagne.

A German machine-gun, recognisable by its slow, steady stutter, rattled away loudly and near. 'Cocoa Tree' is near Farbus Wood and the trenches that we traversed to reach it had notices and signboards suspended here and there directing the uninitiated to various O Pips, water tanks, posts and saps.

O Pip periods of duty range from 12 to 24 hours. Today's vigil was rather uneventful, but returning this evening I met a former Bettisfield Signaller named Salter who also had returned from the Eastern Front and was very bronzed.

15 August (Thursday)

Commenced duties at 'B.C.', the two-gun Forward Section of our Battery. The weather is glorious and during the day the heat scorches. Pale, weather-beaten, German signboards, undeniable proofs of our advance and bearing lengthy names, adorn some of the trenches in this vicinity. The gunners, the other Signaller and I occupy dug-outs, but one man prefers to live up in the trench. He is Lieutenant Cook, who is in charge of the Section. Cook is a dashing, handsome fellow whose fine figure fills his uniform perfectly. He looks better wearing his cap or helmet, as his receding hair gives his forehead too high a dome-shaped look. He is a regular and has served in India. He is variable and devilishly hard to please at times. Some of the men think that as a result of long service in India he suffers from the Doolally Tap.[2]

17 August (Saturday)

Since being here I have finished reading two novels – *O'er Moor and Fen*, by Joseph Hocking, and *The Scarlet Pimpernel*, by Baroness Orczy. Like *A Tale of Two Cities*, the latter has for its background the French Revolution. If *A Tale*

---

2. The phrase Doolally Tap originated among British soldiers serving in India. It is a corruption of the Urdu place name Deolali (location of a large Army transit camp) combined with the Hindustani word for fever 'Tap'. It was light-heartedly used among soldiers to describe anyone acting eccentrically or strangely.

of Two Cities can be described as an oil painting, *The Scarlet Pimpernel* can be described as a fresh and brilliant water colour, and I must admit I prefer water colours.

We have telephone lines to the Battery and communicate directly with Headquarters with an electric signalling lamp, using the 'Don Don' system,[3] since Headquarters are behind us and could not reply without being seen by the enemy.

18 August (Sunday)

The weather has changed, for it is now cold and damp. Sometimes our position is shelled badly, but Lieutenant Cook recklessly sleeps in a dug-out above us which is only proof against the weather.

One night the shells landed particularly accurately and we were surprised when Cook, clad only in pyjamas, tumbled into the dug-out for safety during a vicious bit of shelling. He got up and grinned nonchalantly. The shells falling so near above us exploded with muffled thuds and their concussions kept blowing out our siege candles, the relighting of which used up almost a box of matches. When the bombardment ceased Cook returned to his perilous but airy domicile and as he did not return to us we assumed that it had escaped intact.

19 August (Monday)

A messenger informed me that Lieutenant Cook wished to speak to me. Wondering if I had done anything wrongly, I immediately walked along the trench to his shelter where I found him seated like an animal in a cage. From the Battery he had received instructions to send me to 'Cocoa Tree' O Pip, for the purpose of making a panoramic sketch of the Front for Brigade Headquarters. He started a conversation on sketching in such an amiable and appreciative way that I could hardly believe my ears, as previously I had misjudged him as being incapable of such friendliness.

'D'you know', he said earnestly, 'I'd give anything to be able to draw.' Respectfully I suggested that it was never too late to learn. He agreed, but shrugged his shoulders as if to say, 'It's too late now.' As it seemed that he

3. Messages repeated and must not be replied to because the sender's lamp is facing the enemy.

wanted me to talk about my hobby, I said, 'Apart from its many other uses, sketching develops concentration and observation, for it is impossible to draw anything properly without studying it closely.' He was most interested to learn that I had won several newspaper competitions for painting, including a 'first' in the *Daily Mirror*, and said, 'There's money to be made out of it.' I had approached Cook with some of that fear of him felt by all the men, but this one conversation revolutionised my opinion of him, for I had discovered a new Cook and felt that should I ever require a favour, Cook would be the officer most likely to grant it.

I arrived at 'Cocoa Tree' to find it occupied by 2nd Lieutenant Raines, Robertshaw and another Signaller, who were there on observation duty. To Raines I explained my mission and they grudgingly shuffled along the plank seat from which the Front could be seen through a narrow woodwork slit.

Wedged between this audience, I proceeded sketching a most difficult landscape with the unhelpful advice of the three critics surrounding me. Raines, a shallow, young lightweight, felt in leg-pulling mood and switched the conversation to Wales and the Welsh and I met him effectively and with good humour, but when he expressed genuine contempt for the Welsh language, of which he knew nothing, I stumped him completely by pointing out a few positive things about it, including its wealth of place names and its almost 100 per cent phonetic pronunciation. In spite of these interruptions I produced a fairly good drawing, but never have I enjoyed such a task less than that of today.

This evening I fired one of our 18-pounder guns three times. I had already fired over parapets and at German aeroplanes with a rifle, but never an 18-pounder, so this evening, when I saw Corporal Evans of 'C' Subsection firing a number of rounds on a given position, I asked him if I could fire the remainder. Elatedly I tugged the firing lever thrice and the shells sped forward with a rushing sound, not unlike that of the last of the water to gurgle down a bath pipe. For the remainder of my life I shall wonder what damage those projectiles did.

20 August (Tuesday)

Tonight our position was heavily shelled and about midnight the wires to the four guns of our Battery position in our rear were 'dis'. I tried the receiver again, examined the terminals, but could not alter that hollow sound in the receiver. At some place the wires must have been blown up. At this station there is another Signaller and myself and it was my turn to go out, and after informing the officer, Shaw, who has relieved Cook, I donned my steel hat and respirator, slung over my shoulder a portable telephone and set out. It was pitch dark, but luckily the shelling had lessened and I trailed through my hand the twin wires, hoping the break was near, not because I had the 'wind-up', but because I was tired and yearned for sleep. At last I came to the break, which must have been midway between us and the Battery. The lines had been blown sky high and the other ends were missing, so I tied my white handkerchief to the ends of the line I had found, so as to find them again and walked around searching for the others. I found them without much trouble, but after pulling hard I failed to make them meet. The shell must have blown yards out of them. I followed the lines in the direction of the Battery, came to a trench where some 'slack' wire had been prudently coiled and which I quickly loosened and then returned to the break. With my jackknife I scraped off insulation from the four ends, joined them with reef knots and bound them with insulation tape. From my telephone two safety-pins dangled on leads. With them I pierced the wires and as soon as the receiver touched my ear I knew by the 'warm' sensation that the lines were now OK. However, to be doubly sure, I tapped OK? on the buzzer and immediately received OK in reply.

On returning to 'B.C.' I found that the line had been blown up again, my only relief being to mutter a long string of picturesque curses. This second time there was some consolation in finding the break nearer home, and in the inky blackness of the night I repeated the performance, except that this time there was sufficient wire. I crept back to 'B.C.', wondering how long the wires would now last. I sank down on my rough bed, glanced at my wrist-watch to find it was 3 am and before I knew it I was fast asleep.

21 August (Wednesday)

This morning I walked down to the Battery position to find everyone there looking glum. During last night's shelling, Gunner Ives had been killed, a shell having dropped in the trench outside his dug-out and a fragment shot through the gas curtain and pierced his head while he slept. A Gunner showed me the dug-out, which was about the size of a small coal house. He lifted up the gas curtain for us to see directly opposite two bunks. On the upper one lay Ives, ashen and with the stillness that makes death so unmistakably different from sleep. My companion informed me that the other occupant, also a Gunner, had gone down the Line with shell-shock. He also told me that Ives had only been up the Line a few days and the singular news that until last night he had slept with his head the opposite way. Last night, however, he remarked, 'I think I'll have a change', and by doing so had met his death. Had he slept in his usual position he might have been wounded in a foot. A curious happening of the war, which his comrades will interpret in various ways according to their faith or knowledge.

We are all shocked at the death of Ives. Whenever we see death we are reminded of our own peril, but when it stalks so near as to snatch away one of our pals, it puts the wind up us, though not for long. Personally I felt that I had taken my own adventures of last night, or early morning, too lightly and that in the passing of Ives we had been robbed of one of our best men, for he was a fine, manly fellow, possessing splendid physique and that quiet dignity which is a by-product of genuineness.

This evening I amused myself by drawing from memory a sketch of a soldier of the USA Army. I had seen them at Hancourt where they were employed on the construction of a narrow-gauge railroad. I intend sending it home and hope the censor will not purloin it. After admiring the drawing, one of my mates talked of some 'Yanks' whom he had seen drilling. 'Don't like their words of command at all', he complained. 'Too many words and those too vague. Give me plain English, brevity is the soul of wit. What d'you think they say for shun? Guys stiffen.' I laughed. 'That's nothing', he continued. 'For our brief command, "Slope arms", their equivalent is, "From foot to shoulder rifles put".' To us their short leggings appear peculiar, but on second thoughts, they are more serviceable and hygienic than puttees.[4]

23 August (Friday)
Tonight we've been bombed by a Boche plane. It happened when our 18-pounders were firing, the din preventing us hearing the familiar drone, the machine being above us before we knew it.

Miraculously there were no casualties, though things are in a mess for one of the bombs blew up our latrine.

25 August (Sunday)
Sent down the Line for the purpose of attending a 'Pigeon' course. Leaving the Forward Section this morning, I had a good look at the wrecked latrine. Spent the night at our Wagon Lines near Mont St Eloi. The monastery ruins at which I have gazed hundreds of times from afar seem to be quite an old friend tonight. It looks very large from here and towers above us like a faithful sentinel. Slept the night in a hut with the Drivers of our Subsection.

26 August (Monday)
This morning set out mounted via Villers Abois to my destination, a village called Camblain l'Abbe. I was accompanied by a horseholder who returned with my mount. Out here pigeons are commonly used, chiefly by the Infantry, for carrying messages. To my knowledge we have never used them, but it appears that Artillery Signallers have now to acquire some knowledge of their use. On the Arras–St Pol road I have often seen motor-cycle despatch riders speeding towards Arras with small pigeon baskets strapped on their backs. From the trenches they fly back to Headquarters with messages. Our instructor was a Corporal of the Royal Engineers, a tall, moustached, easy going fellow. We received lectures in the Corps cinema, a large Army hut in which rehearsed simultaneously the Corps Orchestra, the music being more inspiring than the lectures.

The conductor had the expression of a man crucified on a cross of nerves, but he is an artist with a violin and comes from Cardiff.

4. These are the lace-tied canvas leggings worn by most US infantry on their arrival in France. Ironically, given Ivor's comment, many US Servicemen replaced their leggings with puttees.

We became familiar with the message forms, small sheets of tissue-paper which are folded and placed in a tiny aluminium box that is clipped around one leg of the pigeon. Our class numbers about eight and we were taken to the pigeon house, a kind of caravan, standing in a field corner.

Into this the Corporal entered, captured a bird expertly, demonstrated the correct way to hold it and the method of clipping on the message box. Afterwards, in the village, I chose a picture postcard, a silhouette of blue colours, and informed my people at home of my presence in this peaceful and pretty hamlet and how I wished my stay were for three months instead of three days. I concluded by writing that I was just about to have a wash before paying a visit to the cinema – the first for many a long day.

27 August (Tuesday)

We are billeted in a large hut. It is in very good condition and fitted with the usual tier of wire beds. Compared with our Up-Line fare the rations here are splendid, being superior in quality and more generous in quantity. This evening enjoyed a rollicking concert given by a party called 'The Archies', which had recently been to London on tour. Every night, at a reasonable price, we are able to buy from the civilians a good feed of eggs and chips. The house we went to tonight was packed with Tommies, many of whom were teasing one of the waitresses, a very dark-haired, beady eyed girl. Between carrying innumerable dishes of eggs and chips to men with unappeasable appetites and the teasing, she was exasperated and she raged at some of her persecutors with English swear words to which she gave her own special interpretation, so amusing that it brought the house down.

30 August (Friday)

On Wednesday we had our pigeon-course examination and in the evening I went to the cinema again. A horseholder was supposed to meet me at Camblain l'Abbe this morning at an appointed time, but as he did not turn up I foolishly set out on foot and had walked fully half the distance before he, with the two mounts, loomed in sight. Arriving at our Wagon Lines near the monastery I reported to Lieutenant Cook, who to my joy ordered me to return to the Line. I was delighted, for one look at the stables had been enough for me. At dusk I reached the Battery, which had advanced from the former position. The new signal pit shares the same dug-out as the Officer's Mess. It is a large, cavernous retreat. The officers have a Decca gramophone and among the records are the melodious songs, 'Let the Great, Big World Keep Turning', 'The Girl I Love is on the Magazine Cover' and a song of a sailor who in the darkness fell in love with a girl, but when he eventually saw her face in the light, he cried, 'Hurrah for the Rolling Sea'.

7 September (Saturday)

On the right and slightly in front of our guns are two 'Archies' (Anti-aircraft guns) mounted on motor lorries.

We watch them with great interest when enemy planes come over. These guns fire very rapidly, but their swiftly moving targets are difficult, and I have never seen a direct hit, although the planes I have seen under fire might have been hit by fragments, for the small white puff-balls of the shells burst all around them. Also such fire tends to keep them at a respectable height. We often wonder where all the steel from these shells fall. Behind us is a 60-pounder Battery which seems to worry the Germans a great deal since they receive so much retaliation.

Recently we took part in another bombardment which commenced at 6 pm and continued for hours. Just before the appointed time our Gunners were ready at the breeches and with sleeves rolled up they looked as though they meant business. Promptly at 6 pm Lieutenant Sabaston blew his whistle and every firing lever was instantly pulled, but the sound of our guns was drowned in the thunderous, roaring, deafening crashes of guns of larger calibre for miles around us.[5]

We are now attached to the 8th Division of which the Rifle Brigade is one of the regiments. I have read that during the German offensive of last March, the 8th Division kept 12 German Divisions in check for 36 hours.[6]

---

5. Between 1 and 7 September batteries of 311 Brigade were involved in laying down harassing fire on the German lines both during the day and at night.

6. This is a reference to the Battle of Rosières (26–28 March 1918) in which 8th Division as part of the much weakened XIX Corps (also including 16th, 24th, 39th, 50th and 66th Divisions) held 11 German divisions from 7.30 am on 26 March until ordered to withdraw in the early hours of 28 March. During this time 8th Division undertook a counterattack and was the only formation still holding its original position in front of Rosières on 27 March.

14 September (Saturday)

News from home is rather depressing, for I have just read that our friend Captain Will Bowen has been killed in action and that Sidney James, formerly ticket collector at Cockett railway station, has been so badly wounded that a leg has to be amputated.

Bowen, who was in the Welsh Regiment, had risen from a Private to his present rank, while James is a Gunner in the Royal Garrison Artillery. Consolation comes from the knowledge that out here we are advancing slowly.

I share in the general optimism created by these latest events and hope we can keep pushing the enemy before us until he is compelled to surrender. There is not the least doubt that the present 'push' has brought peace much nearer.

20 September (Friday)

This month's weather has been very unsettled. We have had dry periods, but occasional showers have kept the mud in ample quantity. At times it has been quite wintry. We have had occasional hours of leisure during which I have finished reading *Allan Quartermain*, by H. Rider Haggard, and with a few others have done some unofficial rifle practice in a trench, using bully beef tins as targets.

21 September (Saturday)

Our Battery has advanced again and we are now on the crest of some uplands. The Battery Staff are installed in a large dug-out bearing the classical name 'Lancelot'. It is reached by descending 32 steps. You feel your way down and support yourself by a rope handrail, for you cannot see anything until your eyes adjust themselves to the inky darkness. At the foot of the steps is a passage which leads to several spacious, cavernous apartments. In the smallest of them Petherick is in charge of a canteen. To the right is the Signaller's apartment. This huge dug-out has two exits, useful if the position were suddenly attacked.

Here we feel happy and secure. After being down for a few seconds the candlelit interior begins to take shape. It is one of the biggest dug-outs I have ever seen and we feel sure that a coalmine must look and feel something like this. Quickly and studiedly we chose our place among the eight wire beds, which are erected in two tiers and we fling thereon our equipment to stake our claim. I am on the upper tier. At the head of the beds is a long, stoutly built table before which there is, on the wall, a network of telephone wires. Tonight I share duties with another Signaller, so I made myself acquainted with the new stations. Bombardier Cannon is busily brightening the wall with his collection of assorted pictures, postcards and cartoons. The postcards are of nude French females and are placed in the most prominent position. Someone protests, 'Bad taste, Cannon. Too fat, besides like that they leave me cold. Much more attractive chicly or partly dressed.' Cannon, however, thinks otherwise and smiles voluptuously at the photographs. It is midnight and I sit before the telephone exchange listening for any call on the buzzer. In front of me is a message pad and I have reached such a state of tiredness that for a time I have to prop up my eyelids with my finger tips. Even the alluring poses of the nudes opposite have no effect, but suddenly I am aroused into complete consciousness by the sudden plaintive beating of the buzzer. It is Major Hollingworth testing the telephone line before he retires for the night. I have a quiet, uneventful night of seemingly endless duration, receiving only the usual daily weather forecast called a meteor and a map reference of a position with instructions to fire on it some salvoes at a given time.

Chapter 17

'BONES' OBSERVATION POST

22 September (Sunday)

Signaller Oram and I accompanied Lieutenant Harold Sampson to an observation post named 'Bones'. All O Pips have a name and on a small notice-board hanging above the entrance was painted this discouraging name, but through its narrow observing slit the view it affords compensated handsomely for the name. Here we seemed to be perched on a cliff from which we overlooked miles of plains. With his ordnance map spread out before him on the aperture ledge, Sampson gave us a practical lesson in geography. Drocourt is prominent on the left background, Crest Wood in front and Douai right incline. Domed and towered Douai looks impressive. Measuring on the map we found that Douai is 13km away, and we estimated about 21km from the Belgian frontier. The famous Oppy Wood, a thin and blighted remnant of spiked tree stumps, stands in the middle distance straight in front of us; Gavrelle is beneath us to the right and Izel beyond it, each of these places a heap of ruins. The chalk-rimmed trenches ripping the landscape looks like white breakers on a beach. In the distance is the Hindenburg Line and in front of it the Fresnes-Rouvroy Line, then in front of that the German front line, while our lines lie beneath and before us. Bones is an observer's paradise. Teatime Lieutenant Sampson talked of Port Talbot, which he knows well. He shared his food generously with us, his rations including a pot of honey and a large box of chocolate bars which had been sent him from home. He even shared with us his bread and butter, daintily cut slices prepared by his batman and so different from our coarse, thick culfs. From our perch in Bones we can see German working parties busily engaged behind rising land that hides them from the view of our men in the trenches; also reliefs coming into the Line and odd men here and there. Sampson wears glasses and aware of my excellent eyesight sometimes hands me his magnificent binoculars, directs my attention to a particular spot and asks, 'What d'you make of that Hanson? Half a dozen of the Boche there.' He always refers to the enemy as 'The Boche'. 'What are they up to?' I replied, 'One thing certain Sir. They're digging something. Half of them are working with shovels. Could be a gun-pit or perhaps they're putting up another pillbox.' Keeping his gaze fixed on the scene, Sampson observed, 'We observers fight the Boche with our eyes.' Through the binoculars we can tell if the men nearest us are big or small, we can see their bronzed skin and the pastel shade of their field-grey uniforms. With a telescope we explored the background towards Douai, and the farther back you look the bolder and more numerous the enemy are. Occasionally in the back areas we spotted vehicles. Sampson made copious notes in his log book. We studied Douai with the telescope and consulted the town-hall clock for the time. Buzzing Sampson's directions back to the Battery we did our part in registering our guns. The ranges we calculated from the map and the firing was corrected by increasing or decreasing the ranges by distances of 50yd and by switching so many degrees right or left until our targets were reached. There was more unusual movement, which Sampson again noted and which brought from Oram, my fellow Signaller, the remark, 'No wonder they had such a scrap to capture Vimy Ridge.'

All through the night we watched in turns, dotting down even the most trivial happenings. Once an ammunition dump received a direct hit, blowing up, creating a terrific din and illuminating the sky with a vermilion glow.

I watched the Verey lights ascend, now here, now there, right across the Front and in their brilliant lights imagined I saw strange, crouching figures, but the light was transient and I was soon left in impenetrable darkness. At frequent intervals there arose from the German trenches lurid, yellow flares which burst into two green lights, leaving me to wonder what their purpose was. Perhaps they are the best illuminating flares they can afford to produce during the stranglehold of the tightening blockade. I resumed my vigil as the strengthening light of dawn divided earth from sky, suddenly realising that it was extremely cold sitting in this same position for hours. The racket of machine-guns and rifle fire arose from the trenches. Was it an attack, a raid or just the usual defensive measures at this crucial hour? Sampson asked me to awaken him if anything like that happened. I did, to learn from him that it was a British raid. He had been told that it was to take place. Our own field guns assisted in this 'stunt'. We paid particular attention to their vicious snarls behind us and felt proud of our own shells hurtling over our heads. Those of the raiders who are lucky will be back before it is daylight for such events are swiftly carried out and we strained our eyes to catch glimpses of them, but were unsuccessful as the whole scene was enveloped in smoke which, hanging low on the earth, was rolled by a breeze along the trenches to the right.

23 September (Monday)

We have been strictly ordered not to make any new paths in the vicinity of the Battery, as enemy observation planes frequently fly over us during the day, photographing our Lines. By comparing these with previous photos both sides can tell where movements of troops are taking place. The gunners have been plucking grass and shrubs and strewing them over the paths and over the scorched patches of ground under the gun muzzles. Lieutenant Cook caught some men walking over the forbidden paths and he saw red. He paraded all the gunners, gave them a final warning and in the extravagant language common to so many old soldiers he told them, 'Even Jesus Christ, and his twelve holy apostles would be denied those routes.'

About teatime today three of our captive balloons were observing on the right of our Battery, the nearest mooring cable being about a quarter of a mile from us. Diving from a great height a Jerry plane machine-gunned them and set the three afire. The observers leaped out with parachutes, but as they descended the swaying figures were machine-gunned by the hawk-like raider that savagely encircled them, then triumphantly raced for home.

Within seconds there was nothing left of the balloons except black smoke.

Lately I have missed a lot of rest, so that I was glad to get to bed tonight. I am on the upper tier and as the wire netting is rotting, I have to move cautiously or I shall collapse on the Signaller below. If I forget and move suddenly, a mesh gives way and I descend a fraction nearer to the cursing individual below, who is nearly blinded by the rusty dust I have created.

24 September (Tuesday)

Bombardier Kingsland and I were chatting at the entrance of Lancelot. He wanted to read to me some extracts from a letter he had received from home and his large hand pulled from one of his tunic pockets a bundle of letters. Out of them a small ribbon dropped onto the duckboard. I picked it up for him, but before he had time to stuff it back in his pocket I recognised it as the ribbon of the Meritorious Service Medal, awarded him some time ago. Its colours are crimson-lake divided by three narrow, perpendicular, white strips. 'Now the place for this is there', I protested, and I proceeded to pin it on his breast. 'Not worth troubling about,' he said, 'especially up the Line', but he allowed it to remain.[1]

Kingsland told me that after several of our boys had been killed at Arras Major Hollingworth asked him to accompany him up the Line. The Major, aware of Kingsland's religious beliefs, wanted to sound him on certain subjects, and a few very personal things. Hollingsworth thanked him for the help he had given him in this talk, but hoped he was wrong in one thing – for Kingsland had told him that according to his readings of the Bible, Germany would rise again in a few years and make war of a different and even worse kind because of increased mechanisation.

Passing the gun position, I encountered Gunner Turner, who had just hung up the telephone receiver fixed on a pole alongside a gun-pit. Turner's concave cheeks accentuate his protruding chin. A look in his face hinted that I was studying his face rather than listening to his complaints, a rude habit I am beginning to be aware of, and acquired by having studied so many faces in order to sketch them, for whenever I see a face I always imagine how I should sketch it. In future I must try not to be caught staring in this way. Turner was offended by what he imagined had been the effected superiority of 2nd Lieutenant Sabaston, who, watching him use the

---

1. Ivor recalled: 'I was told that he was awarded the medal for crawling into a German trench, tapping a water pipe and bringing back a petrol tin full of water for a group of thirsting men who were temporarily surrounded by the enemy. As the aforesaid trench had been captured from us, we knew of the existence of this water pipe. I presumed that at the time of this daring exploit German Infantry must have thought it safe enough to retire for some purpose, say to the cookhouse'.

telephone, had remarked, 'You take to the telephone like a duck to water, Turner', to which Turner had curtly replied, 'Naturally, Sir. I have one installed in my home.'

I returned to the dug-out, for dinner time was near, and saw, emerging from a trench an officer plastered with mud. Through the mud a bright patch of red cloth was visible on his tunic collar. He was a Staff Officer and must have been reconnoitring the Line. At the cookhouse we found skulking around the Signaller's dog, which is very partial to cookhouses, that being the reason why a recent proposal to train him to carry messages appeared absurd, for the messages would either be delayed for hours in various cookhouses, or reach Jerry's Lines, from where he originally strayed, for I am sure that when he is missing for several days, he is back scrounging Jerry cookhouses. He is a big, brown, wiry mongrel and among the several names he has been given is 'Maconocle', a variation of the name of the popular tinned soup. The cooks have earned our everlasting gratitude by inventing a new dish. The rock-hard issue biscuits, which require a hammer to crack, have been transformed into biscuit pudding. Why did no one think of it before? After being well soaked in water, the biscuits are mashed, fried in fat and served up with jam, a wonderful improvement on the original.

We are infested with rats, ugly, flat-nosed pests. All night in the dug-outs their persistence and daring is amazing. As soon as the candles are blown out they start capering around. One man swears that they go through a series of drills, forming fours and so on. This afternoon we planned and carried out an offensive against them, for the nuisance becomes intolerable.

We armed ourselves with cordite, extracted from shell cases and with shovels. We lighted and laid the cordite in a number of rat holes from which the creatures were bound to emerge to escape the fumes. I have learned what an effective weapon a small, sharp, shovel is, used as a guillotine. Any rats that escaped our guillotines met a more frightful death in the jaws of Maconocle who never enjoyed himself better. A monster rat dodged my shovel and leaped into a hole that did not reach far so that its tail stuck out in the trench. I tugged hard at the tail and the skin slipped off the animal like a glove from a finger, leaving a white, shiny, ribbed tail behind. I left it to Mac.

At dusk we saw another of our balloons 'go west'. We heard the rat-tat-tat of a machine-gun, but couldn't see the plane. The balloon suddenly burst into a magnesium-coloured flame, exceedingly vivid in the twilight, lasted but a few seconds and then nothing could be seen except clouds of spiralling smoke which slowly dissolved into the indigo sky.

25 September (Wednesday)

Today at Bones O Pip with Sergeant Stuart, who was deputising for an officer for an hour or so. I kept watching an opening in a part of the enemy Front Line, where the sandbags had been blown away by our gunfire and where there was such constant movement that I felt sure that a big relief was taking place. I called Stuart's attention to it; excitedly he watched the position for some time through binoculars and then suddenly ordered me to ring up the Battery. The Battery switched me through to the Officer's Mess. 'Is that Major Hollingworth?' Stuart's voice trembled with emotion. 'I thought I'd ring ye up Sirr, as the movement here is abnormal. Must be a relief of some sort Sirr. Right Sirr. Thank ye Sirr.' 'He's coming over at once', said Stuart proudly, and we both felt that we were in for something this day. Soon afterwards Hollingworth arrived and in time to see the activity still in progress, but unlike Stuart he remained as cool as a cucumber, made some rapid decisions and calculations, while I rang up the Battery. Hollingworth took the receiver himself, gave the map reference, some special firing instructions and then said to me, 'Now ring up Brigade Headquarters. We'll have a Brigade Shoot at this.' Soon 18 18-pounder guns and 6 howitzers were pounding the position and blowing it to smithereens. The sound of the guns behind us resembled the barking and snarling of angry dogs. It looked as if the trenches would be levelled out and as for the occupants, I had a feeling that there'll be some mourning in the Fatherland after today's Brigade shoot. In the background some Hun guns became active, some of them firing high-velocity shells which arrived without much warning. We watched the gun flashes amid the distant trees, counted the seconds between flash and report, worked out the range, found the exact positions on the map and reported details to Headquarters who will instruct heavier batteries capable of reaching that range. We hope the 'heavies' will lose no time, for we know the German trick of evacuating gun sites after having done much firing, our retaliation fire often being wasted on empty gun-pits. War breeds deception. In my opinion the Germans are masters of the art of war. In comparison we are amateurs, but necessarily learning the tricks speedily. Also we've got the shells and it's the shells that will win this war. The enemy shells are fewer, but very well aimed, as though they made doubly sure before firing, but although they are still destructive, how long can the enemy withstand the hailstorms we send over?

26 September (Thursday)

At Bones O Pip again, this time with 2nd Lieutenant Gascoyne. Walking along the trench towards our destination Gascoyne noticed that some duckboards were missing and guessing that the Signallers were responsible he lectured me for about 5 minutes. I bore the chastisement in silence, well aware that the real culprit was Brain who had used the boards as firewood, but you can't let a pal down. We sheltered in a small dug-out while a machine-gun swept the trench we were in. The bullets swished to right and left like rain driven by a capricious wind. We had been spotted. After a short time at Bones Gascoyne decided to reconnoitre Gavrelle, which was beneath us and on the extreme right of the post. Occasionally German gunners fire 'five-point-nines' into Gavrelle.

They completely destroy the ruined buildings and send up clouds of white dust. Gascoyne wears pince-nez. I dislike seeing a soldier wearing glasses, which I think spoil photographs of some of the French generals. 'Gassy', as he is known to us, is very reticent. The only words he addresses us with are either orders or reproofs, delivered dryly. He is reputed to be the best scrounger among the officers and I should like to know what he got out of this afternoon's trip. I remembered that it was here at Gavrelle that Hollingworth led the Naval Brigade in a raid when their own officers were killed or wounded and I tried to visualise the venture. We came across an abandoned German gun with elevated piece and obviously *hors de combat*. It was a 'five-point-nine', elaborately engraved, having the design of an eagle inlaid in the piece. A shell was jammed in the breech so we didn't trifle with that.

27 September (Friday)

Tonight, at dusk, our Battery came down the Line to Roclincourt, where we are going to train in preparation for the much talked about big advance. The sight of the horse teams lined up near Lancelot put the wind up me and I had visions of hours of interminable grooming. I'd much rather risk it up the Line than slave at Wagon Line stable work.

28 September (Saturday)

This morning the Up-Line men had a route march to a bath house, a large hut fitted with numerous shower pipes.

We were lousy and dirty and badly needed a bath. Though the water was none too warm we revelled in it. We wallowed in it. Standing in full view of each other's nudity, jokes were rather ribald, but what a relief it was to lather our louse-bitten bodies with soap and then stand under a sharp and plentiful shower of water. Then to dispense with our rotten underclothing and glow under a clean change. After this exhilarating necessity, while waiting outside the bath house before forming up, a French civilian arrived with a small handcart full of tiny but ripe grapes. He did good trade, most of us buying a large bunch and thus on this chilly morning were outwardly and inwardly cleansed, and the uncomfortable, rickety sensations that have plagued us for want of bodily cleanliness and fresh food disappeared. Curious as to why a certain 'C' Subsection Driver went by the name of 'Digger', I enquired to learn that he had spent a number of years in Australia. At the first opportunity I manoeuvred him on to the subject and he told me that when he was about 18 years of age, a quarrel with his father resulted in him running away from home. Eventually he settled in Australia, working for traders of small animal furs. Two years later he had saved £200 and had married the boss's daughter.

29 September (Sunday)

Reveille at the Wagon Lines is still at the heart-breaking hour of 6, but we consoled ourselves this morning with the knowledge that today there would be a half-holiday. We are now attached to the 51st Division, 'Scottish Storm Troops'. They are also training and passed through our Lines today in extended order. Fine, stalwart fellows they looked, with kilts protected by khaki drill aprons. We have noticed that there is a very decided improvement in our rations and the general opinion is that some divisions are treated better than others.

1 October (Tuesday)

Today we did some flag-reading practice, training that fills in the time nicely and reduces the hours of stable drudgery and of miserable fatigue jobs.

Received a letter from Cyril Bunker, who has had his foot crushed by a gun limber. When taking ammunition up the Line they were bombed and the horse team bolted.

2 October (Wednesday)

The Battery had a Field Day. My role was that of a Scout and I was mounted on a chestnut pony from 'C' Subsection called Bobby. It has been a bright, enlivening day and on the uplands we had some exciting gallops. My face tingled after rushing through the keen air.

At one time during the manoeuvres I was alone at a certain position, but was in communication by flag with a group of Signallers under Corporal Swallow, who signalled me to move to the left. In accordance with the rule so thoroughly drilled into us at Bettisfield, I raised my flag and moved to the left, at the same time awaiting their 'Toc' which would signify when I was to stop. This puzzled them and resulted in a deadlock for which Swallow must have reported me, for at the end of the 'stunt' Major Hollingworth made some criticism among which a reference was made to my not responding to the 'Move left' signal as quickly as I should have. Before the whole Battery it was a most humiliating criticism and in true military manner those of us criticised were given no opportunity of defending ourselves. I suspected that Swallow and his group were totally unaware of this orthodox signalling rule. Here at Roclincourt the Signallers are housed in a large hut which is in excellent condition. Water is plentiful and near at hand and that's a big item out here. This locality looks like a vast burial ground, large cemeteries, crowded with small white crosses being numerous and there are odd graves everywhere – alongside roads, in fields and in gardens. When we are suddenly confronted with them we curiously read the inscriptions, but are glad to divert our minds to other things. Recently we witnessed the burial of some infantry lads – a gruesome sight. The bodies were wrapped in blankets and bound with tape. A drum and fife band was in attendance.

Bagpipe bands practise nearby, making an unholy noise, weird and uncanny. One evening I waited with a crowd of spectators at a road junction for the arrival of a kilted battalion, looking forward to experience that thrill that my former north-country friend James Dick had dilated about – the swirl of the kilts and the wail of the bagpipes. Perhaps days of listening to bagpipes practising has ruined my capacity for enjoying them, for when the battalion arrived I thought the music horrible, almost ruining for me the splendid spectacle of the massed swirling kilts. A brass band in front of that lot would have sent shivers up and down my spine, but no Scot would agree with me.

Tonight, in the large YMCA hut a concert was given by the 6th Battalion of the Black Watch. When we arrived the hut was already full, but although we had to stand at the back, we enjoyed ourselves immensely. A Chaplain presided. I was impressed mostly by the singing of Lemon's 'My Ain Folk', a reel accompanied by bagpipes and another song, 'Bonny Scots', the last being sung by a well-oiled Sergeant who almost sobbed with emotion.

5 October (Saturday)

The special training continues. Yesterday we had practice in lamp reading and this morning Sergeant Major Mailey took us (Signallers) at riding drill in a field near the camp. Mailey seems well acquainted with the various drills and we were put through them thoroughly, but he was in a good mood and the contrast to the exhausting Bettisfield riding course and the bad tempers of the instructors there was a pleasant surprise.

During the afternoon I was one of a squad erecting stables. I am now accustomed to all kinds of heavy work and although it has not resulted in making my body any bigger, for I am still between 9 and 10 stone, I am tougher and probably fitter than I have ever been.

6 October (Sunday)

On my return from an after-tea walk, it seemed that the whole Battery had been hunting for me. On reporting to an NCO, I learned that I had been detailed as one of a party to take 'ammo' up the Line. We loaded two G.S. wagons with 18-pounder shells and about 10 pm proceeded up Line, our destination being Arleux, which two months ago we used to observe from Horror O Pip as a possession of Jerry. Before reaching Arleux a wheel of one of the vehicles sunk into a shell hole and we all dismounted, but even then the six-horse team failed, after repeated efforts, to shift the wagon, so we heaved at the wheels while the Drivers whipped up the horses, but 'ammo' is heavy stuff and the shell hole, a new one, was deep. After a succession of ineffective attempts it seemed that the only alternative was to unload some of the 'ammo', until someone suggested we try the mule team from the other wagon. The six horses were unhooked and the six mules put in their place and with one long, stubborn pull, with the help of us all heaving at the wheels they dragged the wagon out on the very first attempt.

The traces would have snapped before the mules would have given up.

The first part of the return journey was done quietly at a walk, but when we had reached a respectable distance from the Line the teams were goaded into a brisk trot, the horses and mules, homeward bound, needing no urging.

The empty wagons rattled noisily along the rough roads and we arrived tired out at the Wagon Lines at 3 am.

7 October (Monday)

Spent the day with a party digging gun-pits up the Line. The weather now is very dry and cold, but this navvying kept us quite warm. The pits open out from the side of the trench nearer the enemy and we had a good view of the Front, though not a commanding one like that seen from Bones, but we could see Douai and the more-noted landmarks. During the afternoon a batch of shabby looking prisoners filed down the trench, not altogether a popular spectacle because we realised that for some time they will be on our ration strength. Returned to Wagon Lines in the evening and read *Tommy Atkins* by Robert Blachford.

Chapter 18

ADVANCE INTO BELGIUM

12 October (Saturday)

Our Battery commenced advancing, passing through Gavrelle, Fresnes and Izel. Rain poured, yet the journey was full of interest, especially for those of us who had observed these places so many times from O Pips. Noticed with pride the devastation caused by our shells. German battery positions are peppered with shell holes and we noticed one gun-pit with a shell hole right in its centre. That certainly was a bull's-eye, though there might not have been a gun in it at the time.

On the roadside saw a number of painted wooden soldiers in characteristic gestures of attack, used by the enemy as a 'blind' on which we probably wasted much ammunition, while the real raiders stormed the trenches at another point. At dusk halted on the roadside, under dripping trees, had a makeshift tea and then went scrounging for German dug-outs. The one I slept in with several other men was a grave-like hole about 7ft square and a yard deep.

14 October (Monday)

Battery advanced through Quiery-la-Motte and Escquierchin. The retreating Jerries mine bridges, crossroads and dug-outs, but the Royal Engineers do valuable service in finding many of the charges before they explode and also by speedily improvising bridges and repairing roads. The undiscovered mines cause many casualties and we cannot help feeling a bit apprehensive, for there are so many places where they could have been laid. Our camp for the night was in the open with no shelter whatever. I was detailed as a horse picket, a job I did not relish as I did not get much sleep the night before, when we had to dig ourselves into a bank and cover the opening with our groundsheets. During that night the rain was torrential and water, accumulating in one place, flooded in on us while we were asleep and soaked us to the skin. Last night the horses were tethered to a rope and when they broke loose, as they often do with that rare skill for which they are notorious, they had boundless space on these plains for providing us with some long and weary chases.

18 October (Friday)

Still advancing, we passed through Flers, Auby and Roost-Warindin. For souvenirs I cut off some buttons from a German soldier's tunic. The metal is a very hard alloy. One button has on it the design of a bursting bomb and another a crown, the same symbols as ours, but the slight difference in design gives them an appearance quite foreign to us. On entering their towns and villages the civilians gathered in groups to wave an enthusiastic welcome and sometimes when we halted they brought to us coffee in tiny cups. Those civilians who remain in their homes are lucky, for when a locality comes within the fighting zone, the civilians have to evacuate and flee behind the Lines, taking with them as much as they can carry.

19 October (Saturday)

Passed through Raches to Flines-lez-Raches where a few of our 'B' Battery men were killed by the explosion of a mine. Gunner Scott, quite a young fellow, is one of the victims. The civilians were terribly shocked and took the bodies into their houses which we visited in the evening, to see for the last time our dead comrades lying in candlelit bedrooms.

Billeted for the night with a Royal Horse Artillery Battery in a large building, which we learned had been a hospital. We slept on the floor of a large, draughty ward from which everything moveable had disappeared.

The glass of the large windows had been completely shattered and the floor is littered with the splinters.

20 October (Sunday)

Awaken this morning by Reveille beautifully blown by a Royal Horse

Artillery trumpeter. At breakfast time, standing in the hospital yard, I watched curiously a squad of RHA men being marched into the building. One of their own men laughingly told me they were defaulters. 'Hell of a mob this,' he added, 'but damned good gunners all the same.' Then a miracle happened. One of their Corporals asked me if I wasn't from Port Talbot. I instantly recognised my questioner as Dick David of Taibach, Port Talbot. 'D'you know that this is the Port Talbot RHA?' he continued. To think that I had slept alongside so many acquaintances and not to have been aware of it. He carried a trumpet and not a bugle. So he was the trumpeter who had sounded the Reveille better than we had ever heard it before. Rather strange to see a Corporal acting as a trumpeter though, but formerly he had been a cornet player in the Taibach Temperance Brass Band, and it seemed that in addition to his duties as Corporal, his trumpeting was so good that it was retained in order to add a bit of glory to his Battery. After a few words of greeting he strode away and brought back with him several Port Talbot 'boys', including Bert Cope, who told me that he himself had risen to the rank of Corporal but had been stripped for some offence or other. Among them I was surprised to meet a Bettisfield comrade named York, a quiet, mischievous-looking fellow. In their horse lines I recognised more familiar faces, and one or two men suggested that I apply for a transfer to their 'mob' as they called it. For a time I toyed with the idea, but thought it safer to endure the ills I already bore than fly to those I knew not of. Besides, their Battery Commander, Major David, affectionately known to his men as 'Tom', is at present home on leave. This afternoon warned that I had to report to Brigade Headquarters as Mounted Orderly (Dispatch Rider). Before leaving I bade goodbye to my Port Talbot comrades, among whom I recognised a fresh face, that of a man whom I had seen behind a gent's clothier's counter in an Aberafan shop. His parting advice to me was 'Never say die', delivered in rather dramatic fashion. I was given a big, black, nameless mount, known in his subsection as Number 63, that number being cut out from the hair on his left flank. A Corporal Shoeing-Smith accompanied me most of the way to Headquarters. During the journey Number 63 dropped a shoe, but by good fortune we found an Army smithy, and half a franc did the rest. Rode on through Bru and Le Catelet to

Bovignies where Brigade Headquarters are billeted. Just outside Bovignies a bridge had been destroyed by the Germans and I had to ford a little river. Arrived at Headquarters to be told to join a troop of horses being led to the aforementioned stream where, with canvas buckets we watered them. Under the surveillance of my namesake, Regimental Sergeant Major Hanson. I feel rather proud of being a member of Brigade Headquarters Staff. There is a Mounted Orderly from each Battery. We are among a small army of batmen, grooms, Royal Engineer Signallers and clerks, all buzzing around the Colonel. My duties will be to carry despatches between Headquarters and 'B' Battery. They will have to be taken at all hours of the day and night and we are advised to sleep whenever we can, and clean our appointments and groom the horse during spare hours.

21 October (Monday)
We are continually advancing and today I rode with Headquarters, a column of G.S. wagons and outriders, through Beavry, Sars-et-Rosièrs to Alene Dor. About 1 am I was roused unsympathetically from my deep slumber by a clerk who handed me a letter for 'B' Battery, which I knew to be several miles away, but which I found without much trouble. However, on the return journey I lost my way, which is an easy matter out here, for there are no lights, and landmarks are more often than not blown to pieces. No wonder my mount had obeyed my reigning so grudgingly. I slackened the reins and allowed him to wander his own way, and it was not long before I recognised familiar paths. It is only necessary for a horse to traverse a route once for it to be able to instinctively find its way back to the stables. I felt a strange tenderness for animals in general and for horses in particular. Horses are very sensible. During this journey, at one place I was impatient with the animal for persisting in walking in a zigzag manner, until in the darkness I was able to make out a group of new shell holes around which he was picking his way. At times we have to work them very hard, and it cannot be wondered that occasionally they pretend lameness.

22 October (Tuesday)
Entered Brillon, which must have been an enemy base camp, for on

numerous buildings there are German words such as 'Keller fur nach', 'Commandantur' and, over a cellar, '20 Personnen'. A slight twist to a letter here and there gives to the signs an unmistakable German look. During our advancing the sign 'Achtung Eisenbahn', which confronted us on several occasions, set me curious, until I noticed it always preceded a railway crossing.

24 October (Thursday)

Arrived at St Amand, one of the largest towns we have been in during the advance. Late at night a message was handed me, and feeling rather tired, the thought of having to deliver it went badly against my grain. I knew that 'B' Battery guns were situated outside a cemetery, not very far away, so I set out on foot. 'B' Battery Officer's Mess was in a house, presumably the former residence of the sexton. The walk among the gravestones at this dark and chilly hour was bewitching. A batman answered my knock, ushered me into Major Hollingworth, who, lying on a camp-bed, lit a siege candle and read the despatch. Except for odd parties of soldiers the town is deserted, for all civilians are somewhere behind the Lines, and a town without people or traffic is like an empty container and reverberates. On my return journey through these dark and silent streets in which the only sound was that of my own footsteps echoing in various locations, 'Jerry' started shelling. Now a town under shell fire is about the unsafest place in the world to be walking in, for in addition to shell splinters you have about a thousand times as much stone, brick and mortar flying about. Some of the shells were plunging very near too and I had the unpleasant sensation that they seemed to be following me. Large quantities of masonry crashed all over the roads and pavements. I started running, diving for shelter into doorways when a shell burst very near.

Panting, perspiring, but relieved, I reached the cellar at Headquarters in safety.

25 October (Friday)

Headquarters is billeted in a fine house in its own grounds. On some of the buildings there are printed notices warning troops, 'Looters will be shot'.

Nevertheless, looting does take place, for today we met some fellows who had been at it. One of them had a gold watch and another had some old medals. Personally I thought that was going too far.

The silver wrist-watch presented me by the Fforestfach friends last year has proved invaluable. It has kept good time in spite of much rough treatment, though sometimes the concussion of gunfire dislodges the second hand. I fully realised its value today when it went out of order, but one of the Royal Engineer Signallers here understands the mechanism of watches and quickly set it going.

26 October (Saturday)

Finished duties as Mounted Orderly and returned to 'B' Battery, passing through Rosult to Lecelles where we have settled down for a short rest. We are billeted in the barns of a farmyard, and entering our loft is a gymnastic feat since half the ladder rungs are missing. In the loft we are among huge, rough-hewn timber beams that bear the barn roofs. The joints are secured by wooden pegs. The amount of the French language that we unconsciously pick up is, on examination, surprising. It is impossible to see repeatedly so many shop signs and notices of all descriptions without getting to know what most of them mean. From one of the drivers I have bought a pocket French and English phrasebook, have learned quite a lot from it, and also from the tiny phrasebook given with packets of Black Cat cigarettes.

29 October (Tuesday)

Yesterday we were re-equipped and issued with new clothing. I was determined to have some kind of bath before donning the clean underclothes. This was difficult, for water was scarce and there is no suitable place to perform such ablutions. However, a few of us solved the problem by carrying a tub over to a little river nearby, where we had a cold bath behind a hedge. Sabots[1] add to the picturesque appearance of the few civilians clinging to the hamlets in the vicinity. One old peasant man spends most of his time chopping firewood for the cooks, for which I guess he is paid with an occasional good feed. The French think our bread wonderful.

1. A French clog. The shoe is hollowed out from a single piece of wood and was worn by French peasants.

We only see aged people and children. The young men are all in the fighting forces, but we often wonder where all the young women are, for they are conspicuous by their absence. Probably they are engaged on war work. One very attractive young woman passed the camp recently, so unusual and pleasant a spectacle that we stared at her until she was out of sight. She was pale, dressed neatly in black and probably a war widow.

The faces of the elderly are networks of wrinkles and their hands are gnarled. They seem to work from dawn to dusk, and they live, I should imagine, as did our people a hundred years ago.

1 November (Friday)

The weather is very cold, but dry with sunny periods. On Wednesday I was on guard, and today I was inoculated. I noticed that my fellow victims were members of the squad I arrived with at Hancourt last Christmas. Operations took place in a field. The doctor pinched up the flesh on our arm and punctured it in no uncertain manner.

2 November (Saturday)

Our 'rest' was ended, for this morning we commenced advancing again. We who were inoculated should have been granted 24 hours excused or light duty, but now we're on the move there's no hope of that materialising. My arm was very painful, and dressing was most difficult and so was putting on equipment. Tin hats, worn on the march behind the Line, are carried over the left shoulder, but mine rubbed against my sore arm, so I transferred it to the other shoulder. An officer and a few NCOs, at different times, spotted this breach of discipline, but their remonstrances collapsed when I explained the reason.

During long marches the weighty equipment hangs like lead on the shoulders, and sometimes gives me a slight internal pain in the region of the heart. I recall the freedom that I never appreciated in 'civvy' life where you may move about without all your possessions dangling from you. Passed through Alene-Dor, Sars-et-Rosièr, Marchiennes, Brillon, Waraing, Somain, arrived in the afternoon at Bouchain where we settled for the night, fixing the horse lines in a square which we overlooked from our billets on the second floor of a business premises with white plastered exteriors. Opposite our billet was a church, and after tea I was thrilled to hear wafting from it the sweet strains of its pipe organ. I hurried across, meeting Kingsland in the street. 'Grand isn't it?' he exclaimed, beaming. I was curious to know who the organist was and to hear the music better, for music sounds even more enchanting when you haven't heard any for months. The organist was a Driver from our Brigade, and as I entered he was playing vigorously 'We Plough the Fields and Scatter'.

Could anyone think of a more appropriate hymn for an artilleryman to play? The church floor was strewn with stones, plaster and broken roof slates, and one naturally looked up to the shell hole in the roof through which were now visible the twinkling stars. While enjoying this stirring harmony of sounds, a man with his arms full of long, red, twisted candles slunk down from the altar. He was my old Bettisfield hut mate 'Fish', who said as he hurried away, 'We're short of candles in our billet.' With some others climbed to the organ loft, a difficult task as portions of the stone steps were missing. One fellow told me that this church tower had been a German machine-gun post. I thought it must have been an excellent though risky O Pip. By the time we reached the organ loft the volunteer organist had been persuaded to play a few ragtimes which sounded ludicrous in such a setting. The organist played in the light of a few siege candles carelessly stuck by their own grease to the unstained woodwork on which the flames had scorched black, perpendicular columns. He was now playing 'Oh! You beautiful doll, You great, big, beautiful doll.' And the eight Gunners, including myself, standing behind him sang it lustily.

And then back to our billets for an early retirement, for by so doing our next meal, breakfast, will appear to arrive so much quicker, for tea is the day's last meal, and this 100 per cent open-air life makes us ravenously hungry.

Recently we made a supper out of boiled cabbage alone, which was all the food we possessed and which some hero had scrounged. He is a looter who should not be shot. The cabbage would have tasted nicer had we salt to add to it.

3 November (Sunday)

We are continually moving forward, and doing a little firing now and again. I was told that during my absence at Brigade Headquarters, our Battery, under Lieutenant Sampson at the time, had a duel with a German field-gun battery which we put out of action, but in the mean time they had communicated with their 'Heavies' who afterwards gave our people a very warm time of it. Hitherto we have only seen cavalry in action dismounted, in the trenches, but now we see them at their own game, for they are very busy nowadays, do much skirmishing, and capture many odd prisoners. Recently, while on the march, we were amused to see a few German prisoners being chased ingloriously by a gang of small French schoolboys, brandishing huge staves and shouting abusively. The prisoners were hatless and their captor, a smiling cavalryman, trotted behind nonchalantly. Occasionally we meet big batches of prisoners, some of them big, sturdy fellows, but others freaks. Their shabby, dowdy, long-coated field uniforms do not improve their appearance, which contrasts in a marked way with that of British and French soldiers, who, whenever possible, preserve a certain amount of smartness, even in the trenches. Some of these prisoners cast wondering eyes at our polished guns and well-groomed horses. As they retreat the Germans continue to destroy the main bridges and crossroads, and our progress is made over the pontoon bridges and temporary roads so swiftly improvised by the Royal Engineers. Today we passed through Douchy, Croix-Ste-Marie and Rouvignies to Herin. This is a coalmining area with pit shafts and colourless slag tips so reminiscent of the coalfields of South Wales.

Here there are no civilians, and one window bore a pathetic appeal, hand-printed in English – 'Please do not loot our homes'. The watering of our horses and the quenching of our own thirsts were delayed today by a rumour that the enemy had poisoned the wells. We are now attached to the Canadians again.

Riding on the gun limber today a Gunner told me that from what he had heard the Canadians are a tough lot, used to roughing it, very resourceful, and always springing some surprise on the Germans.

5 November (Tuesday)

The long column of our Battery moves forward at a sharp walk-march. Guns and limbers first, then GS wagons, vans, cooks' cart, and water cart in the rear. The steel wheel tyres grind along the cobbled highways. This morning, seated with the Gunners on the limbers, I saw the frightful havoc wrought by German machine-guns. In the distance a particular expanse of land looked like a turnip field, but when we drew near we found the objects were not turnips. There the tragic, lifeless corpses lay, the price of our advance. The nearest corpse laid on his back with arms flung out and knees drawn up. He stared at the sky with glassy, questioning eyes. He seemed to be asking 'Why?' Farther on we came to the outermost building of the village. It was whitewashed and looked like a barn. From the wall, near the floor, some bricks were missing.

Through that gaping hole a machine-gun had spat death most effectively. Later we entered Valenciennes, one of the largest places we have yet been in. The railway station had been wrecked and the railroads too, for in frequent places the rails point fantastically skywards. The German dead were dragged unceremoniously from the road to the pavements for us to proceed. Their faces are lurid, amber-coloured, and the bodies stiff like waxworks models. Disgusting, disturbing sights. How cheap human life can become. The Canadians were the first to enter Valenciennes, though the British troops shared in the fight for it. Billeted in a factory in which lay stretched, bayoneted German machine-gunners. What a hope they had of being taken prisoners. The nearest one had received it in his stomach, for we inspected the wound. He looked exceedingly tall in that position, but righteous as our cause might be, it is a shameful sight.

'Digger', the Australian, and another Driver have already relieved two German corpses of their boots and socks and are wearing them. They are boots of a size midway between ankle boots and knee boots. Steel helmets and tunics have also been stripped off some corpses as souvenirs.

Dinnertime some 'C' Subsection men staggered in, amid roars of laughter, with a small harmonium which was hauled up to a platform where we were subjected to some miscellaneous music played for the most part indifferently. On the keyboard I have only reached the hymn-tune stage of playing, but for a brief time I amused myself, if no one else.

6 November (Wednesday)

Arrived at Onnaing, where we were billeted in a large building that resembled a riding school. There was generous headroom, and on its ample brick walls the Huns had painted in large white figures:

1914

1915

1916

1917

1918

191

In commencing the figures for next year we wonder if they have presumed too much. Detailed to take a sick horse to the Sick Lines, situated a considerable distance away. The poor beast must have been very ill for I had to lead and goad it along the whole distance, an exhausting task for us both.

7 November (Thursday)

Moved forward through Quarouble, Quievrechain to Quievrain where we assumed that a local industry was clay pipe making, as the civilians presented each one of us with a sample. Some cute devils had more than one. It is an odd sight seeing everyone smoking a clay pipe. Out here a widespread superstition exists among the troops regarding the number of pipes or cigarettes one match could light. Frequently one witnesses two lights made, the match thrown away, and a fresh match struck for the third smoker, for it is considered unlucky to be third man. This practice is undoubtedly good for the match trade, and the cynics suggest that the manufacturers are responsible, but I have heard one very interesting and reasonable explanation of the superstition's origin. During the Boer War a light would just have to last long enough to fire three British pipes or cigarettes for a Boer marksman to score a bull's-eye.[2]

2. One of the most enduring anecdotes of the First War came from the practice of sharing cigarettes in the front line. It was said that it was unlucky if three people shared the same light. When the first soldier lit his cigarette, the sniper would see the flame. When the second soldier lit his cigarette, the sniper would take aim. And when the third smoker lit his cigarette, the sniper would fire. No doubt superstition raised its head here, but assuredly events such as this did occur in the trenches. Also, after the First World War it was usual to see men who were smoking hold their cigarette cupped in their hand, rather than the usual stance of slotting it between the index and middle finger. The cupping action would be the one they learned to use in the trenches to shield the burning tip of the cigarette from view.

8 November (Friday)

Advanced to Elouges where the water pump at our disposal delivered small results for the expenditure of energy required to work it, so that the endless refilling of the canvas buckets for our many horses and mules was hard labour. Rumours of a coming Peace are plentiful and Sergeant Stuart seems confident that the war will end very soon. The pickets have received instructions to awaken the Battery should peace be declared during the night. Most of us treat such rumours and hopes with doubt as we have so often heard them.

10 November (Sunday)

Having spent the night on picket duty I felt very tired this morning and could have slept very well on the gun limber, for our restless march still continues. We have passed through Dour and Warvignies and we must have crossed the frontier, for the Belgian flag with its sickly combination of black, yellow and red is now most prominent in the decorated streets. To enter Belgium has been my secret ambition for a long time, and I feel rather proud of having lived in two foreign countries. Our column rumbled briskly along to Frameries, a fair-sized town buzzing with military activity. We halted for some time in a street, and sat motionless, for three whistle blasts had warned us of the presence of a 'Jerry' plane overhead. It was a very sunny day and we had to shade our eyes to gaze up at the tiny silver speck travelling at a terrific speed high up in the sky, cloudless except for the tiny white puffs of shells from the anti-aircraft guns, the barks of which resounded loudly through the town.

The plane, looking like a dangerous and deadly insect, raced out of sight and hearing, and we reached the outskirts where we halted again, for the road that stretched beyond and below was being heavily shelled. A man approached with his hand bandaged. 'You're right for Blighty', someone shouted enviously. He looked up and smiled happily in agreement and walked by. It was decided that the Battery should run the gauntlet as there was no sign of the shelling ceasing, and as we were probably blocking the road for the traffic behind us. We moved forward one vehicle at a time, and at a brisk trot, the whole column arriving without any mishap.

Rumour spread that we were making for a place called Noirchain which we learned was near. As we neared it, Mons, which today had been captured by the Canadians, could be seen on our left. We are now passing over historic ground. Arriving at our destination we were billeted in a barn of a large farm. The farmhouse, barns and outhouses have been recently white-limed and dazzle our eyes in the brilliant sunshine. During the afternoon the mail arrived and there was a letter for me. In the yard stood a GS wagon against which I leaned and read the latest news from home. Suddenly there was a whine and a shrapnel shell burst above the barn. One of its small splinters shot between the spokes of the tall wagon wheels and grazed my left thumb. Belief in the quick cessation of hostilities increases now, although I still remain among the sceptics. Of course I realise with some astonishment that the enemy is crumbling up, but I fancy he may hold out for a long time yet, and possibly spring some surprises on us.

11 November (Monday)

After breakfast, about 8 am, while having a clean up, we suddenly heard a burst of cheering from behind the Lines, followed by a band striking up a rollicking march. We knew something good had happened, but that the war was to end seemed unbelievable. Rumour circulated that an armistice was to be signed at 11 am. A mounted officer proceeding up the Line had broken the news to one of our men, but we still had our doubts. A little later we heard that the band was that of the Canadians, and that, on hearing the wonderful news, it marched up and down the streets preceded by Tommies and civilians dancing. At about 11am we were ordered to 'Fall in' on the roadside at the farm entrance. We were given the 'Stand at ease' and 'Stand easy', then Lieutenant Cook said to us casually, 'Well boys, I'm pleased to inform you that the bloody war is over.'

Was ever an adjective used so fittingly? Consternation was followed by hearty cheering after which Cook instructed us to carry on as usual until we were drafted back to Blighty, which would probably take place in the near future. Our thoughts flew homewards. What would they think of it? Their uncertainty as to whether we were alive or not must now be agonising, so one of the first jobs for those of us who possessed a field card was to fill it in and post it immediately. The formal sentence 'I am quite well' and the date will relieve their minds until I find time to write a letter. I was detailed for horse picket and was glad to find Bombardier Kingsland in charge. The horses were in a field surrounded by a high wall. We walked to and fro, discussing the wonderful news, and Kingsland shared with me a huge slab of delicious chocolate. He spoke very kindly of Gunner Page. During the German offensive last March, Kingsland, owing to his duties, was separated from his kit and took it for granted that it was lost, but at the end of the retreat, Page turned up with his (Kingsland's) kit in a waterproof sheet. He had even saved his books.

Right up to 11 am normal fighting took place on both sides. One of our Gunners told me that his gun crew fired as many shells as they possibly could in order to have that much less to carry about afterwards, or to use his word, 'hump'. As the historic hour passed our air squadrons returned, but at about 11.15 am we were astonished and dismayed to find that Jerry was still firing at us. The shells burst on our flanks and we had the 'wind up' badly, and worse, doubted the authenticity of all this talk of peace. Later in the day we heard the explanation of this dangerous incident. The shells were fired by a German battery that had been surrounded by our troops, and which was therefore out of communication with its headquarters. We also heard that the German Battery Commander was speedily made acquainted with the news by a 'streamer' message dropped from one of our planes.[3] Just before the great hour silenced the cannonading a young Canadian infantryman was killed near us. I judged him to be about my own age, 19. What rotten luck to be killed at the eleventh hour. The civilians laid him in the church. Bombardier Kingsland asked me if I would accompany him in the church for the purpose of offering to God a prayer of thankfulness for Peace and for our own escape. Being undemonstrative in such matters I was not very keen on going, feeling also that I could express my gratitude silently, quite as well outside, but I consented to go with him. The sexton was slow in understanding the reason for our visit and kept glancing at the dead Canadian covered by a blanket and lying on a stretcher

---

3. The message was placed in either a screw-capped box or a bag to which long coloured streamers were attached. The streamers help stabilise the fall of the container as well as enabling those on the ground to track more easily its descent and recover the message.

in the aisle. He must have thought that we either meant to remove the corpse from its sacred resting place or loot the contents of the pockets, and he watched us suspiciously until we knelt in a pew where Kingsland offered up a prayer for the soul of the departed soldier and afterwards a prayer of gratitude for having been kept unharmed through so much danger. We learn that we shall have to follow the enemy, while keeping at a prescribed distance, right into Germany. In the evening we set off on a trek and journeyed all night. It rained a great deal, but it would take more than rain to damp our spirits this night, and we sang and we whistled as we lumbered along, passing through Asquillies, Ort Harvengt to Harve. During this march we encountered a large number of men of the Naval Brigade, their battalions bearing the names of such renowned old sea dogs as Anson, Hawke and Hood.

At Harve we were billeted in houses emptied of all their possessions. The ground-floor room that I shared with half a dozen others was scrupulously clean and the walls had been newly papered. We slept on the flagged floor, a luxury compared with some of the places where we have had to sleep.

12 November (Tuesday)
Today we were surprised to find some civilians walking around our billet. They must have been the former dwellers.

I noticed a pained look on the face of one of the women when she discovered some soot marks on her new wallpaper. Some careless vandal had stuck a candle by its own grease on the wall. I felt ashamed and hoped reparation would be made to these refugees for any damage done by us.

13 November (Wednesday)
Mons lies behind Harve and we have longed to pay it a visit, partly to see civilised life again – civilians, children, shops and tramcars. Such a place seems like heaven after the unspeakable hell we have had to endure. We welcome a visit there too, partly because of its renown, and lastly but not least, for the probability of a good feed. Each day Hollingworth is granting a half-holiday to 12 men, for the purpose of a visit to the city. In 'C' Subsection we tossed up a coin for turns and I was among the lucky ones

to go today. We went mounted, having an enjoyable ride, and a bright sunny day. On entering the city we espied a canteen. It was run by the Canadians who sold us some large packets of good-quality biscuits.

We stabled our horses in a street called La Rue d'Harve. We were thrilled to see shops and traffic in full swing. Presently a procession approached solemnly. It was a funeral – that of the last men to fall in action.[4] It was a long procession, with civic representation and civilians in large numbers. The floral tributes were remarkable. Jocks and Canadian soldiers, the former probably Canadian Scottish, marched behind. Resuming our walk we traversed the town well, finding interest everywhere. We admired the fine Gothic cathedral, and observed that the prices of commodities were extraordinarily high. I bought a book of picture postcards of Mons. We were due back early and we returned to the stables (in Mons) to find that one of our horses, that of a Driver, had broken loose, eaten a packet of precious biscuits and half a sack of linseed belonging to the stable. Trotting happily home in the cool evening we could not realise that Peace had come, for it seems too good to be true. Instead of the terrible din of war we now enjoy quietness and calmness, and the feeling we have is akin to that relieved sensation experienced after the passing of a violent thunderstorm or a bad dream. There still exists among us a slight fear of unexploded or undiscovered mines, but the old gnawing fears that more or less haunted us have ended.

16 November (Saturday)

I remember being taught in school that Belgium is the world's most thickly populated country, and am now seeing visible proof of it. Towns and villages are in close proximity to each other and often there appear to be no division whatever. We have had another night march, but such marches are infinitely more interesting since the Armistice because lights are now permitted. The streets of Jemappes, which we passed through tonight, were illuminated, and we heard loud rejoicings taking place in some of the houses. We passed through Quarengnon and Hainin, our journey ending at Crespin where we were billeted in unoccupied houses.

4. This was Private George Lawrence Price, 28th North West Battalion, 6th Canadian Infantry Brigade, 2nd Canadian Division. He and two other soldiers crossed the Canal du Centre on an unauthorised patrol. Price was hit and killed at 10:58 hours on 11 November. It is probable that Price was the dead soldier seen by Ivor and Bombardier Kingsland in Havre church on 11 November.

17 November (Sunday)

Heard that Bombardier Wraight of our 'C' Subsection wanted a pair of slacks (trousers). Wraight is a slim, bony, ungainly chap with a thin, drooping moustache. He was formerly a Driver and well used to horses, I believe, in 'civvy' life. Having a pair of slacks I seldom wore, and which took unnecessary space in my kit bag, I was glad to sell them to him for 5 francs. This evening went on guard, the Guard Room being the parlour of an empty house. In a cupboard we found a bag of white powder which we guessed was maize flour. With it we made a cake, baked it, and although the other ingredients were missing and it tasted insipid, our terrific appetites were appeased. Across the road lived some civilians. On guard I longed to see what was going on behind that kitchen window blind through which the light shone dimly. During one of my stationary periods on guard a woman emerged from the front door, glanced right and left, was obviously unaware of my presence, for she lifted her skirts, squatted in the space between the door and the window and pissed. Perhaps after imbibing freely she had found the toilet engaged. Between duties wrote a postcard to my parents.

20 November (Wednesday)

Received a letter from Private J.E. Rogers of the Royal Army Medical Corps written in North Russia (Murmansk I learned later).

Being so far away from the old country he often goes back in thought to the happy little spot – my home – where as a theological student he spent so many happy weekends during preaching engagements, as my parents provided such hospitality for our church free of charge. He arrived in North Russia on 2 November after a pleasant voyage, and he writes that the weather there, at the time of writing, is wonderfully mild, whereas only a few days before they arrived it had been very cold – below zero. They are well supplied with warm, fur clothes and snow boots, and he adds, they need be, for the winter temperature goes 40 degrees below zero. He wonders where I am and how I fare, and hopes that I shall soon be home. Nearly a year ago, and only a few hours after I arrived home on leave, I answered the door to find him grinning at me.

To my great pleasure he was also on leave and had decided to come and stay with us for a few days. We enjoyed many walks together. He was home on leave again in October. He enjoys many leaves, being lucky every time his ship coals in Britain. He appears to have had a great time last month, and paid a visit to my uncle and aunt at Fforestfach. He adds that mails out in North Russia are irregular, and warns me that I might have to wait for his next letter. He asks me to omit the name of his ship which is the *Braemar Castle*.

Sir Ernest Shackleton is in charge of this expeditionary force in North Russia.[5] He goes aboard their ship and J.E. says that he looks the picture of robust health. He has given them a lecture on his Antarctic voyages. Ashore, Eddie has seen sleighs drawn by reindeer. The peasants will give them anything for our English cigarettes. Some of them had exchanged furs for them.

21 November (Thursday)

The weather is frosty and foggy. This afternoon we were granted another half-holiday, and with several Drivers from 'C' Subsection I relieved one of the excellent but ownerless local gardens of some of its vegetables. The place is deserted except for a few of its citizens.

Spent the afternoon peeling potatoes and turnips, and the evening consuming them in the bedroom that is our billet. The only meat available was bully beef, but even that tasted well with the fresh vegetables. What a feast we had, ending in the feeling of peace and contentment resultant on a full stomach which until now has been for us a rare treat.

24 November (Sunday)

Half-holiday today, which I was forced to spend polishing-up, as I am again on guard tonight. We have to parade on guard immaculately, in order to bear a most exacting inspection by the orderly officer who spends about a minute scrutinising each guard, front and back, from head to foot.

5. Given his experience as a polar explorer, Shackleton was sent as an adviser to the Allied expeditionary force at Archangel in North Russia. This army of some 30,000 men was commanded by General Sir Edmund Ironside.

26 November (Tuesday)

Our Brigade Sports took place today. They must have known it was my birthday, for today I am 20. For days we had looked forward to this event and the interest and excitement was intense. Our Lieutenant Sampson was prominent in the jumping competitions and we had great hopes of him bringing lustre to 'B' Battery. How well he rode his mount, but there were better horses than his in the competitions, so that he had little chance. One officer was thrown, being dragged along the field for yards through not being able to disentangle one of his feet from its stirrup. He showed great presence of mind and miraculously escaped unhurt. 'B' Battery team lost in the wrestling on horseback event, but did well at tug-o-war, reaching the final, only to be beaten after a long and hard struggle.

Metcalfe, our talisman, had the rope looped around his body. I think it nearly broke his back, for afterwards I heard him complain, 'Well that was beyond a joke anyway.' Lieutenant Cook has been badly kicked by a recalcitrant mule which he was determined to ride and tame. While on guard sent Pa a picture postcard of Eglise Sainte Waudru, Mons, and on which I informed him that the weather keeps fine but very cold.

29 November (Friday)

We are again on the move, today passing through Quievrechain, Quarouble, Onnaing, St Saulve, and halting for a few hours at Valenciennes, where we draw water for the horses in the usual canvas buckets from the River Escaut. We were able to have a stroll into the town, where, in a large, sunlit square were arrayed a large number of captured German machine-guns and trench mortars. We proceeded through Raismes, La Foret, Moulin-des-loup, which we parodied into 'Looping-the-Loop', St Amand, Nouveau-jeu and Alene-Dor to Rosult.

1 December (Sunday)

On Saturday our Battery moved via Alene-Dor and Beavry Toovignies, but today we realised that this was not to be our permanent camp, for we shifted about half a mile to a large farm in the neighbourhood of Orches, where we are likely to be settled for some time.

The farm, which is to be our home, lies alongside a main road. The officers are quartered in the farmhouse, the Signal Pit is in the house adjoining, and above the very good stables are the men's billets. This morning Bombardier White and I went mounted, hay scrounging. First we tried Orchies, but without success, so we rode farther afield, and getting off the beaten track had some exhilarating rides over the fields. Jimmy, my chestnut mount, was quite spirited and seemed to be thoroughly enjoying himself, as did his rider. Once or twice I held him in – a difficult task until White was about 200yd ahead. This teased him very much, he neighed, cocked his ears, then, when I released the reins he galloped at his utmost speed. I could feel his body surging and straining beneath me.

What an exhilarating sport riding is. At a large farmhouse, surrounded by tall barns full of hay, we dismounted and White made our business known to the farmer who did not seem enthusiastic about the transaction, but dare not refuse fodder for British Army horses. We were invited into a bright living room and served with coffee by two young ladies whom we guessed were the daughters. They seemed very well bred, and there was an atmosphere of prosperity about the farm. One of them reminded me of the woman in paintings by Burne-Jones.[6] While we sipped the coffee, they displayed a fine German helmet. White and I pooled our scraps of French language and managed to keep the conversation going. They were particularly interested to learn that White had served on the Eastern Front before coming to the Western Front. The old man occupied the time in what appeared to be the hopeless task of cleaning a very rusty shot gun, which they explained they had buried during the German occupation. Riding quietly back, Bombardier White told me of a remarkable feat he had unwittingly accomplished as a Mounted Orderly during the advance. 'Bobby', a 'C' Subsection horse we both knew well and which he was now riding, one night carried him across the high narrow wall, which was all that remained of a bridge the enemy had mined. It was not until he saw the wall in the light of the following day that he realised the risk he had unconsciously taken.

6. Sir Edward Coley Burne-Jones (1833–98), British Pre-Raphaelite artist and designer.

Back at the camp, found Kingsland, with his usual beaming smile, unobtrusively doing some missionary work for a church service at Bouvignies YMCA. Three of us consented to go with him, though I must confess that the motive, in my case, was not devotion, but diversion. Several representatives from other batteries and units occupied the few front rows of chairs. I listened respectfully, sang moderately, observed how Kingsland loved and revelled in every minute of it, but I was unmoved. I cannot recall one military church service that has genuinely inspired me. Kingsland remained to take part in the Communion Service.

2 December (Monday)

On guard again. One of my fellow guards was in civilian life a coalminer and he is very excited at the prospect of his early demobilisation. Particulars have been taken of our civilian occupations and we learn that coalminers are among those to receive the first consideration.

3 December (Tuesday)

We have settled down in a pretty place, on this farm outside Orchies. Nearly opposite us are a few cottages skirting the road to Orchies. Here and there a windmill improves the landscape.

In the direction of Orchies, but slightly off the main road there is a spacious building that has just been evacuated by a section of the Chinese Labour Corps. After the Chinamen left, we Signallers, armed with axes, raided the place, and as it was only a temporary structure, we easily dislodged a few doors and beams and also a quantity of wire netting with which we have each made a bedstead. In our room, which adjoins the signal pit, there was no fireplace or stove, so with bricks we have built a huge hearth which resembles a small furnace. We feed it with wood and sometimes when it smokes badly, it brings tears to our eyes. Bastow was the chief mason.

He is a hard-boiled Yorkshireman with so deep and resonant a voice that if it were trained, it would equal that of an operatic bass I once heard. He sings sentimental ditties, staccato and with a catch in his voice, like a third-rate musical-hall artiste. He is a Signaller, yet since I have known him he has been the driver of the cooks' cart and probably he prefers that role.

He pronounces horse as 'Hoss'. Occasionally he recites his creed: 'Hear all. See all. Say nowt. Sup all. Pay nowt, and if thee do owt for nowt, do it for thesen.' He is blunt, unimaginative, tells you to your face what he thinks of you in monosyllables, and is inclined to treat outsiders like myself with scorn. He doesn't think much of Wales and the Welsh. Sometimes I think he hates the Welsh as some hate foreigners, the Irish or the Jews.

For my benefit he described some rough houses between men of the Welsh Regiment and an English regiment in which, according to him, the Welsh always came off second best. To Bastow, Wales is a long range of mountains with a railway station about every 50 miles. When I told him that Port Talbot had some of the most modern steelworks in the country, he stared at me incredulously. Were I, a Welshman, to excel Bastow in every way, you would never convince this son of the West Riding that by some Divine Right I was his superior. Stuart, our Scottish Sergeant, carries his 'Burns', but I never heard Bastow even mention the Brontes, yet I a Welshman have already read *Villette* and part of *Jane Eyre*. Lying in the darkness on his newly made bed before going to sleep he thaws a little when he talks of 'Bradfoord', for which he craves, and then we are treated with some vivid little descriptions of the intimacies of married life. We single men are left to imagine the agonies of married men such as he, doubtless used to regular and frequent sexual intercourse, and now through war, separated from their wives for periods of 12 months, for leave is not granted for less periods than that, except for special circumstances.

5 December (Thursday)
Lieutenant Sampson has been awarded the Military Cross, and the neat, white-purple-white ribbon adorns his breast.

He deserves this honour, if only for the way he commanded 'B' Battery during the German offensive of last March. Our Major was killed during this battle, and Captain Hollingworth (as he was then) was home on leave, which left Sampson as senior officer. Signallers Brain and Pomeroy have each been awarded the Military Medal, not for any conspicuous acts of gallantry, perhaps, but for good general service. To those of us who asked Brain for what he had received his decoration, the sheepish answer was, 'Now, how the hell do you expect me to know?'

6 December (Friday)

This evening a letter from Dad. They have all been down with the flu, but recovering, although Granddad is still very weak, but he is now over 80 years of age.

Aunt Fanny has done great work for soldiers and sailors with her flag-day efforts. She and Mrs McRitchie, wife of the medical doctor of Fforestfach, hired a barrel organ for one of the flag days. Their last effort was on behalf of the Church Army, which has a hut near us here in Orchies. There we may read or write or buy light refreshments.

9 December (Monday)

To use the Army word, I am 'sweating' terribly on leave now, for I expect to be notified any day. The thrill of the Armistice has worn off, and grousing, the soldier's privilege, is again universal, since life here is now exceptionally dull and monotonous. We have to make our own fun. For days such mock arguments as 'Are there ponies down a pit?' and 'Is there such a thing as a one-man band?' have been raging, until some of the uninitiated participants have nearly come to blows. One is forced to laugh at the sheer absurdity of it all and in doing so we forget for a time our boredom. Sometimes our bodies have an uneasy feeling, a restless, nervy sensation, produced, I believe, through lack of fresh food and fruit and insufficient baths. My teeth too feel tired and ache faintly, due to insufficient cleaning, for water taps and toothbrushes cannot be obtained at will as in civilian life. In view of this and the other multitudinous discomforts, what a prospect leave becomes. The thought of leave has kept us alive on many an occasion and made this life more bearable at all times.

Leave is a way of escape, a safety valve, a release from miserable routine, discomfort and squalor, for at least a brief period of bliss among those we love, who understand us and whose anxiety, prayers and tears have not ceased since the moment we wrenched ourselves from them. We dream of a hot bath, a feather bed, 'civvy' clothes and good food.

Tonight I am 'Waiting Man' of the guard, the coveted role, competed for by each member of the squad, first because one is relieved of guard duties and secondly there is a certain amount of pride in being judged the smartest man on parade. Except for fetching the grub, carrying any odd messages or temporarily relieving a guard to go to the latrine, there is nothing to do and plenty of time to do it in. But what preparation going on guard entails. For every parade we have to turn up spic and span, but for guard the standard demanded is perfection. Lieutenant Sampson inspected the squad and after a meticulous scrutiny of each candidate from cap to boots, front and rear, commanded me to 'fall out', so that for me all the scrubbing, brushing and polishing had been worth while.

10 December (Tuesday)

I have learned something new about myself. I am supposed to possess a vivid personality and am either greatly liked or disliked. This applies to November-born people according to a newspaper horoscope I alighted upon recently in our draughty, communal latrine.

Chapter 19

LEAVE

11 December (Wednesday)

With several others left the Battery for leave at Home. We had walked a considerable distance beyond Orchies, along a tree-flanked highway and had been refused a lift by a few French Army lorries before we were overtaken and picked up by a British lorry, which bore us through Coutiche and Flines to Douai. Being assured of a long wait we strolled through the town, which we had observed so often from the slopes of Vimy Ridge. Darkness was approaching before our train arrived, the hours having dragged very slowly. On the railway station was a good canteen where we were able to buy ample refreshments. We were to travel as usual in goods vans and my pass was routed via Boulogne. I had boarded the train when Gunner Turner rushed up excitedly and holding out a haversack. Turner's route was via Calais and in the excitement we had taken each other's haversacks.

Our train had ambled along for some time before we clanked into a big centre which turned out to be Arras. The station looked very familiar, even from this new viewing angle, but as we knew it when our Battery was in action nearby it was of course derelict and without all these lights. Aubigny revived pleasant memories of my meeting with W.T. Davies and then we passed through St Pol and Ligny St Fechole. It became so bitterly cold that some Army Service Corps occupants kindled a fire in the centre of the van floor this being fed with fuel filched from the locomotive tender during halts.

One of these ASC men possessed a good voice. He was a lorry driver and wore an astrakhan-collared greatcoat. He sang aptly:

I love that dear old home of mine,
I love that dear old home of mine.
I love that dear old place where I was born,
I love that dear old home of mine.

Our train was picking up speed after a halt when loud thumps on the van door could be heard, accompanied by excited ejaculations in French.

No one seemed in a hurry to open the door, room already being limited, and there was also murmuring about the indifference shown by French lorry drivers to British Tommies. However, the thumps and shouts increased, as did the speed of the train and as the fellow must have been growing desperate, someone opened the door through which leaped in a big, handsome, French poilu clad in dark-blue uniform with a beret of the same hue. He had dark hair and the fresh complexion of a healthy child. He was very relieved at being admitted and made a speech in French too rapid for anyone to understand and to which little attention was paid. He settled down near me and we gathered that he was returning from leave. We carried on a conversation by picking out a familiar word or phrase here and there, gradually arriving at his meanings. Later I got him to give us the correct pronunciation of such place names as Arras, St Quentin, etc. By this time the fire burned and collapsed through the van floor and instead of heat we were plagued by a new and sneaky draught. When nearing Etaples, the train jolted badly and stopped abruptly. Evidently something was wrong so we hastily jumped down to the track and ran towards the engine to find that our train had run into a stationary light engine. The buffers had been knocked off one locomotive and the other was slightly damaged. On such journeys urgent urinating has to be done through the van doors and we heard that a few passengers had suffered slight injuries and bumps during this performance, but that no one had been seriously injured. The accident was caused by our engine driver falling asleep. Not only on grounds of propriety, but also because of the space it would entail, I withhold the colourful opinions of the driver expressed by men anxious to go home safely on a well-earned leave.

12 December (Thursday)

Arrived at Boulogne and stayed the night in a large and up-to-date rest camp. Climbing up on my wire bed, I was very anxious to sleep so that the morning would appear to arrive quicker, for this slow travelling speed became irritating.

13 December (Friday)

Marched to Boulogne Docks where French souvenir sellers, of both sexes, pestered us to buy their trifles. Having nothing French to take home I bought a flimsy, silk kimono and a brass and copper crucifix made from cartridges and fragments of shell cases. We had a very pleasant crossing in a speedy little steamer. Very few were sick and I wasn't among them. There was plenty of singing. At one time I felt a slight queerness, but escaped sickness and when the white cliffs of my homeland loomed in sight, I understood that oft-repeated remark about a lump coming to one's throat. The London express awaited us at Folkestone Quay and how comfortable the upholstered seats felt and how swiftly the train sped. Judging French railways by the speed their troop trains travelled, someone in the compartment said, 'If a Froggy was on this train now, he'd jump out of the window, thinking the engine was out of control.' Even winter cannot rob the landscapes of Kent and Surrey of their beauty. The country slid past us like a well-kept park. How we have missed those hedges across the Channel.

Then came the soot-soiled, yellow-bricked buildings of London, where we were able to raise from our Army Pay Books adequate sums of money from the capital which has quietly accumulated during our long sojourns in places where opportunities for spending were reduced to a minimum. At Paddington the excitement of the occasion was beginning to make me slightly light-headed. There at the bookstall I bought a copy of *Nash's Magazine* and its delectable short stories and its equally delectable black and white illustrations annihilated the distance to South Wales. At Port Talbot I was met by my father who was on night-shift duty and who greeted me with a proud beaming smile and a vigorous handclasp. Then he led me down to his office where I plumped on his table my pack and there in the light of the gas lamp he had a good look at me, observed that I had returned in one piece and that my only defect was the broken front tooth, which a flint-like Army biscuit had halved early in my service abroad, that being the only part of me the war had succeeded in breaking. Anyway, I was now in a position to repair that defect at the earliest possible time. Arriving home I found them all in good health and all anxious to give me a glorious meal. More important to me, I had a hot bath and a clean change of underclothes before going to bed. My mother, thinking I must be tired, tried to dissuade me from bathing until the morrow, but I insisted.

And so to bed, which sinking under me with exquisite softness, bore me instantly into the land of dreams.

14 December (Saturday)

Today my dreams came true, for I changed into 'civvy' clothes. What a luxury, although one feels a bit chilly in them after the thick Army clothes.

From Pa I heard some revelations concerning the Port Talbot man I met so fortuitously near Hancourt. He was drunk when he presented himself to my father at the railway station last January and among other foolish actions had displayed some obscene French photographs. Pa didn't quite know what to make of him, but in order to gather some information concerning my whereabouts, invited him to our house. One evening he came, to frighten the life out of them by telling them that in the sector where I was there would take place shortly one of the worst 'smash-ups' of the war. This of course was true, for everyone knew of the forthcoming 'stunt', but how tactless of him to tell them.[1]

They imagined that I was on that same front for weeks after the German offensive of March and were greatly surprised to learn in June that I was on the Arras Front. Of course I hadn't been allowed to mention Arras, or any other place, but in a letter they had told me that W.T. Davies was at Arras and I had promptly replied stating that I was in the same place.

15 December (Sunday)

Read a short biography of David Livingstone and felt inspired by the determination that this great and practical Christian showed in pressing

---

1. Ivor notes: 'His name was Donald Ace, and he was brought up with his grandmother and uncle in Water Street. He worked first as a gardener under my father's brother in Margam Park, entering the Forestry Department of Glamorgan after the war.'

forward to his goal in the teeth of terrific obstacles, such as repeated attacks of fever and hardships of all kinds.

Today I learned how my cousin, Arthur Harries[2] was killed by a shell on the 31 October, so near the Armistice. Destined for the Church, he was the favourite of the six sons of my uncle and aunt, who are almost broken-hearted.

Tonight I attended a service at our church, which, until it is financially in a position to erect a building of its own, holds its meetings in the 'Upper Room' of the Carnegie Free Library. I sat in the centre of the hall and among the friends who greeted me was a former companion, Brinley Singleton, who is a Victualling Petty Officer in the Royal Navy. Curiously, he fingered the blue baize bands fixed on my tunic lapels, which is the distinguishing mark of Signallers overseas.

16 December (Monday)

The green woollen gloves issued us wear out quickly, so today I have been trying to procure a pair of leather and astrakhan gloves in local clothing shops, but was unsuccessful. From Aberfan, Nellie and I strolled out to Baglan Road, where I was at once struck by the resemblance to the scenery of Flanders of the strip of moorland stretching from Aberfan to Briton Ferry.

My friend Dan Evans is also home on leave. This afternoon I went with him to Neath on a bus, as he wanted to make a call at Penrhwtyn Hospital, where he had been confined for some time with pneumonia. When I offered our fare money to the conductor he said, 'A lady at the back has already paid your fares.' We looked back to see smiling at us Miss Annie Davies, Headmistress of Eastern Girls School. Dan looks very pale and thin. During the March Retreat, when he was at the offices of the Supreme War Council at Versailles, he spoke of not being able to change clothes for days owing to the frequency of telephone calls. I nearly laughed in this face. He also told me that during one aerial bombardment of Paris one of his mates sought shelter up a tree.

2. Recorded by the Commonwealth War Graves Commission as 131639 Gunner Arthur Lynton Harris, 268th Siege Battery, Royal Garrison Artillery, aged 20. Son of David and Mary Harris, 24 The Promenade, Swansea. Undergraduate of London University and Scholar of St David's College, Lampeter (Theology). Arthur is buried in Vichte Military Cemetery, 25 miles east of Ypres.

21 December (Saturday)

Visited my uncle and aunt at Fforestfach and received a warm welcome. In the evening they took me to the beautiful house of their friends, the McRitchies, charming Scottish people. Mrs McRitchie is a relative of Bonar Law. One of the two daughters is very attractive and has skin like pale, transparent alabaster. On my arrival, Dr McRitchie drew me aside towards a lamp and scrutinised my face professionally.

When he pronounced the verdict, 'You're all right', he squeezed into my hand a packet of cigarettes. After a tea and a talk, Mrs McRitchie put on a gramophone record of herself and my aunt singing a duet, but there was more laughter than song in it. When we were leaving, the parrot, who up to now had stubbornly refused to talk, bade us 'Good Morning.' He was nearly right.

26 December (Boxing Day)

All good things come to an end, but returning today goes against the grain, though I do feel thankful for having spent Christmas Day at home. My mother began to weep hours before I left and my attempts to console her by reminding her that the war was over were futile. Nellie came with me to the railway station and there were tears in her eyes too as I left Port Talbot with the 'Mail' at 9.35 pm. As for myself, I had that terrible 'sinking' feeling always felt when leaving the comforts of home for life in the Army. However, I was lucky in having as a travelling companion, as far as Paddington, Davy Sheppard of the South Wales Borderers, who was returning to his Depot for his final discharge. Davy has a gold watch which he pinched from a German prisoner.

27 December (Friday)

We arrived at Paddington at 3 am, where a Free Buffet yawned a welcome to us all. It was run by some titled lady – bless her. After refreshments here we were packed like sardines into an open lorry which bore us swiftly to Victoria railway station. The streets, which were decorated for the visit of President Woodrow Wilson, were deserted and the polished highway reflected the long avenue of street lamps.

One might quote Wordsworth and say:

Dear God! the very houses seem asleep;
And all that mighty heart is lying still!

At Victoria station there was another Free Buffet. From Folkestone Harbour, the sea, grey with white foam, looked wild and forbidding and when we embarked the weather was so rough that we were all ordered below. Unwisely, I watched for some time the pronounced see-saw movements and the rolls of the little ship until I began to feel a bit queer. The majority of us were sick and everyone was morose and silent, for returning from leave is a miserable business at the best of times, but a journey like this after a fortnight of heaven is wicked and it was a relief to reach Boulogne.

One fellow was so ill that during the whole crossing he writhed on the deck and groaned terribly. At Boulogne we marched along the cobbled quayside, past a forest of masts and up steep alleys to Telegraph Hill, where our camp was situated. This long and hilly march, immediately following an exhausting Channel trip, half killed us and we were glad to flop down in the snowbound bell tents, where we were to stay until our particular train was ready to take us farther. Lying in this cramped and draughty domicile, I felt for hours the swaying of that wretched little ship and my misery was complete. When I recovered enough to be sufficiently interested in external matters, I found that my tent mates were swarthy ANZAC soldiers.

30 December (Monday)
I am back with the Battery at Orchies, and being on guard tonight have ample time to live over and over again my wonderful leave. I left Boulogne on Saturday and arrived here yesterday by the same route, namely Douai, Raches, Flines and Coutiche. I found my wire bed broken. During my absence a whist drive had taken place, to which a number of civilians had been invited. I was told that one of our Signallers had enticed a girl from the whist drive into the room, had tried to make love to her, not on his own but on my bed, but the wire netting had failed to hold the weight of them both. Whether this was the truth or a leg-pull I failed to prove.

31 December (Tuesday)

Most of the men celebrated New Year's Eve by getting drunk, a disgusting and degrading, though at times humorous sight. 'H', one of the Signallers, who is younger even than I, got tight for the first time. He had been drinking vin blanc, which made him very sick afterwards and caused him to mislay his cap. He was greatly concerned for his cap in that exaggerated way produced by booze, and continually like a magnetic needle finding the north, his mind returned to his missing cap which he suspected had been hidden. His countenance bore an expression of unspeakable grief. The effect of wine on Bombardier Clarke was quite the opposite, for he stepped about sprightly, as if on air, his eyes glowing like stars. He was determined to recite a poem and after he had gained his poise on a box in the centre of the room, he recited in dramatic fashion a poem he had found in a page of that soldier's and sailor's guardian journal, *John Bull*.[3] The verses described trivial war services rendered at home by patriotic people, each verse ending in a tone of amazement: 'And he, By God! got the OBE.' Since most of the audience agreed emphatically with the sentiments expressed in this recital, Bombardier Clarke was rewarded with general and prolonged applause.

1 January (Wednesday)

2nd Lieutenant Shaw gave me his notebook in which I have to copy names and ranks of men, particulars of horses and personnel of the Centre Section of the Battery of which he is in charge and to which I belong. I interpret this as a compliment to my penmanship and being granted unlimited time in which to write it out, I very much enjoy doing it.

Kingsland, very upset, told me that Sergeant Major Mailey, catching him standing with his hands in his pockets, reprimanded him in what was an apt, but exceedingly vile way. 'Take your hands out of your pockets and stop scratching your balls.' What would have made another man grin made Kingsland wince, and after brooding awhile, he sought Mailey and told him that he intended reporting him to Major Hollingworth. At first the Sergeant

3. A patriotic journal started by Horatio William Bottomley in 1906. The journal was a favourite among servicemen in the First World War as Bottomley was very much on the side of the fighting man. He flouted regulations by setting up a column in the magazine where servicemen were encouraged to air their grievances, upon which a company that advertised in the paper would send a parcel to them. The government thought about prosecuting Bottomley for this but did not bring proceedings against him because they saw the usefulness of such a 'safety valve'.

Major pretended not to care a damn who he was reported to, but he must have reconsidered the matter, for shortly afterwards he returned to Kingsland, apologised and begged him not to take the matter any further.

This evening went to an orchestral concert at Orchies. We had to queue up and soon after the doors were opened the hall was filled. Near the pay box I recognised the Cardiff man whom I had seen conducting the orchestra in the cinema at Camblain l'Abbe and I had the pleasure of exchanging a few words with him. His sensitive face had a tortured expression, as though this brutal world exasperated him. He conducted this orchestra of the 8th Corps which performed so beautifully tonight. He played a solo too, exquisitely, on the violin. It was Raff's 'Cavatina', which thrilled me to the marrow. Towards the end of the programme the orchestra rendered Elgar's 'Pomp and Circumstance Marches', we in the audience being encouraged to join in the singing of 'Land of Hope and Glory', during which we recaptured some of that feeling of love for and pride in our grand, old country, which Elgar expresses so admirably in this composition.

3 January (Friday)

Censoring of our correspondence has been discontinued. What a relief. Now we can let ourselves go and our friends will get some real news.

The French may beat us at cooking, they may be more economical and their women might be the finest shoppers in the world, but among the things they could learn from the British is our love and care for animals. Thus, our Drivers especially have mixed feelings as their horses are being sold to the French, whom, they say, will work them to death. At least one Driver wept when his pair of horses were taken from him and another was overheard whispering, 'Goodbye old pals, I hope they'll give you plenty of hay, and green fields to graze in.' You cannot work daily with these wise and patient dumb friends without getting to love them. Besides, some of them have saved our lives on more than one occasion. Quite recently we saw on the road outside our billet two French horses, each drawing a cart, the reins of the second horse being tethered to the first vehicle, so that occasionally his bit was jerked violently. We'd be court-martialled for such an offence. Gunner Page, who was near me at the time, observed, no wonder Swift placed horses above men. Also, the French harness large dogs to small carts in which the owner sometimes rides.

4 January (Saturday)

Tonight in 'B' Battery we had an all-male whist drive in the dining hall. Officers, NCOs and men took part and I found it quite a novel experience to partner Major Hollingworth, who made himself exceedingly pleasant. I did fairly well, came among the winners, but my score tied with another man's and in cutting for the prize, I lost.

7 January (Tuesday)

Some provision is being made for the education of the troops, who, now that hostilities have ceased, have so much time at their disposal.[4] In our Brigade, classes have been organised for the study of various subjects. I have chosen shorthand and attend classes once a week in a second-floor room of a house in Bovignies. The tutor is a Royal Engineer Corporal. Since schooldays I have maintained a speed of about 50 to 60 words per minute, but in this class I am not revealing that, as I wish to start from the beginning and relearn every rule thoroughly. Sport too is being encouraged and in a field between our Battery and Bovignies, goal posts have been erected for association football matches between the Batteries.

I am now Line Orderly in 'C' Subsection. Six subsections comprise our Battery, and ours, together with 'D', forms the Centre Section, which is commanded by 2nd Lieutenant Shaw. The duties of a Line Orderly consist in carrying from the Forage Department to the stables, hay, chaff and oats, preparing the feeds in nosebags and all the stable work, excepting grooming. The feed for each animal consists of a nosebag filled with chaff over which about a pint of oats is poured. The oats trickle to the bottom of

---

4. The Army Education Scheme was viewed by even the War Office as part of the overall plan for Britain's national reconstruction after the war. The plan was to prepare men for civilian life and employment after demobilisation. Under the scheme they could brush up on their former trade, learn new skills or simply improve their general education. Of course it was also hoped that by attending classes men would be kept occupied and not have time to dwell on their wait for demobilisation. The scheme was entirely voluntary and open to all ranks. Education Officers were appointed at divisional level and officers, NCOs and men with trades or academic skills and qualifications encouraged to volunteer as instructors. Practical subjects, such as plumbing and carpentry were undertaken at 'technical' units, in this case workshops of Royal Engineer Field Companies or RFA batteries. Theoretical subjects, including modern languages and shorthand, were often undertaken within units by the formation of 'study circles'. Elementary and advanced levels were catered for with the Education Officer being responsible for securing books and equipment. Those involved were excused many military duties and there were even classes for convalescents in hospital. A similar education scheme was put into practice at the end of the Second World War.

the bags which the horses toss upwards, press against the wall, or, if they are not watched, step on in order to get at the oats. Consequently, the average life of a nosebag is short and holes that soon appear in them have to be constantly stuffed with wisps of hay to stop the oats trickling out.

9 January (Thursday)
Finished reading *The Waters of Jordan*, by Horace Annesley Vachell, whose successful novel *Quinneys* I so much enjoyed a few years ago.

The weather is fine, but the landscape now looks colourless. The bare trees in the distance are silvery and grey and when you get near them you find the ground under them thickly carpeted with russet leaves. The southeast wind blows these crisp leaves along the roadsides, where biscuit-coloured toadstools stand amid the blades of grass.

13 January (Monday)
Two events have happened to relieve our existence of its complete boredom and given us something fresh to talk about. Friday night the second Battery whist drive took place, and tonight a concert party from the Labour Corps entertained us in the dining hall. Admirably they performed several short sketches and in between rendered a few musical items. One of the sketches dealt with espionage causing so much laughter by a sentry bringing in a German pigeon which he said he had bayoneted while it was flying with a message. In the playlet one of the characters was a most attractive WAAC cleverly impersonated by a male. Another of the party, a Captain I believe, had a superb bass voice being able to descend to the depths of the song 'Drinking' with ease. This concert has had the happy effect of inspiring some of our colleagues to form a 'B' Battery concert party.

14 January (Tuesday)
Food, or the lack of it is still our obsession. Tea being our last meal, we are by supper time ravenous for something to eat. Some fellows actually go early to sleep to escape hours of hunger and in order for breakfast to appear to come quicker. To me, sleep, other than the bare hour's necessary, is a

shocking waste of time. Smoking is about the best alternative to supper and we draw generously from our Army issue of cigarettes and tobacco. The cigarettes are packed in thin paper packets and the most common brands are named, 'Haversack' and 'Red Hussar'. Pipe smokers receive tobacco named 'White Cloud'. The United States and French tobaccos are abominable stuff. We are used to milder brands, but many prefer these more powerful mixtures. In a recent issue of cigarettes distributed to us, we received some paid for by the proceeds of a performance at the Adelphi Theatre, London. They were labelled to that effect and were quite aristocratic cigarettes.

Tonight the mail was very late, and disappointed, we were all abed before we heard the welcome sound of the two mules and the ration cart, which also brings the post, clattering over the cobblestones into our yard. One of the company volunteered to go and see if there were any letters or parcels for us and clad only in his shirt and boots, he braved the cold night and was rewarded, for he brought back a parcel for me containing a cake and a small Christmas pudding. I divided the cake between them, suggesting we keep the pudding until tomorrow when it could be warmed to advantage, but one fellow said generously that he had not the slightest objection to eating it cold, so not needing much persuasion myself, we ate that also. During this glorious meal I heard an account of one of our Corporals who, having received a parcel, made up his mind to give none away. He retired early to bed, taking with him his parcel, the contents of which he ate under his bedclothes. 'He'll hold an auction sale on his death bed', someone observed. Unexpectedly appeased, we slept in peace.

21 January (Tuesday)

Mr Charles Routledge, the Head Stocktaker in the Plate Mills of Port Talbot Steelworks, has been kind enough to write me several breezy letters during my active service. The last letter contained an offer of a clerical position in his department, which I readily accepted. Promptly, and in his usual magnanimous way, he applied to Major Hollingworth for my release. Summoning me to the Officer's Mess, the Major pointed out that the application had not been stamped by the local Advisory Committee, but he had replied to the 'firm' requesting them to forward another stamped application. I am very elated at the prospect of a return home to 'civvy' life, feeling as though I were about to be released from a prison.

Tonight 'B' Battery concert was held in the dining room, the large, ground-floor apartment of one of the barns. A stage had been erected and Army blankets, skilfully hung, served as curtains. In the party were Lieutenant 'Jack Holt', 2nd Lieutenant Raines, Sergeant Major Mailey, Corporal Swallow, the Battery tailor – a Welsh tenor named Hughes, and Driver Petherick. They had been rehearsing for days and had scrounged the surrounding villages for costumes.

Signaller Oram and I were detailed to manipulate the electric signalling lamp, which was to serve as the limelight. Before the performance Petherick came to us, told us that in his 'turn' he would be making a number of chalk cartoons on a blackboard and begged us not to focus our light on the blackboard as the shine would not only be bad for him but for the audience too. The cook, a stolid fellow with a good bass voice, sang 'Absence' and Mailey, who's a splendid baritone, sang 'My Old Shako'. Then followed 2nd Lieutenant Raines, who, smiling wickedly, sang, 'Another little Drink wouldn't do us any Harm', and although his voice was rather thin he brought down the house, so naively did he interpret it, the packed audience yelling the chorus after each verse. We followed each artiste about the stage with our improvised limelight, which made their eyes gleam brightly and made the show more like the real thing. Then the person we had all been most anxious to see appeared – Corporal Swallow, dressed as a girl. He wore a wig with long curls, ginger coloured, the same as his own hair. He was very self-possessed, demure, but rather too big and dowdy for a girl. The 'girl' in the Labour Corps party had looked more like the 'flapper' type. Still, Swallow did his difficult part splendidly and sang very nicely. First, he sang with Lieutenant 'Jack Holt' the popular duet, 'If You were the only Girl in the World', and then he sang alone in his usual precise way:

Sergeant Brown, Sergeant Brown,
Keep your eye on Tommy for me.
For he may go wrong on the 'continong'
When he reaches gay Paree.

He'll want to parlevous, as they always do
When the French girls they see.
But if my boy Tommy wants to parlevous,
Let him come home and parlevous with me.

'Bonny Dundee', rendered by the quartet, was followed by a pirate song sung by a Driver appropriately attired. The green disc we placed on the glass gave him a lurid, sea-sick look. Petherick, the Battery cartoonist, took the stage next and with rare skill chalked rapidly some clever, humorous sketches of Army mules on the blackboard. Another cartoon was entitled 'The return of the Beaters' and represented Major Hollingworth, who had recently been game shooting, being borne home on a stretcher by weary beaters. At first the drawings were difficult to see and there were impatient whispered demands for 'Light! Light!' from several parts of the hall, but acting on Petherick's request we ignored them all until Major Hollingworth, sitting in the front row, prompted by the men surrounding him, turned around and quietly commanded that the light be switched on. This order had to be obeyed, but it didn't matter so much by then since Petherick had come to the end of his turn. Amid rousing cheers the 'pirate' reappeared, without his make-up, to give a few excellent impressions of an angry lion's roar, the uncorking and pouring out of a bottle of beer, then had the audience shrieking at a number of risqué yarns. A long delay preceded the next item which afforded a splendid climax to the programme. In a state of curious suspense we were suddenly startled by loud and unearthly yelling from the back of the hall. It was the concert party completely surprising us with an attack from the rear. Nude except for loincloths and war-painted like redskins, they danced towards the stage, screeching and brandishing huge bones, the largest the cook had for days been preserving. There was loud laughter and applause.

22 January (Wednesday)
Conversation keeps reverting to last night's concert which everyone considered excellent. Signaller Robertshaw, with a slight smile hovering over his small, weak mouth, said, 'It wor alreet except for one thing. The

men at the limelight let Petherick down.' I said, 'Now look here Robby, it would take that slow brain of yours about six months to guess that Petherick begged us to withhold the light from the blackboard, because he couldn't see to draw on a shining surface.' My opinion of Petherick's work has gone up. He is quite an accomplished cartoonist, doing his sketches with the rapidity of confidence. He specialises in mules whose long ears, brush tails and general awkward appearance intrigues him immensely. He can draw a mule almost in any pose and one sketch of his depicted a mule semaphore signalling with its ears. Petherick has had a few cartoons reproduced in a Yorkshire newspaper, winners in a competition, the prizes being hampers of victuals. At Arras he showed me one of those reproductions which was entitled 'Tales of Hoffman' and represented a wounded German soldier, swathed in bandages, 'telling the tale' to a spellbound boy. Appreciation of each other's work is mutual, for he has complimented me on my own work, admitting that fine art was beyond him. He could not do the landscapes I draw from O Pips, and also would be too timid to go up there, for he is a very timid individual.

24 January (Friday)
Had the gratifying experience of being warned by Bombardier Clarke, the Battery Clerk, that in a few days time I would be demobilised.

25 January (Saturday)
This morning the six of us who are to be demobilised were medically inspected and passed by the Brigade Medical Doctor. This afternoon Major Hollingworth sent for us and we appeared before him in the gloomy officer's mess. He addressed us very nicely, shook hands with each of us, wished us all the best of luck and handed us each an Army Form (Z 18), which is a certificate of employment during the war. My regimental employment has been of course as a Gunner at first and then, from March 1917 as a Signaller. In the space for special remarks Major Hollingworth has entered in small, bad handwriting, which slopes the wrong way, the flattering but generous sentence, 'A thoroughly efficient man, with a sound knowledge of telephony and signalling.'

Bombardier Kingsland arrived about teatime and said, 'I'll be over to see you later. We'll have a nice little supper together. Just you and me. I've got some stuff specially for it.' Some hours later he arrived, wreathed in smiles, with a parcel under his arm. We dined on tinned herrings and biscuits, a rare treat from the limited choice to be had in an Army canteen. Compared with bully beef, flint-like biscuits and plum and apple jam it was a banquet. What a generous and friendly gesture. Kingsland is one of the very few real friends I have made in the Battery and on parting we pledged a life-long continuance of our friendship forged in wartime, exchanged our home addresses and intend to keep in touch by corresponding, at least at Christmastime, with hopes of meeting in the future. He lives in Lewes, Sussex and reminded me that Brighton was not far away from his home town, so I look forward to a holiday in Brighton and to meeting him in that vicinity.[5]

The men of Bettisfield Park Camp, many from Wales, Cheshire and Lancashire, provided for me a soil in which I thrived. I don't appear to have mixed so well with Yorkshiremen, but this may not be their fault or mine and could possibly be due to the differences in our make-ups. Out here I learned that Bradburn came from Lancashire, Oram from Bristol, Kingsland from Sussex and Page from Folkestone, they were my most intimate friends.

5. This holiday took place in 1929. Kingsland, Ivor and their families later met in London in 1959.

Chapter 20

GOODBYE TO ALL THAT

26 January (Sunday)

Those of us who left today for Blighty were issued with a clean set of underclothes and any other clothes the worse for wear. I am going home in full war paint, with steel helmet, a chevron on my sleeve qualified for by having been in the Army two years. Since the date of my Attestation it is actually two and quarter years. Also two small blue chevrons on the other sleeve, one for having landed in France and the second for a year's service and as my withdrawals have been few and small, there being no opportunity for spending during most of the time, the balance to my credit must have accumulated to a useful sum of money. I have been too indolent to ever think of checking the amount due to me, but I must see to it now. When slinging on my haversack, Gunner Page arrived to bid me goodbye and I was very glad to see him, for always there has existed between us a mutual respect and understanding. I felt flattered when he asked me quite seriously, 'Are you returning to College?' We exchanged addresses and he reminded me that Folkestone, where he lives, is well worth trying for a holiday.

Leaving 'B' Battery for home and demobilisation, I couldn't have mustered any feelings of regret had I tried. Active service has caused me so much misery, frustration and discomfort that I am delighted to escape from it and to return to civilian life. I enlisted underage, and as a volunteer as happily and as enthusiastically as anyone, am proud to have done my bit, but I leave the Army with equal enthusiasm and I wouldn't voluntarily remain in it for any price. The only feelings of regard I harbour are for the few men in the Battery without whose friendship I cannot conceive what life in France and Belgium would have been like. I must keep in touch with them.

Almost since my arrival in France my one consuming yearning has been for the war to end so that we can all go home.

Early this morning one of our GS wagons took us via Bovignies to Raches. A thick layer of snow covered the earth. We picked up a few men from the other Batteries, going on the same happy journey and altogether we numbered about 12. Somewhere on the road we passed Gunner Black, an elderly and rather cantankerous member of 'B' Battery, who seemed to be engaged on a fatigue job. He waved a farewell, but when he spotted me, he shouted, 'Hi! Hanson! Where the hell are you going? You haven't been out here 5 minutes yet.' I am not quick at repartee and by the time I had calculated that had I been abroad only 5 minutes, then his service amounted to about 7 minutes, he was well out of hearing. However, it would require a good many Gunner Blacks to upset me today, and his failure to get released is not my fault. At Raches we 'whipped round' in a cap for the Bombardier in charge and the Driver of the wagon and then bade them goodbye. At Douai we entrained in vans and travelled as far as Somain, where we spent the night at a large rest camp. In the centre of our commodious hut a group of feverish gamblers bent over a 'Crown and Anchor' cloth spread on the floor. Having nothing to do, I joined the crowd which watched them for hours and it was evident that the banker consistently raked in most of the tinkling cash, this doubtlessly being the reason for his extreme unpopularity among his clients.

I consider myself lucky in getting my 'ticket' so soon, but I am on pins to be on the move homewards. These long waits torment us.

27 January (Monday)

Entrained into familiar and friendly looking Great Western Railway coaches which must have been borrowed by the French railways. I don't suppose it occurred to the authorities that soldiers hardened to trench life needed heated water pipes, still the cushioned seats were something new and to be thankful for and a great improvement on the hard floors of the goods vans. We rumbled through Montigny, Sin-le-Noble, Arras and Dainville and sometime during the night we were prevented from being frozen stiff by a tin of thin but warm soup, this being our first meal since breakfast.

28 January (Tuesday)

We travelled all last night and after short naps awoke as stiff as pokers. The train lumbered along at about the speed of a slow tramcar and appeared to grudge having to remove us from France. This morning we stopped for a few hours at a place that seemed to be a large railroad centre and when a canteen was discovered near, there was a general stampede towards the hut. Running hard, I found myself in the hut amid a surging sea of khaki-clad figures, struggling for the counter.

How the hut sides survived this scrimmage will forever remain a mystery. An irate counter hand at first refused to serve us until we queued properly, but this was now impracticable and he compromised when the din had abated. After another vigorous struggle to the door I emerged triumphantly with some very acceptable though limited provisions. Grimy locomotives, with intricate external machinery, stood in steaming readiness on the numerous tracks. Continuing the journey, the train glided through St Pol, Ligny-Pernois, St Leger, Flexicourt, Hangest and familiar Picquigny.

I jotted down these placenames seen at railway stations, for the future tracing of my routes will be a fascinating pastime. On we went through Ailly-Surr-Somme to Amiens, near which a fellow traveller pointed out a horse-racing course. Next came Saleux, Namps, Poix, St Segree, Famechon, Fouilloy, Bures, Osmoy, Aroues, Neufchatel and Abancourt. We ended our train journey near the coast in the neighbourhood of Dieppe and found it a tonic to be back in civilisation. Also it was something new for me to see members of the WAAC on active service. Those I have seen have been employed as chauffeurs. Alighting from the train we had a long and tedious march to Martin Eglise Camp, which we reached by nightfall. After tea and the usual waits we were all marched through the camp, which was brilliantly lighted by electricity, to a bath house where the water was gloriously hot and we were issued with a clean change of underwear. German prisoners attended on us and in exchange for our clothes and valuables, which they pigeon-holed, gave us a wooden, numbered receipt. After drying ourselves we filed one by one into a room and stood completely nude in the dazzling and warm rays of a powerful electric lamp, similar to a small searchlight, while three or four medical men scrutinised us professionally. To me they said, 'Right', and I hastily made way for the next. To the waiting Germans I shouted out my number commandingly and a short, grinning fellow of about my age trotted up with my belongings. The man dressing nearest me told me that the MOs had detained the fellow who preceded him. He had attempted to conceal a venereal disease.

31 January (Friday)
Among the German prisoners working here is one exceptionally fine looking NCO. He is in charge of a squad of labouring prisoners, he is well over 6ft tall and holds himself beautifully erect, without being too stiff. I guess he is a Prussian Guard and I think he is the smartest soldier I have ever seen. These hours of waiting seem interminable and it was teatime before the order came for us to leave Martin Eglise Camp for the long march to Dieppe. The officer in charge of us was elderly, fidgety and exacting. He might have relaxed a little on an occasion like this, since from his attitude one would think we were moving up the Line instead of homeward. Our quay was so powerfully lit up with electric lamps that it was almost like daylight. Waiting for the order to march up the gangway of the ship, I enjoyed looking at the ruby, green and golden lights reflected in the smooth, oily dock water. At about 7 pm we embarked on the *Prince Albert*. On board I met a Bettisfield Driver with whom I spent an hour exchanging experiences. Sitting opposite us with his legs drawn up was a soldier wearing kilts beneath which there was no other clothing, so that his pendant genitals were fully displayed to us during our conversation. The sight reminded me of a plucked goose I had once studied when it was hanging in Swansea market one Christmastime. With water drawn from the ship's boiler, tea was made and served out. It contained a generous amount of grease and was the most revolting brew I ever sipped.

1 February (Saturday)
Awaking to welcome daylight, peeped through a scuttle to see land in the distance. Surely this must be England. We learned that we were anchored in the Solent. At 8.30 am we arrived at Southampton, disembarked and

were marched into a room near the landing stage where there was a buckshee buffet. Travelling along what appeared to be a specially laid track we reached Chiseldon in the afternoon and there at the double had to pass through about a dozen huts. They dealt with us as quickly in England as they were slow in France.

We did this 'doubling' willingly and with enthusiasm. One hut dealt with pay and gratuities, another with food-rationing tickets, others with railway vouchers, vermin certificates, the dumping of surplus kits, etc., etc. After this unusual experience of efficiency was ended we were informed that we had barely time to catch the train for Swindon. Grabbing our belongings we made for the road, which was covered with ice, and running half the way and sliding the other half, and never looking back in case they changed their minds about us, we reached the railway station as the train came in, and panting and sweating, but supremely happy, we squeezed into a compartment. At Swindon I had to change trains, and I was pursued the whole length of a platform by two urchins who repeated in turns, 'Master, give me your steel hat.' To my immediate regret I parted with my faithful and dented head protector, remembering with belated gratitude how often shell splinters had ricocheted off it and how often it had shielded my head from low beams in deep, dark dug-outs.

I arrived at Port Talbot at 11.30 pm.

2 February (Sunday)

Sitting with my family at our cheery hearth tonight I learned a few things about the war, news which in order not to discourage me my people had withheld until now.

For instance, when Abram came to bid my people goodbye in the autumn of 1917, he behaved as though he knew he would never come again. Just before he left our house he asked Nellie for a keepsake and she gave him the nearest article to hand, an embroidered facecloth. In return he stripped off his lanyard and presented it to her. Outside our front door he surveyed our house for a few moments, then departed. My grandfather, with the experience of an octogenarian, said to my mother: 'Nid wyf yn meddwl daw Abram yn ol' (I do not think Abram will return), while my father quietly pocketed the sealed envelope secretly handed to him by Abram. On the envelope was written, 'To be opened in the event of my death'. In the following December, while on night duty, my father was appalled when Mr Marienberg brought him the fateful telegram, briefly and with regret informing them of Abram's death in action. Abram's will was a revelation. In it he confessed to having been, for a long time, secretly in love with Nellie. Nellie was astonished, for although they had been such staunch friends for years, he had never suggested, nor had she suspected, that he felt such affection for her.

He divided his earthly possessions thoughtfully and methodically between his relations and best friends. The document begins with instructions that it be delivered to his mother, or nearest surviving relative, one month after the report of his death. In it he writes that his will was prepared and written a day before his entry into the British Army; and that although he could have been exempted, he enlists to satisfy his conscience.

To his mother, whom he describes as the first women in the world, he leaves his Railway Clerk's Association and Railway Superannuation benefits and all his other money. Specified small personal gifts go to his father, brother, sisters and his aunt. To my mother, whom he claims to be 'his truest friend and the second woman in all the world, her character being most beautiful in all respects', he leaves his book of poems. He describes my father as 'one of the finest optimists I ever knew and a man whose greeting is always cordial', he leaves his treasury note case and (1,000) razor. My sister Nellie, 'who still remains the most ideal girl I have ever known and whom I have loved unselfishly, ever since I knew her. (By unselfish I mean I loved her silently, and without expecting reciprocation); I leave the books entitled "It's Never Too late to Mend" and "Quinney's", and I wish I could leave her more.' Out of modestly I omit the complimentary ways he refers to my friendship with him, except the supreme one of calling me his brother, and to me he bequeathed his cigarette-card album, No. 2, his postage-stamp album, a book on swimming and a brooch (I assume it was from a society to which he belonged). My grandfather Daniel Harries is left *Prophets, Priests and Kings*, by A.G. Gardiner; and to J.E. Rogers, whom he describes as 'a man with a woman's heart', goes his best green wallet. To his friend, Miss Mabel Hughes, he leaves the books, *Freckles*, by Gene Stratton Porter, and *Some Old Love Stories*, with the hope that his affections shall be replaced by his friend Ivor and accepted by Mabel. Other gifts, chiefly books, are bequeathed to his favourite schoolmistress, Miss Gwladys Penry Edwards BA, Kenneth Revell, 'the finest boss he ever had', and Mr R.S. Rees.

The document ends with thanks to everyone who had been kind to him, and forgiveness for everyone who had wronged him. Also a declaration of his belief in a hereafter in which he hopes to meet the greatest man he has known, his uncle L. Raphael. The final paragraph states that 'Religion should not be a barrier to true love', but that born a Jew he dies a Jew, Jews being the best people in the world; and ends with the valediction 'Farewell to all and may the Lord have mercy on my soul.'

Abram's death was a stunning blow to my family and they shrunk from the ever recurring thought that 'Ivor might be the next'. My parents were often unable to sleep thinking of me, and when they succeeded in doing it were wont to awake in the early early hours of the mornings. During wet, cold and stormy weather their feelings were indescribable, their only consolation being in their deep religious faith. Many times they gained sleep by reciting biblical psalms. The March Retreat of 1918 reduced them almost to complete despair. On the 11 April 1918 Sir Douglas Haig had issued to all ranks of the British Army in France and Flanders his famous special order in which he had said, 'There is no course open to us but to fight it out. Every position must be held to the last man. There must be no retirement. With our backs to the wall and believing in the justice of our cause each one of us must fight on to the end.'

My people did not receive a line from me for six weeks during this battle and their despair was only slightly relieved by the kind visits of the Revd David John BA, the minister of the church to which my grandfather went. Revd John revived their hopes a little by explaining the unparalleled nature of the offensive and that postal services there were in a state of chaos. One day, however, he arrived with a genuine glimmer of hope. Some friends, similarly situated, had just received a Field Card from France, and he added reassuringly, 'You too will probably receive a similar communication in a day or two.' He was right, for in two days time three Field Cards arrived from me with all lines crossed out except the simple, vital sentence, 'I am quite well.' One of those Field Cards was dated 11 November and must have reassured them for it was written just after the cessation of hostilities.

On the 10 April, the day before Haig wrote his historic 'Special Order', my father's eldest sister's son, Private Ernest Moger[1] of the Suffolk Regiment, was killed at Fleurbaix, France. He was only 19 years of age and from the fragmentary account of his death, it seems that he was blown to pieces by a shell.

At my request, Nellie has kept all my military correspondence, which fills a portmanteau. There the pencilled letters lie with the censor's signature on the envelope. Some of the pages have portions torn out of them leaving me wondering what forbidden news I wrote there. I look forward to the pleasant task of weaving the information contained in that pile of letters to the brief but uncensored entries of my Walker pocket diaries.

3 February (Monday)

Before I returned, permanently I hope, to civilian clothes I thought it advisable to have my photograph taken, and on my father's suggestion we were taken together in uniform, he being dressed in the uniform of a yard or traffic inspector of the Great Western Railway. The photograph was taken by W. Newark Lewis.

20 February (Thursday)

Presentation of gifts to returned sailors, soldiers and airmen at Gendros chapel, Fforestfach. One officer was presented with a sword. When my name was called out and I marched up to the front, I was a bit embarrassed by Aunt Fannie's too enthusiastic hand clapping. From the set fawr[2] an attractive young lady who had acted as accompanist to the musical programme presented me with a handsome, gilt-edged, thumb-lettered Bible with maps. On a flyleaf is written, 'Presented to Gunner I. Hanson, RFA by the inhabitants of Fforestfach and District on his return home from

---

1. The Commonwealth War Graves Commission records that 42147 Private Ernest Henry Moger, 12th Battalion, Suffolk Regiment, died on 12 April 1918. He is recorded on Panel 3 of the Ploegsteert Memorial.
2. Set fawr – Welsh for big seat – an enclosure around the pulpit of a Welsh chapel for the elders or deacons.

the War. Signed on behalf of the Committee by Wm Jas Taylor (Police Sergeant) Chairman'.

24 February (Monday)

From the Army Pay Department I have received a voucher for £44. This is the accumulated capital of my undrawn pay, plus various gratuities for my military service. Quite a nice little start for 'civvy' life. With the exception of a few pounds for gifts and expenses I have deposited it all in the Post Office Savings Bank.

4 March (Tuesday)

Received from the Colonel in Charge of Royal Horse and Royal Field Artillery Records, Woolwich, my Certificate of Transfer to the Army Reserve, information that amuses me. I thought I had done with the Army but it seems they still have a claim on me. Not discharge or demobilisation but transfer to the Army Reserve. They even state the name of the Depot for rejoining, in case of emergency. It is Preston, Lancashire. This document states that my medical category is A1 and that my medals are to follow.

At later dates, which I failed to record, I received the ribbons of the British War Medal and the Victory Medal and some time afterwards the medals, the edges of which are stamped with my regimental number, rank and name.

IVOR HANSON'S TRAVELS WITH THE RFA, 1917-1918

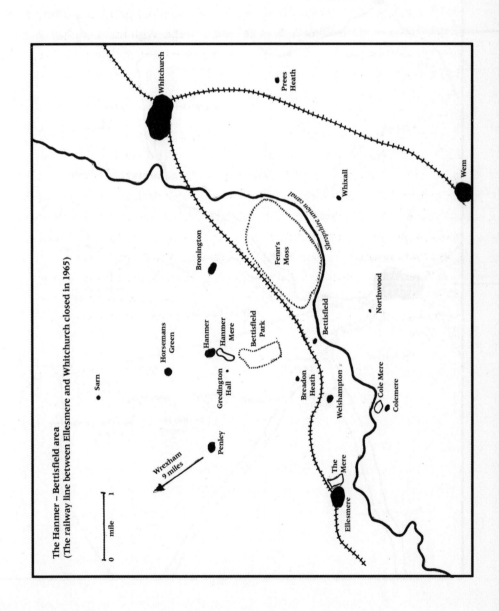

The Hanmer – Bettisfield area
(The railway line between Ellesmere and Whitchurch closed in 1965)

Whitchurch
Prees Heath
Wem
Whixall
Shropshire union canal
Bronington
Femr's Moss
Northwood
Bettisfield
Horsemans Green
Hanmer
Hanmer Mere
Bettisfield Park
Sarn
Gredington Hall
Breadon Heath
Welshampton
Cole Mere
Colemere
Penley
The Mere
Wrexham 9 miles
Ellesmere

mile
0   1

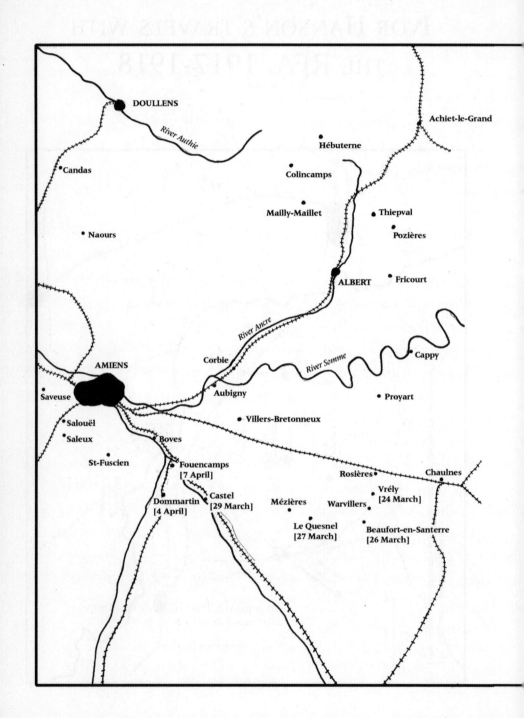

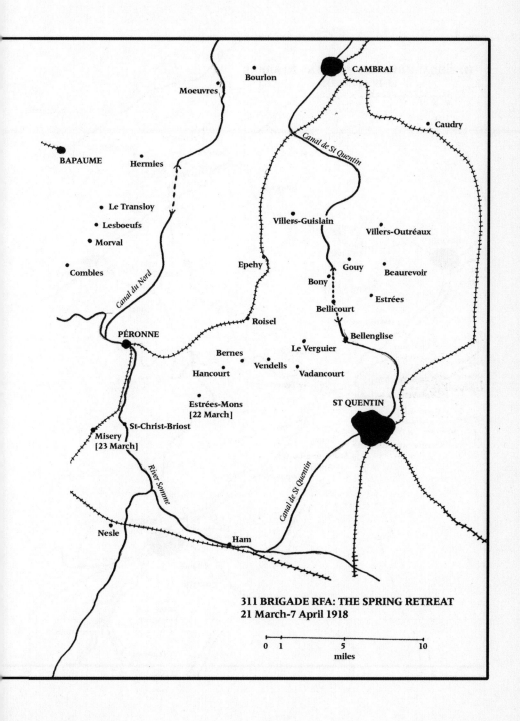

311 BRIGADE RFA: THE SPRING RETREAT
21 March-7 April 1918

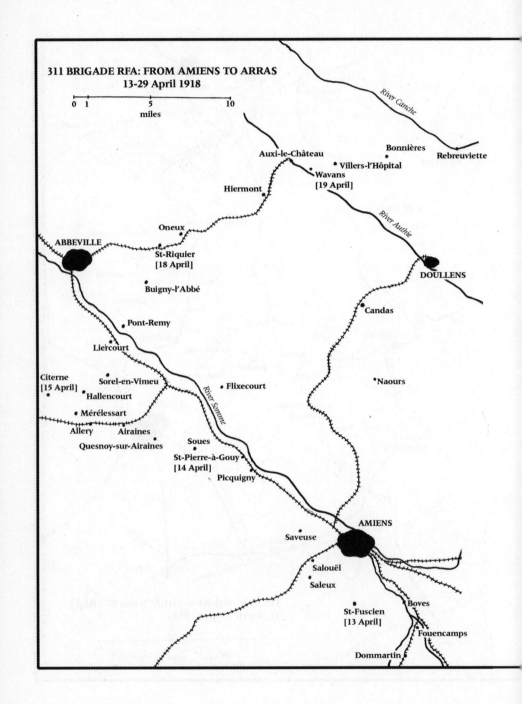

311 BRIGADE RFA: FROM AMIENS TO ARRAS
13-29 April 1918

0 1   5   10
miles

River Canche

Bonnières
Rebreuviette

Auxi-le-Château
Villers-l'Hôpital
Wavans
[19 April]
Hiermont

River Authie

Oneux

ABBEVILLE

St-Riquier
[18 April]
DOULLENS

Buigny-l'Abbé

Candas

Pont-Remy

Liercourt

Citerne
[15 April]   Sorel-en-Vimeu   Naours
Hallencourt   Flixecourt
Mérélessart
                    River Somme
Allery
Airaines
Quesnoy-sur-Airaines   Soues
St-Pierre-à-Gouy
[14 April]
Picquigny

AMIENS

Saveuse

Salouël
Saleux
                                Boves
                St-Fuscien
                [13 April]   Fouencamps

Dommartin

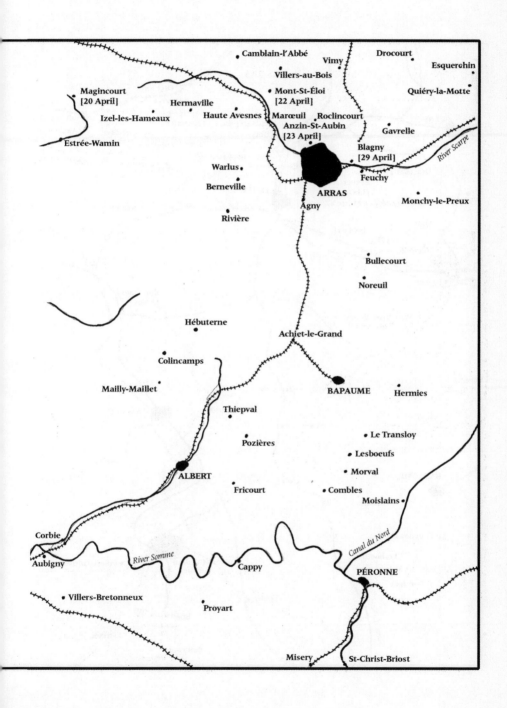

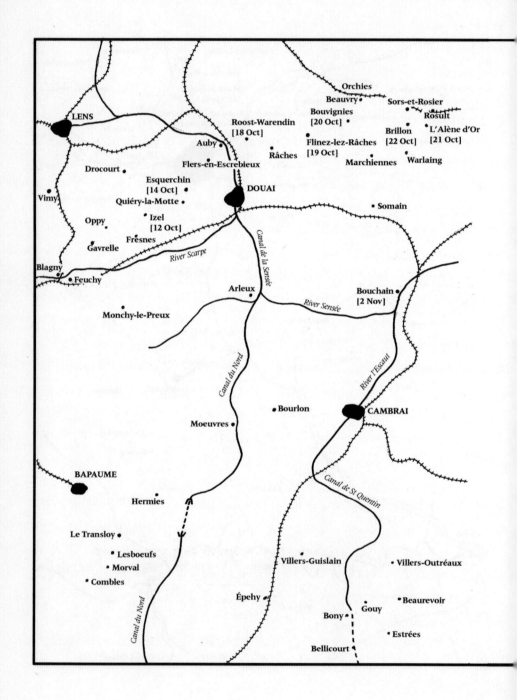

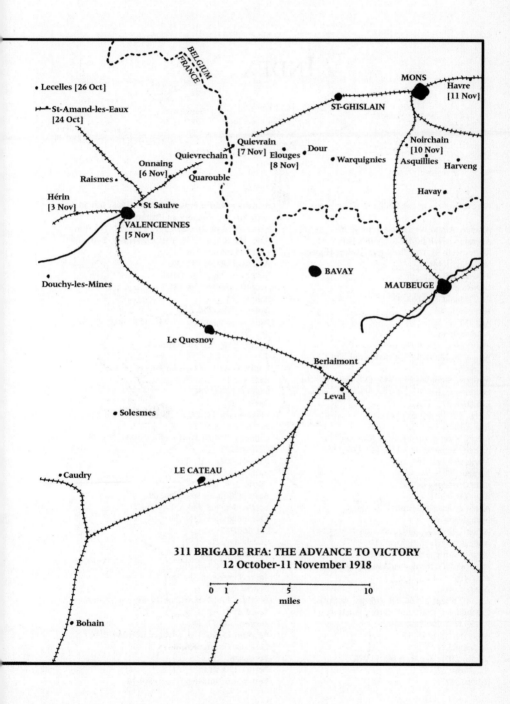

311 BRIGADE RFA: THE ADVANCE TO VICTORY
12 October–11 November 1918

INDEX